I0612768

Written by Carolyn R. Parsons

Cover Photo by Tenisha Saunders

National Library of Canada Cataloguing in Publication Data

Carolyn R. Parsons

The Secrets of Rare Moon Tickle

ISBN 978-0-9865006-1-9

ENNA Imprints is a Canadian publishing company

This book is dedicated to

Kent Chaffey

My love stories are all for you.

Carolyn

Prologue

The three stained glass panes formed an arch of violence behind the red-faced pastor who issued his message of defiance against Satan. His face bore the confidence of his faith, his lips spewed the words of his heart, and his body was rigid in his pride that he was one of the chosen ones. He was an unworthy sinner who had overcome and you could be too if you just obeyed and feared his God.

The window on the left had a picture of a lambs-blood stained door painted to protect the faithful on the day of the Passover. They were frail doors but the babies were safe from the genocide that threatened them by virtue of those sheep plasma splatters. The window to the right showed a battle between demon-like creatures coming up from the pits of hell's flames and being fought back, defeated by the white-winged angels of heaven bearing golden swords and determined expressions. The larger centre window depicted a man hanging by cruel nails hammered through his tender flesh.

The smack pushed Christianna forward with a jar, her forehead stopping just short of hitting the back edge of the pew in front of her. She didn't need to peer up, nor would she dare. Her mother had seen her looking up instead of bowing and she would pay for that later. She stifled a sob.

Christianna kept her head low, her curly bangs touching the edge of the pale wooden pew back. She swallowed. The pastor droned on and the congregation mumbled agreement and "Thank-you Jesus" on cue. A smile tickled her lips under the veil of her long hair. She was safe now hidden from the judgement by the blanket of curls.

She was going to hell. Non-believers would burn in the fiery pits. She had read the Bible as her mother had insisted so Christianna kept her secret sinful thoughts to herself. She did not let on that she was anything other than what her parents expected her to be. She learned to keep her secrets close and to live with her silent wrongs. It was the only way to be accepted, to be loved, to be at peace.

After all, how could she tell her parents, that for the most part, the only words from that monstrous tome that spoke to her twelve year old heart, were the words of Jesus in the Gospel of John 14:27. "Peace I leave with you; my peace I give to you; not as the world gives do I give to you. Let not your hearts be troubled, neither let them be afraid." She wouldn't dare but it was this verse she repeated to herself as the noise of the congregation grew into a frenzy of righteousness and violent protest against the evil outside the doors of the sanctuary.

Mercy Cormack looked at her daughter and caught her chanting under her hair and breathed a sigh. Her daughter was praying! She would understand soon. God would save her girl. The water she'd forced her to be washed in, had been successful. She had seen the whispering and chanting of the Bible enough to recognise it and she'd seen the holy spirit in the bodies of enough of the members of her church to recognise its work and it was present now in her daughter and she was overjoyed by it and shouted, "praise Jesus," and listened for it to echo back to her from the congregation.

Christianna jumped at her mother's voice then relaxed when she realised her tone was a happy one. Yes, this was the easiest way to peace, pretence and secrecy. Christianna returned to her meditation. **My peace I leave with you** *she thought and the peace she so desperately needed came upon her simply because she believed it would.*

It is a common belief throughout humankind that the universe operates as a coincidental mechanism without reason and that all of mankind wanders helter-skelter with no particular path. Yet all the major world belief systems speak of a force, a divine map, some mysterious energy source that makes sense somewhere in infinity. What if they are all right? What if all of our lives are predetermined in the heavens and we simply get to live in the details? What if the stars, the moon, and the sun all shine in perfect rhythm with our lives, counting our days, watching our nights, determining our every step though we count it as accidental? What if there are no coincidences?

Christianna Cormack
Punt Cove, NL, 1987

1

The kitchen smelled of turkey-neck soup and fresh-baked bread. Mercy Cormack had no idea that her daughter would never eat that meal—her favourite—again for many years. She rubbed cream into her red-skinned hands with a furious motion as though it irritated her to take the time. She sniffed her hand, inhaling the scent of the lotion. It wasn't a fragrance so much as a really nice smell, she thought. She made a mental note to order some from Betty when she came by with the Avon book. Then, not trusting her memory, she placed the plain white, almost-empty tube back in its spot over the sink. She took a pen and made a note on the little pad near the phone. She smiled at the slip of paper next to the note pad. Mercy kept it there so she wouldn't make a mistake when she read the results to inquiring callers, though there were few left who didn't know.

"Honours," she'd repeat with more smugness than pride. "She'll be going to MUN in the fall." Mercy bragged to her friends at church and her relatives who lived in other small towns not far away including her sister Maisie whose son David had gone straight to the mainland out of school.

Mercy was proud of her accomplishments as a mother. She had not spared that rod and Christianna hadn't caused any problems for her. *That was the problem with kids these days*, Mercy thought, *the parents were too soft*. She went to check on her soup, a Saturday tradition. She still had cleaning to do, that was a Saturday tradition as well. She untied her apron and poured Mr. Clean into a bucket of hot water. It smelled better than the hand lotion to Mercy Cormack as she bent onto her prayer-worn knees to scrub the floor in front of the kitchen cupboards. While she was there she sent up a quick devotion out of habit and then turned back to her cleaning with a furious motion.

Christianna Cormack sat up in the front seat, laughing at the close call. Betty was the local Avon lady and would be on the phone to her mother in an instant if she saw her in Greg Kennedy's shiny maroon Chevy Nova. Greg hadn't noticed and didn't seem to hear her laughter. She stifled her smile and folded her hands in her lap as they reached the edge of town. The sky was dark in the distance, the grey-blue ocean reflected on its surface giving it a shiny purple bruise at the horizon. The road wound along, trees on the right side, ocean to the left and Christianna let out a breath when they turned off onto the road that headed towards the Trans-Canada Highway that would take them to Port aux Basque. They had plenty of time to make the ferry but Christianna wouldn't relax fully until it pulled away from the dock, heading into the Gulf of St. Lawrence.

Greg's hair was immaculate as usual and he was clean shaven. He wore a trendy shirt and tight jeans. He stared straight ahead as they headed out of Punt Cove on the dusty gravel road. He was still irritated by the dust that was messing up the car he'd spent hours shining. He'd stop somewhere and clean her again before they got to Kitchener. He certainly didn't want his friends to see the car he bragged about in such a mess. He'd have to deal until they were in Ontario. He sucked in his breath and remembered they cleaned underneath the car on the ferry. That would help a little.

Excitement welled up in Christianna. They were doing it, they were leaving. She looked at the road ahead of her, the promise of freedom; the promise of something new and different lay before her, stretched out for miles. The car bumped as they hit the pavement that started up about two miles outside of the community she'd grown up in. She laughed and this time Greg glanced over at her. She leaned over close to him and kissed his cheek and he glanced at her with a smile. His hand slipped between her legs and rubbed the tight denim of her jeans. Chris snuggled closer, happy with their decision. She looked at the ring on her left hand. She had only been able to wear it when she was with Greg though he was often angry if she didn't. Until now they had been forced to keep it a secret in the glove compartment of his car. She hoped he would feel more secure now that she could wear it all the time.

It was a promise ring and she loved it not only for the promise from Greg, though he'd sworn that within a year he'd buy her a beautiful diamond to replace it. It was because it promised her freedom.

The packed car, full of all of their belongings, including packages of Mount Scio savoury and Tunnock's Caramel Log bars, was her getaway vehicle. This man who loved her was taking her away and from now on freedom would be hers. She would now be able to go where she wanted to go, do what she wanted to do and she'd do it all with Greg.

Greg Kennedy was five years older and a recent graduate from University. His job waited for him in Ontario and she was thrilled to be going along, flattered that he'd chosen her and she was ready to live with him and eventually marry him. He was an engineer, precise and detailed in his thinking. He'd planned this entire trip and advised Christianna on what to pack.

Christianna glanced in the rear view mirror and watched the road disappearing, the line between the gravel and pavement signifying the separation of her past and her future. She felt a lump in her throat that she didn't expect and swallowed it down. Her parents would be hurt and they'd waste a lot of their prayers on her. They already had. She looked away from the mirror and back again at the road in front of her, beckoning, welcoming. The regret waned and her excitement returned. She would be across the gulf before her family received the letter she'd mailed to them. She pictured the confusion on the postmaster's face as she put the letter in her parent's mailbox. Then once the word spread she'd tell the whole town she'd known all along.

But Christianna and Greg wouldn't witness any of that. They were on their way beyond the reach of her parents, beyond the reach of anyone. It was finally happening, she was going to escape and she owed it all to Greg! She promised herself she would do whatever it took to make it up to him. She faltered for a moment in her happiness. A frown wrinkled her brow and she worried her lip with her teeth. It would be easier, she thought, if she were actually in love with him, she owed him so much. She scooted over closer still and held his hand on her lap, laying her head on his shoulder. He wrapped his right arm around her shoulders. She remembered them then, the six jars lined up under her bed in a bright yellow row. She'd forgotten to pack the pickles and Greg would be furious. She hoped he was mistaken and they actually did sell sweet mustard pickles in Ontario.

Christianna Cormack
Kitchener, ON, 1989

2

The diamond on her left hand was nearly flawless. It was a cushion cut set in an eighteen karat gold setting that had been custom designed. It had cost a fortune, and as she was often reminded, was one of a kind. It sparkled and reflected the light of the room and twinkled at her, mocking her. She had nice hands and the ring suited her long tapered fingers. It had been made for her and she should have appreciated it. The ring was pretty and traditional and exactly what she would have chosen for herself. In reality though, it was simply a perfect recipe of carbon and time. It was a crystal, no more complex than quartz or water. Diamonds weren't even rare; every woman she knew had one, though none was as large or flawless as hers.

What *was* rare was love. This stone was as common as the dirt it was mined from and as evil as those who mined it.

She stared into space, in meditation, the daily practice that brought her the only moments of peace in her life. The perfect stone of love would be a blue-purple gem she thought, the colour somewhere between amethyst and sapphire, a perfect match to the Atlantic Ocean surrounding the coastline of the Newfoundland outport community she had grown up in. A stone of such depth, such unusual colour, such beauty must be as rare as the love she longed for. Christianna hadn't ever seen such a stone but surely nature had created one.

Maybe rare wasn't even the ideal. Another memory of home, of love, of nature, moved in, that of the ever constant sunset that had dipped behind that indigo ocean with a gentle crash in a scarlet blanket of night sky. A stone of deepest scarlet, red, steady and hot would perhaps be more appropriate. Maybe the sunset stone was preferable to the rare indigo stone, beautiful and dependable. A love like that would be perfect. She breathed, relaxing into her fanciful musings but reality penetrated her peaceful thoughts.

The diamond *was* a perfect representation of the way she felt. She was empty and cold, her truth only told through the colours reflected in another's eyes. Perhaps the diamond did suit *this* relationship. It mocked her as it bit into the flesh of her palm, reminding her of the promise that wouldn't be kept.

Her body tensed as Greg walked into the apartment, closing the door closing behind him. He glanced at her a moment and then his eyes moved around taking in its immaculate appearance. He walked over to the dark wooden shelf that sat underneath the window and picked up a picture of the two of them, stared at it a moment and then put it back, careful to place it in exactly the same spot. He whistled happily, a familiar tune. Christianna felt her shoulders soften. Finished with his inspection, he went to the radio and put on a station. He played country music. She hated it. She said nothing. Chris picked up her book instead.

"Pizza for dinner?" Did he plan that? Did he always have to jump in when ever she started to do something she enjoyed?

"Sure," she answered attempting to sound enthusiastic but her fear made her voice sharp. Her eyes flicked at her mistake, looking away from him and then back.

"I said I was sorry." His voice hardened at her tone.

"I know, sorry, I'm distracted, tired," she lied and faked a smile. "Not you, me," she added. It was, in effect, the truth.

"Did you make any plans?" He asked, expecting her to know what he meant.

"Yes, I looked at flowers and invitations." The lie dropped like another fragment chiselled from her soul. Her secrets demanded these lies.

There are two kinds of secrets. The first kind plagues on its keeper, like so many unrepentant termites biting and chewing at the base of an ancient oak until, under the furious storm of time, the mighty tree is felled by the weakness eaten into its roots. This is the secret of shame.

The second kind was the kind that Christianna kept, the kind that protected a person from the danger that would destroy them. This secret, if revealed, could end her life. A secret she had to keep until she could escape. Her secret filled her with fear and she shared it with no one, not even those who might rescue her, for surely they wouldn't, or couldn't protect her from the danger she was in from the man who claimed to love her.

"David's party tonight?" He asked, his voice interrupting her thoughts yet again.

"Do you want to go?" She managed to keep her voice level this time. Chris waited for his answer, this was his decision.

"Should be good," he said. "Yeah, we'll go, order pizza for dinner."

"Ok." She agreed in a dull voice and went to the phone to place the order. That was her job. Chris ordered the usual, loaded with meat, though she didn't particularly like it. It didn't matter to her; she would eat what he wanted as she always did. She surveyed the room as she spoke into the telephone receiver.

The house was spotless, the floor was vacuumed and every surface was clear and shiny. Dust didn't dare live with them. This apartment was as cold and sterile as the steel bank vault that held the means to her escape. The sun filtered through the space between the custom-made curtains. Silvery particles hung suspended there, still as though they dare not move. A picture of him in her mind vacuuming the air out of the room to get them tickled at her sense of humour. Her serious expression didn't change.

"Be ready by eight," he advised.

She would be. She dared not do otherwise.

3

The smoke rose in grey cancerous swirls from the table in front of her and joined the thick cloud that already hovered in the room. The smell was cloying and claustrophobic. Christianna picked up her cigarette and took a long deep drag. Her shoulders relaxed a little when the chemicals hit her blood stream. A deadly relief, the nicotine gave her a rush of pleasure. There were so few moments of that in her life these days that she was grateful for this small measure.

The thumping of the bass from the stereo jarred the walls. The system was located in another area but her cousin had screwed shelves on the walls of the dining room and the large speakers shuddered and spit out their noisy offerings. Mick Jagger irritated her with his lament that he could get no satisfaction repeating the problem to the drunken eardrums of the crowd. Nobody else seemed to mind. Christianna furrowed her brow in annoyance and took another pull of the cigarette then placed it in the little foil ashtray.

Her perfectly manicured nails pulled at the label on her beer bottle, picking it off and rolling the bits of paper between her fingers and flicking them in the ashtray that held her latest smoke. She picked it up and inhaled again.

The droning conversation of girls at the table was mind-numbing. Chistianna's preoccupation went unnoticed. Someone had been dumped by a boyfriend. Lucky girl, Christianna thought.

"Greg is smoking weed upstairs," she answered Carol, a big-haired blonde who noticed her there and asked about him. Tension coiled like a snake in the pit of her stomach. He usually didn't leave her alone this long. The party swirled in a frenzy of smoke and activity. A girl squealed, guys bragged of their beer drinking abilities, determined to prove them, as the tempo of the party increased. Chris chatted a little more, laughing at their jokes, participating as the beer and cigarettes relaxed her further.

"Beer?" Someone offered. Chris took the cold brown bottle, twisted the cap off and drank from it with a casual thank you. At each passing moment without Greg's presence a little of herself bubbled up and spilled into the night air like the beer had when she'd opened it.

Time blended into a confusion of loud music and laughter. The group at the table moved together as one into the living room where some over-drunk partiers were dancing. One girl, her blonde hair hanging like wet straw and smelling of the beer that had been tossed over her head, undid her shirt one button at a time, her antics the cause of the excitement.

Christianna backed away from the spectacle and walked over to the dining room table and sat back down in the chair opposite from where she had been sitting earlier. She picked up her package of cigarettes from the table, tapped one out and looked around for her lighter. David's roommate noticed her with the cigarette in her hand and came over and held his lighter up, she lit her cigarette, exhaling her thank you.

"You're welcome," he hesitated for a moment and she looked up at him with her large blue eyes, waiting, but he closed his mouth as though he had second thoughts and left her there alone.

Christianna jumped at the crash, the wetness on her shoulder and left side of her face baffling her. She looked to where the bottle had hit, her eyes blinking at the amber liquid that flowed in several streams down the wall. The drywall was dented from the force of the attack and Chris reached up to pull something off of her shoulder. She held her hand flat, displaying the sodden mess from the bottle that had rebounded off the wall. Several dangerous looking shards of glass were still attached to the label.

Chris stared at it for another brief moment before looking up, shock in her eyes. Through the hazed glare of smoke, the buzz of the alcohol and the shock of the attack, she saw a movement in the kitchen door from where the bottle had to have been thrown and she caught an unmistakeable glimpse of the retreating back of her fiancé.

4

The fog dampened the night creating a break from the smothering humidity that had defined the day. It was clean and cool and filled with mystery. Christianna had never seen David's backyard in the daylight and wondered what was hiding out there in the mist.

The fog could hide all sorts of things and she wondered if it could hide her from the prying eyes in the house. Chris had always liked that when you were in the fog you didn't know you were in it. It surrounded you and held you close like a loving friend. She was grateful it was there, it represented her only hope yet she was reluctant to go.

A green Coleman cooler sat on the edge of the deck, against the brick of the house. Christianna opened it pulling out a Coors Light. Wrinkling her nose, she decided it would do. She yanked open the twist off cap with a quick movement and pulled her jacket over to sit on it. The beer was cold from the ice in the cooler and the label slipped around on the bottle. It came off and she reached over and stuck it to the top of the textured surface of the lid. She pressed it with her fingers as she let the cold beer slide down her throat.

"Greg went home." David popped his head around the door. It was a statement but his eyes held a question. She looked okay but she always seemed that way and now he knew it wasn't the truth.

"He's gone?" Her shoulders softened.

"A cab was dropping someone off and he jumped in." David sought to reassure her. David had suggested he leave. He wanted to kill Greg Kennedy and a few drinks more and he might have.

"Why?"

"I told him to go."

"You saw? She had thought no one had. She didn't know how to explain the fact that he behaved this way or that she put up with it.

"No Sid did." Sid was his roommate who had lit her cigarette. He must have still been close by.

"We'll talk later." Christianna's eyes dismissed him. She needed to be alone for a while.

"Yeah, ok." He needed to know what was going on, but he understood and slipped back into the house.

Chris looked back at the grey dense blanket of fog, thinking.

There *was* hope, yet no immediate solution. She was defeated by her own stability, her own sense of responsibility.

What her heart screamed for was rescue. What her body needed was solace and sweetness. She had once had an impulsive nature, but she'd tamped that out a long time ago. Still it took all of her willpower not to go screaming into the fog like a lunatic or even better, to slip into the fog like a fox, stealth and free.

Her mind bounced back to the rational. She did have a plan. She *would* get out but she needed time. She rubbed a tender spot on her upper arm. A bruise? It was from the rebounded glass, a painful reminder of the danger she faced.

Like the proprietor of a convenience store, she took inventory. Did she love Greg? No. Did she hate him? Close. Did she have a way out? Not yet. There was a lease, jobs, responsibilities. Her body tightened as she swirled the pretty little diamond ring on her finger with her left thumb.

Mindful she stopped, willing herself to be still. She closed her eyes and whispered the words that usually brought her solace, words she had used to keep her soul intact as her body was being battered.

Peace I leave with you; my peace I give to you; not as the world gives do I give to you. Let not your hearts be troubled, neither let them be afraid, my *peace I leave with you, peace.*

She picked up the bottle again and took another long drink.

The bars of her trap moved closer and her body tensed with the emotional claustrophobia as she slipped further into despair. The noise of the party dulled behind her as did the roar of a motorcycle that pulled up to the front of the house.

Instead of the elusive peace that she prayed for, the force in the universe that decides such things sent her something more substantial. It sent Christianna her destiny.

Joe Indigo
Angell's Cove, NL, 1980

5

Joe avoided his parents as he made his way through the kitchen to the cozy little bedroom at the back of the house. He opened the door, hitting the heater that warmed the little room, scraping it across the floor. The small lady on the bed looked past him, then as her eyes focused better, moved down to his face and she smiled. She was happy it was him and she nodded as he came forward.

"How was school?" She asked him the same question every day. Her black hair was as dark as ever with only a sprinkle of grey at the temples. The tidy bun on her head was a masterpiece, accomplished with no mirror, yet perfect and elegant. She touched it, patting it, waiting for his answer.

Joe could have lied. He was pretty sure she couldn't see details well enough to see the bruises on his face. He sat on the chair by the bed pulling it forward a little.

"Shitty, got in a fight." He winced a little, more from the disappointment he knew he would hear in her voice then the pain of his injuries.

"The girl?"

"Yeah?" He shook his head and grinned though it hurt. Aunt Mae just knew things somehow.

"Not worth it, girls aren't worth fighting over."

"I thought I loved her."

"People are worth fighting *for*, not fighting over," she revised. Joe grinned again. His aunt was full of these little wisdoms.

The words tumbled out of him then as she listened, her nearly blind eyes seeing the fight, seeing the slap he'd delivered across the petite blond girl's face and watching as though she'd witnessed it first hand as another, bigger boy, had stepped in and fought for the girl. She saw his desperation and felt his pain and it hurt her heart to know he'd been wounded. This boy was her closest kin and she loved him more than his own parents did. They didn't see what she saw in him. He was special and capable of great things but their neglect inflicted greater injury than a school yard fight ever could.

"You don't hit girls ever, promise?" She said to him in a firm voice. She struggled not to be angry with him and it shook him.

"I promise," he said and he meant it. Aunt Mae had never been angry with him before.

"Good." She was satisfied. "You know you're better than that, Joe Indigo, you are a *protector*, you were sent to protect people not to hurt them." Aunt Mae patted his hand with her soft frail one. He liked it, her touch held forgiveness and understanding.

"She'll come along," she continued and she asked him then to pass her the little brown leather book that she kept on the window sill between her geraniums where she liked to sit and look out the window in the summer. He'd read the book to her before, when it was what she requested, and couldn't help but wonder who this Fred had been who had given it to her in 1967. Whoever he was he'd not kept his promise to *love you forever* as the salutation before his name said.

"Who'll come along Aunt Mae?"

"Your grand love, my son, she'll come along," and she pressed the little book into his hand with a smile. She always gave it to him to read when he was sad. Funny thing was it always cheered him up. He would read it later alone in his room and then return it to her.

Then she directed him to the mystery story she wanted him to read to her. One good thing about his aunt

Mae, Joe thought, was that she didn't dwell on things too long. He put the little book in his back pocket. Aunt Mae spoke often of this grand love everybody was to have once in their life. As a child he'd been fascinated but now he was starting to doubt its existence and he began to read as his Aunt Mae sat herself up and tucked the shabby red and yellow quilt around her legs and smiled as she closed her eyes, soaking in the sound of his newly deep male voice.

In the deepest secret places of his soul, while his teenaged body lived in angst and anger most of the time, a spark of hope had been lit that indeed, at some point, he would meet the girl that would be this special grand love his aunt spoke of so frequently. Meanwhile he would work towards escaping the extreme poverty he lived in day by day. Aunt Mae wanted him to go to University and study English Literature and he thought that he would when he graduated. With her help, he'd managed straight A's and in three years he'd be free to leave. As much as he would miss his aunt, he longed for that day.

Joe Indigo
Kitchener, ON, 1989

6

The party was well underway. His old school friend David greeted him at the door and handed him a beer with a welcoming smile and a thump on the back.

"Hey Joe, beer?"

"Hey buddy, thanks," he tipped the beer and allowed its mellow flavour to slide into his throat. He was too sober and the beer was cold and bitter. He sighed and took another chug.

"So, you come on bike?" Dave asked moving to the side to place his empty in the nearby beer case leaving the sliding patio doors in Joe's line of vision. Joe made a whistling sound under his breath, seeing her long, tanned legs first. She held a beer and stared, unmoving, like a statue. She wasn't warmly dressed and though it wasn't a cold night, there was a chill from the damp fog, yet she was still.

"Yeah, foggy night." Joe answered, distracted. Brown curly hair fell down her back and when she lifted the bottle to her lips he was almost surprised at the movement. Dave looked to where Joe's gaze had gone and he grinned and shook his head. He really couldn't blame the guy. His cousin was a good looking girl.

"Almost time to head back uh?" Dave tried to redirect his friend. Chris had enough trouble in her life right now.

"What?" Joe looked at David but his mind remained on the girl outside on the patio as he tried to recall the question.

"Back to the rock?" Dave repeated. Joe went home every summer.

"Leaving Sunday night on bike as usual." He always rode the bike home too.

"Who *is* that? She yours?" Joe nodded towards the patio, the tactic working only for an instant. He hoped not but he was getting the sense David was attempting to keep him away from her.

"My cousin, Christianna." David answered and he gave her a quick worried glance. Joe caught the look and chose to ignore it.

"Good stuff." David went on relieved that Joe was going home. He could tell he was interested in Chris, hell all of his buddies were, but Greg kept her on a short leash. His stomach knotted in anger. Greg Kennedy was a jerk but Joe Indigo was just as dangerous, in a different way. As far as David was concerned, none of his friends were in her league.

"Dave." The high pitched female voice called from the living room and then she entered the kitchen. It was April, the girl David had been seeing lately. She was motioning with her hands in an agitated gesture for him to come.

"We have a huge mess," she informed him staring at Joe.

"Shit," said Dave, irritated at the interruption. He knew Joe would make a move at the first opportunity.

"Hope not," Joe joked tipping the rim of the beer forward in front of his lips before taking a drink. He swallowed and grinned. His dimples flashed and April smiled at him, her face brightening at his joke.

Dave rolled his eyes as he walked away. *Could be shit*, he thought, anything was possible, and he left Joe with a resigned shrug. Perhaps April could at least keep him busy until he got back. He glanced at Chris once more then hurried towards the living room.

"Joe, hey," April spoke to him. Then she stared, her mouth slightly opened, she could think of nothing else to say.

"Shouldn't you go?" Joe motioned to where David had disappeared, anxious for her to leave. April hesitated and then reluctantly turned to follow. Joe watched her departing ass for a moment. It *was* pretty nice and she was deliberately swinging it for his appraisal. He chuckled, a low sound under his breath, then looked back to the place where his mind had been almost since the moment he'd walked in the house.

She still hadn't moved other than to lift the beer to her lips. He didn't hesitate.

"Hello." Joe spoke from the opening of the sliding glass door.

Chris tilted her face around and up, curious. If she had nice tits she'd be perfect, Joe thought, when he saw she was prettier close up.

His black leather jacket made a soft squicking sound as he stepped on to the back porch and lifted his hand in a little wave. Chris took in his jet black hair that was pulled back into a tight ponytail that didn't look like a ponytail from the front. His eyes were dark too, almost black and his face was tanned and masculine. His square jaw would have been harsh but his entire face was softened by a mischievous grin that tickled the corner of a very sexy set of lips. He was tall, filling the frame of the door completely.

Joe grinned then, his eyes dancing with a light that Chris felt immediately connected to. It was familiar and warm and she was mesmerised by it.

"Can I sit?" He asked. His voice was deep and had an element of complete confidence. He moved to do so a millisecond before she answered.

"Sure." She patted the wooden boards beside her in invitation. Her large blue eyes looked boldly into his, searching for something. He looked into *her* eyes disturbed by the hint of pain he saw in their depths and, though she appeared happy in that instant, he sensed she was very troubled. He liked blue-eyed girls. He liked troubled girls too.

"Joe Indigo." He held out his hand to shake hers as he lowered himself into the narrow space between her and the beer cooler. She moved just a little to make room.

"Chris Cormack," she replied, taking the hand he offered. He stared at her for a long moment, his black eyes penetrating, confused. They didn't speak yet the silence wasn't awkward. *I like her* Joe thought then shook off the silly fancy and broke the trance with a grin.

"So what are you doing out here all by yer lonesome?" He asked glancing around at the empty night.

"My asshole fiancé kind of ruined my party," she replied. She looked down at her hands and twisted the beer bottle in a clockwise motion. She didn't talk about her life to people. She looked back up at him.

"You want me to kill him?" Joe's eyes held a glint of sincerity though his grin was light-hearted.

"Yes please," laughter burst from her, a pretty sound that chimed like church bells in his ears. "I'll give you his address."

His laugh harmonised with hers composing a melody. Their song erased the brief hint of danger and mellowed her fear. It was a delightful instrumental tune that needed no lyrics to tell its story. It was a tune they would grow to know well and recognise as their own. It was a song of laughter, a song of nature, a song of love. It would play for a lifetime and beyond. It was the song of soul mates.

"You're too pretty to be out here by yourself, you want to go back in?" He didn't, he realised, no longer interested in partying.

"Nah, they're all talking, I don't want to hear it. He's gone though, Greg, my fiancé I mean." It consoled her to say that out loud.

"You wanna go for a walk?" He nodded to the grey night.

"It's foggy." Chris said. Yes, she wanted to walk into the fog, she had wanted to all evening.

"Come on," he said standing and reaching out his hand, assuming her answer was yes.

In spite of the mist it was a mild night and she walked where he led. The fog itself was familiar and thick and she walked into the grey sanctuary. Alone she had been able to resist the temptation of its pull but at his invitation she went uncaring of how she would emerge. She had promised herself that never again would she act on an impulse as she had when she left home with Greg Kennedy two years prior, yet something inexplicable was tempting her to follow a man she had met moments before, into the dark mist.

There were no parallels between the control Greg had tried to exert over her and the control of the forces that led her to follow Joe Indigo into that dark night. The former was a selfish, cruel control, the other a loving guiding force that led her to follow the rhythm her heart played with every beat. There was choice here, within the celestial control. Her choice was made on that dark foggy evening. She followed the lead of her heart.

7

Joe's dark brown eyes, the gateway to a cynical soul, not expecting love, not really believing in the falling into of it anymore stared into Christianna's. They were large and blue and he saw his reflection in their depth. He blinked it away. He looked different in her eyes somehow and it disturbed him in a place he didn't care to explore.

"Cold?" He asked but she was warm though it was a damp night. He held her close. Her hair was messy, completely curled by the damp. He touched it fascinated by its shocking wildness.

Then he tucked her arms inside his leather jacket with his hands and she embraced him around the back, her hands almost coming together at the fingertips. She felt the heat from his back against her palms and moved them to massage the strong tight muscles there.

"Where did you come from?" The connection to her was unfamiliar and mystified him. Her hands on his back released a stress he hadn't been aware existed. He understood the sexual need and it was intense but familiar.

It was the mysterious other need that tickled at the surface of his soul, teasing it, stroking it, comforting it, that confused him.

"Newfoundland, Punt Harbour to be exact," she answered not getting the deeper question.

He laughed tossing his head back, his white teeth flashing for a moment. His joy was like sunshine, hot and soothing. She laughed with him, his mirth contagious.

"No, I mean you look like you showed up, like magic, just for me," he explained. He was embarrassed by the words. It sounded like a line.

"Hocus-pocus?" Chris thought his corniness endearing. The nurturing the impulsive part of herself had exploded as though someone had pulled the little metal tab on a shaken cola can. Under pressure for so long, when released it bubbled up and surfaced, overtaking all rational thought.

Having arms around her, even the arms of a stranger was oddly comforting. The saying out of the frying pan into the fire flickered in her mind for a moment and she liked the fire. Beyond the heat, beyond the danger she sensed something more. She saw something hidden and unnamed in the depths of his dark brown eyes and felt something warm and familiar in his firm embrace.

"Abracadabra," he grinned and he held her a little closer. She felt the heat from his body outlined in his jeans, his t-shirt. This timing was perfect and he was a perfect distraction. Right now in this moment Christianna felt free to make her own decisions even if tomorrow things were exactly as they were yesterday. She heard the message that broke through loudly from her sensible self that this was dangerous. She ignored it for the softer message that whistled through the foggy night telling her that this was right.

His lips were on hers then and her body reacted as a blue heat soared through her veins. She kissed him back. It was novel to her to kiss someone she actually *wanted* to kiss. She needed him closer, enveloped in a wave of sensual need that was almost unfamiliar. It was a first kiss but it felt like coming home.

The map that had been laid out for her, weighted down by the expectations she'd placed on each corner, curled up slowly into a roll. The directions that showed marriage, children, a home was completely ready to be tucked away forever. It was useless to her now. This was uncharted territory. Here she was with a beautiful stranger that tempted her and caused her to risk her plans and her life. And she felt more comfortable with this man than she was with her own fiancé. In the cocoon of the passion she followed her stifled impulses.

Christianna lost herself in his essence. She felt the raw physical nature of the kiss and set aside all thoughts of anything beyond enjoyment of the moment.

Joe dropped his head against the top of hers when the kiss ended.

"Wow, where *did* you come from?" This time it wasn't a line.

It was the first time since he was a young teen man that Joe felt more than attraction. He loved women and he was excited to find this one. He ignored the little tingle at the back of his brain that said this wasn't going in the same direction.

Christianna looked at him, her face flush, lips full from the impact of their kiss. She pulled her arms from underneath his jacket and ran them up his chest. They rested around his neck and she smiled at him. Her large blue eyes disturbed him in an unfamiliar way. He looked away for an instant, the connection too much. Then he looked back, compelled to do so by something stronger than his own resistance to intimacy.

Joe always felt attracted to needy girls. A bad home, a bad marriage, he was their white knight, their rescuer, and then, when the fire was out, the dragon slain, he would cause them further pain with his departure

Was he rescuing this girl too? That was what he thought he was doing when he had approached her on his buddy's back deck. He sensed somehow that beyond her immediate situation that she was strong and able and ready for the challenges of the world. She was warm and sexy and something about her eyes held an unfamiliar curiosity that looked for answers to questions most people were afraid to ask of him. Tonight though, she needed a hero and that was a role that was familiar to him.

A little dimple played underneath her lip on the left side when she smiled and he bent forward to kiss it gently before moving back to kiss her fully on the lips again. She tasted of fruity Chap Stick and beer and something else he had never tasted before, something distinct and potent. He wondered as he kissed her how it was possible for someone to be new and familiar all at once.

Had the couple been able to see, through the dense purposeful fog of the night, they would have noticed that a full and powerful moon hung low in the sky. Had they believed, they would have known that great powers had conspired to connect them forever in the moments that their eyes first met. They could not see that they were held, suspended from cosmic puppet strings, that something divine determined their first meeting, designed their lives, made them fall in love. In spite of the fact that they couldn't see it, they could feel it and eventually their hearts would be able to name it. They would call it destiny.

8

She'd introduced herself as Chris but Joe decided he preferred her full name, Christianna. It was a somewhat unusual name, simultaneously spiritual and earthy. He liked the way it sounded in his mind. It flowed through his consciousness as if it were a thought that belonged there, that was supposed to have been spoken by him at some point in his life, meant to flow through his lips and hang in the air a moment, sweet, uncommon, special.

"Let's go Christianna," her name on his lips as sweet as it had sounded in his mind. Recoiling at his use of her full name, she hesitated for a moment then felt unexpected pleasure. For the first time in her life, her name sounded beautiful. It *was* a beautiful name when not being spoken in her mother's or Greg's disapproving voice.

Joe led her around the outside of the house hoping to leave unseen. He seemed to have sonar as he manoeuvred through the fog. Chris picked up her red leather jacket from the deck along the way. The fog hid them until they reached the front and she was struggling with the helmet straps when her cousin David appeared, his eyes full of concern.

"Come on," he pleaded. "P'raps you'll work things out with Greg." David regretted the words once they were out. He didn't want her with that asshole either. But he was scared of what Kennedy would do to her if he heard she had run off with Joe Indigo.

"He's an idiot," Chris said, shocked that he cared so little about the fact that he'd almost killed her with a beer bottle earlier.

"What, I'm not good enough for your cousin, buddy?" Joe interjected in a hard tone moving closer to David. He realised he likely wasn't and it made him defensive.

"No, man, not that at all, but Kennedy will kill her if he finds out," David *was* concerned for his cousin's safety but the truth was that although Joe was his friend he didn't like this. Joe was a womanizer and Dave had always been protective of Christianna. Now here was Joe putting her in greater danger just because he wanted her. Chris was so pretty and smart and deserved so much better. He liked Joe, he was his friend, but he was using her and it rankled. David also knew Joe could kill him with his little finger and wisely, he stepped back and watched helplessly as she climbed on the large bike behind Joe Indigo and he chewed his lip as the Harley roared away with his beloved cousin on the back.

Joe was troubled at David's words. Was she in that much danger? Was he endangering her even more by taking her away tonight? He'd have to make sure that wasn't the case. He pulled the bike out of the driveway, well aware of the woman on the back who leaned against him as though she belonged there.

The fog held the street in its grip, revealing it as a narrow pathway unfolding like a dull carpet, rolling out to welcome them. The street lamps had an eerie yellow glow and Chris held him tightly relaxing into the seat of the motorcycle once she decided she was not afraid.

Christianna's hands dropped eventually to his thighs and became mesmerized by the taut denim jeans he wore. She stroked along them, feeling absently, enjoying the texture against her fingers. Chris had no concern for how much she was distracting her driver.

Joe steered slowly through the blinding fog, forgetting David. His body pushed against her hands. He concentrated on his driving but all that was male in him wanted to pull over in an isolated spot and take her right then and there on the motorcycle. He cursed his decision not to when they reached their destination.

"Shit," he said pulling the bike into a parking space. There was a light on in the third floor apartment window. The guys were home.

"Watch the exhaust," he warned then. "Don't burn those sexy legs." His grin flashed as she carefully dismounted. They took off their helmets and he took her hand and led her across the parking lot.

The apartment building was dark brown and disappointed. Cloaked in fog it reminded Chris of a grand duchess who has fallen in the world. The former grandeur of the once magnificent home was still visible in its ornate cornices. But its ghosts were unmotivated to haunt and the tenants were equally unmotivated to care.

The development company that had converted this beautiful old home into haphazard units, forced by statute to install a herring-bone pattern of fire escapes from each apartment to the ground, destroyed any hope for the return of the duchess to her past glory. But, ever a lady, she welcomed them warmly.

The buzz of acid and beer hummed in the eyes of the 5 guys and Chris and Joe quickly joined them. The smell of weed from the balcony was strong and familiar and lingered in the apartment although the door remained closed. They were soon enveloped in a wrapping of chemical pleasure.

Chris sat on his knee though there were other seats. No one seemed surprised to see her there. She was a little prettier than Joe's usual girls and the guys were interested in her.

"When did you meet?" The big guy with laughing bloodshot eyes asked.

"Half an hour ago." Joe answered with a wink and a glance at his watch. Chris giggled at the truth of it.

"How?" This question was asked by a guy she knew a little and who knew Greg as well. He wouldn't tell though, Joe had warned him.

"I stole her." Joe Indigo grinned at this truth.

"I let him," Chris said and his eyes met hers and held. Her intellectual side screamed that this was a one night stand and she wasn't supposed to become attached. There was a danger here she hadn't considered before beyond Greg's anger. She *liked* Joe Indigo.

As the party wound down the guys left the apartment to find women or drifted off to couches and pass out. The unwritten code that says that whoever has the girl gets the room applied so it was the natural course of things that Christianna and Joe ended up in that dingy bedroom decorated only by the ambient glow of new lust.

The lights were still on when he undressed her. She stared at his body when he undressed himself. He was muscled, lean and dark. Though the details of the night were blurred and the memories somewhat vague the impression was permanent.

In later years they would remember things differently. Christianna remembered his starving eyes and male strength. Joe remembered her breasts in his hands and the fading bruises he discovered on her tender flesh that made him wince in anger and kiss them as a mother might kiss a child's hurt. Both remembered that they had thoroughly enjoyed each other, touching, tasting, teasing and stimulating.

Hours passed. They would doze and resume where they had left off. Booze hazed and bold they experimented and sampled and tasted a new vintage and found it was exactly to their taste. It was a night that lasted forever and ended too soon. It was a night that was a beginning and an end for both of them though they didn't know it as they laid there curled together in spite of the humidity and heat that came with the dissipating fog. As their bodies grew to know each other their spirits rejoiced in a reunion that their minds were unaware of and when the hot sun rose in the morning, it was to an earth that existed exactly as it was supposed to while they lay in their peaceful and destined embrace.

9

In a stupor of dehydration and morning breath Christianna made her way to the clothes that were scattered around. She tiptoed out to the bathroom in the dawning light. The cloudy mirror revealed no bruises other than the ones that had already existed. It was good to look for bruises for a different reason.

I look like a woman who has been thoroughly fucked. Chris grinned at the thought and it hurt. She pushed gently on a plum-coloured spot on her lower lip loving the tenderness of it. Her first *love* wound. Her eyes sparkled with a glint she hadn't seen in a long time. It was happiness.

Chris dabbed at the smudged mascara around her eyes with a piece of dampened toilet paper. A one-night stand, cheating on her fiancé, she was officially a fallen woman, though her parents had already branded her that when she ran off after graduation with Greg. She imagined a scarlet letter sewn to the front of her tank top and smiled.

Make it an F for fucked she thought feeling decadent and rebellious. She checked for shame and found it lacking. Maybe she had some sociopathic tendencies that prevented her from feeling remorse. But then, would a sociopath even check for shame? Were there degrees of hell? Would the flames burn hotter for a Jezebel than a simple non-believer? She was already lost by her parents' standards for living with Greg before the actual marriage.

Of course she could always ask for forgiveness. The thought made her smile. She didn't remotely feel repentant.

She'd managed to take out her contacts in the blur of her drugged-out daze the previous night. She popped the case opened and inserted them back into her eyes, left side first as usual. Nothing changed in minutia yet everything had somehow changed.

Chris stared at the young woman in the mirror and wished for a toothbrush. She made do with her finger and some toothpaste. A pony tail band from her purse tamed the wild curly mess that was her hair. She tiptoed back. Sneaking into the bed beside the man, Chris stared at him.

Joe's skin was smooth and dark except for some acne scars from his teen years along his cheek and the shadow of whiskers sprinkled along his square jaw. His long, shiny dark hair was wild on the pillow. He smelled good in a salt-earth way. The skin on his face was oily in places, shiny with it and his features indicated some native background. She carefully settled into the crook of his arm but her caution was wasted. He stirred and became aware. He pulled her closer speaking only one word as he held her in his strong, now familiar, arms.

"Wicked," he whispered, the heart-stopping grin touching his lips just before he kissed her. Christianna smiled at him and agreed with her eyes and then drifted again into a light sleep in the dawn of the new day.

The sun lifted itself over the earth to shine hot rays on the couple through the dirty window with its cracked pane held together with a wide strip of greying masking tape. But even in these dingy and dirty surroundings, there was great beauty in the new love that was dawning, hot and as breathtakingly common as the sunrise.

10

"Bring me something to wear," Christianna said into the phone. Joe was sprawled on the bed beside her grinning and stroking her thigh. She rubbed her eye where her contacts had irritated it. She regretted putting them back in and then falling asleep again.

Grabbing the phone from her, he spoke into it, "bring her something sexy," and she swatted him. He wrapped her in his other arm and held her as he spoke to April. His eyes twinkled with a blue light as he spoke into the phone.

"Tell her to bring me some make up," Chris asked, fascinated by those eyes. They were a dark brown yet there was blue in their depths that flickered in the light of the early morning. She forgot she was staring until he looked away. He finished the phone call and then grabbed her, unnerved. Could she see straight to his soul? He kissed her and that same soul stirred along with his body and he pulled back and peered into her blue eyes to see if he could see into hers. She smiled at him. Unnerved he went back to what was familiar, kissing her again. He was astonished at how much he wanted her, not understanding yet. It was new and intense and he was determined to enjoy every moment.

Still dripping, wrapped in a large towel Joe had provided, Chris came out of the bathroom. April was already there with her things. Chris thanked her, wondering how fast she'd driven as she grabbed them and scooted back to the bathroom, avoiding Joe who tried to yank the towel off as she walked by.

His grin turned her heart to molten lava. She chided herself for being smitten with him as she dressed. This was a one night stand and she had to get over this infatuation. He was a guy on the make and she was the *girl de jour*. It needed to be enough.

She changed into the clean mini skirt and tank top April had brought and slipped into the clean blue cotton bikini underwear with a satisfied sigh. Her legs were smooth from shaving them with Joe's razor and they were soft and tanned. She knew Joe liked them by the way he kept touching them. She smiled as she applied a bit of makeup, blending it near her bruised lip before going back out to the kitchen.

Joe was sitting on the kitchen counter and April stood there across from him leaning against the refrigerator. She looked at him with obvious adoration and Christianna understood. She was relieved it wasn't just her who found him so incredible. She was starting to feel like a groupie hanging outside of David Lee Roth's trailer. Chris stood back, watching, her big blue eyes alight with curiosity.

Joe wore only his jeans and he was bowed forward, his back against the lower edge of the upper cupboard. His body was chiselled but not from working out. He was naturally fit and strong, sitting on the counter, smoking a cigarette, long black hair tousled, jet eyes glinting, grin threatening.

He laid his cigarette on an empty plate and picked up the coffee cup in front of him and held it out. Chris took it, looking into the cup. She sipped and recoiled from the flavour. It was instant, yuck, but still, caffeine. She sipped again and then looked up into his eyes, searching for the blue mystery she'd seen earlier that morning.

He picked up the cigarette, lit a second with it and handed the new one to her. He had a delicate, almost feminine way of holding objects that was at odds with his entirely masculine essence. She thanked him and took a long drag.

"Greg came back," April told them. "He went ballistic when David said you were gone, he wanted to find Joe and kill him with his bare hands he said."

Chris laughed, tossing her head back and April joined her, nodding.

"I know eh?" April said shaking her head with a grin.

"Is he a fighter?" Joe asked and they shook their heads no.

"That's why it was so funny."

"Only with me." There was a flash of pain in Christianna's eyes. She sipped her coffee again wishing she hadn't said that. It was as weak as this horrible brew.

"I had no idea he was like that." April said in a soft voice. She'd thought Greg odd but violence hadn't been on her radar.

"Mostly he's controlling but he can't handle the drugs and booze and gets like it after he drinks, perfect when he's sober." Chris stopped. He was too perfect but that was a bit hard to explain.

The cigarette trembled in her hand as she brought it to her lips. The nicotine did nothing to wash away the sudden fear that enveloped her. In the magic of the previous night with Joe, the buzz of the alcohol and half a hit of acid she'd taken, she had been able to disregard the fact that Greg was violent and dangerous. He was enraged and rightfully so this time.

"Are you going back?" April asked. Joe was watching this exchange between the women. He saw the fear cross Christianna's pretty face and immediately sensed that it was all coming at her now, in the sober light of day. He was overwhelmed by an urge to pull her close and reassure her.

"I have to go back at some point." Chris replied looking at Joe and there it was again, confirmed in her eyes. The fear that he'd only caught the edge of the night before, and he knew she was terrified at the thought.

"You tell him if he touches her I'll fucking kill him." Joe said in a cold quiet voice to April. "You tell him that for me?" His voice held the tension of cold hard steel. April was still at his words. She would have David tell him. He'd believe David over her. She also didn't want to get in the middle of this. She wasn't sure for a moment who was more dangerous, Greg Kennedy or Joe Indigo and she didn't want to get caught in the crossfire finding out.

"I'll have David let him know." She said nodding. "But I'm not sure it'll be enough."

Joe's eyes narrowed and his lips sealed in a line. He searched April's face. April started at the hardness she saw and knew that Greg was now the one in danger instead of Chris. She had shifted things with her observation and it would cause Joe to react. She tried to retract her words, not wanting the responsibility.

"He knows about you now Joe, David told him about you, I don't think he'll kick up too much fuss and David won't side with him because he's buddies with both of you so he'd pretty much be on his own, I think Chris'll be safe."

Joe caught a hesitation in April's voice. She couldn't be positive and neither could he.

Christianna watched him in wonder. Would he hurt Greg? She was torn between hoping he would and knowing it was wrong. Either way, he had a quality that she admired. He was a man who made decisions and followed through. He was a man who took care of what had to be taken care of. He had violent tendencies though he was as gentle as a kitten with her but the violence wasn't directed by cruelty or possessiveness but by a fierce need to protect those who were in danger. He would kill for what he believed in and she realised that without a doubt, he'd die for it as well.

When the door closed behind April, Joe's black eyes narrowed and looked into Christianna's blue ones. The fear he had seen earlier had dissipated, and instead there was a new look. It wasn't the fawning adoration he saw in the eyes of many girls, that he'd seen in April's eyes as she worked to stop staring at his bare chest while she talked to him. This look was new and unfamiliar.

He took a sip of the vile coffee in his hand and put out his cigarette just as the realisation hit him. The look that Christianna was giving him was something he didn't see very often from the girls he dated, even the ones he rescued. It wasn't hero worship or infatuation or even gratitude. She was looking at him with something that was akin to respect and admiration. He wasn't sure what to make of it but he decided he liked it. He only wondered what he had done to deserve it.

11

After April left, Christianna moved to stand in front of him where he sat on the counter. She looked up into his granite eyes. She was not afraid of his anger. He kissed her, looking into her eyes until their lips met. When he pulled back the anger was gone, dissolved in the magic of the kiss. She wondered if he planned these things or was he unintentionally sexy and romantic. She sensed a depth in him that was as rare as the blue flecks that flashed from the depths of his ebony eyes. She was compelled to know more about Joe Indigo.

"I had a girlfriend once." He said surprised at his own words. "I thought she was the love of my life."

"Yeah, I know," she replied. His eyes widened. How would she know this?

"You're famous." Chris grinned adding. "I spent a lot of time at David's in Angell's Cove when I was a kid. I know Terri so when I heard your name…" She shrugged. Everybody knew each other in small towns.

"Tricky," he poked her ribs and she wriggled and laughed.

"What were you going to say?" She held his hands trying to stop the tickling, enjoying the brush of the soft dark hair on them against her palms when he stopped.

"I loved her, it didn't work out, I wasn't good enough for her," he said exactly what he was thinking.

"Why are you telling *me*?" Her eyebrows went up.

"I'm not good enough for you either," he said soberly.

"You're bad," Chris agreed with a serious nod, teasing him.

"No seriously, don't go falling in love with me or anything." He thought he should warn her and realised it was a bit self important to do so. He'd never warned a girl away before.

"Ok well don't you go falling in love with me either," she joked "Because I'm fantastic and it's going to be hard for you to resist" She preened and moved the hands she had stilled with her own up to her breasts covering them with his large, brown ones.

He tossed his head back and laughed a deep delighted sound that thrilled Christianna.

"You know what, I just might," he joked and he leaned forward and kissed her gently still holding her breasts in his hands.

He jumped off the counter.

"Never mind the coffee, let's go!" He pulled her along by the hand.

"I need coffee or I'll commit murder," she grumbled pulling her hand away. Chris picked up and held her cup against her chest.

"Then let's go to Tim's," he said and she quickly put the cup down and agreed. She grabbed her jacket, though it felt too hot to wear , she wouldn't ride on the bike without it. He grabbed his leather jacket as well and hung it over his shoulder with one finger as they headed out the door, helmets in hand.

She followed him to the motorcycle, leaving behind the Duchess. The early morning sun had burnt the fog from her shoulders, and the old building appeared to have reclaimed some of her former beauty. She did not appear quite as forlorn to Christianna as she mounted the motorcycle. Excitement rushed through Christianna stronger than any drug she had ever experimented with. How could going to the Tim Horton's be this exciting?

Being with Joe was like standing in the centre of a storm. The clouds hovered, the thunder shouted and the lightening burned and sizzled through her body, charging it with an irregular pattern that confused and excited her all at once. But peeking through, in that grin that threatened the corner of this mouth, was the bright beautiful sunshine. Christianna was discovering that the sunshine that comes with the storm is the hottest.

Humidity in Ontario in the summer is a barricade. It holds people inside. Desperate for relief, they huddle in malls and air-conditioned homes and restaurants. A lucky few have pools or time for beach trips. Still others sit in Tim Horton's and drink their hot coffee and complain about the heat outside.

Fairway Road, one of Kitchener, Ontario's busiest uptown arteries, was buzzing with mindless traffic, loud with humanity and its toys as they walked into the parking lot. Chris hung out by the motorcycle as Joe made his phone calls on the bell phone in the booth near the McDonald's next door. He was intense. The sweat on her forehead beaded and trickled down her body as the temperatures rose with the ticking minutes of the day. She looked at the motorcycle longingly. All you needed to fight the humidity was a fast bike to slice into it she'd discovered.

The phone call ended and he came out of the phone booth. He took the helmet off the seat and put it on his head, strapping it expertly. With a quick grin he straddled the bike and Chris followed him. He reached back with his hands and pulled her closer with her thighs and then pulled her arms tight around him.

"Hang on real tight this time," he said. He meant nothing by it. He just liked her arms around him.

Chris felt herself tense at his triggering words. She held on to his waist and tightened her legs on the seat. Was he planning on doing some fancy tricks on the bike? He felt her tightening around him and sensed something had shifted. He carefully pulled the bike away merging into traffic as she held him more tightly. He had no idea what he'd done wrong.

She had jolted back in time to a trip with Greg that had the car hurling at a heart-stopping velocity as she screamed and cried for him to stop.

"Hang on really tight this time." He'd said. Her heart remembered his cruel laughter and then his anger when she was still shaking after it was over. She needed to trust him he had told her with angry eyes. He would never hurt her. And she had wanted to believe him but her heart still beat at an outrageous speed, frantically sending her the message that he couldn't be trusted. She should have listened to it.

She knew that Joe was a good driver. He'd been careful this morning. But those two words made her nervous in light of her experience in the past. She only wore a leather jacket and a mini skirt and the stories she had heard stories of terrible scarring from a skid on asphalt came to her. What if he was warning her as Greg had been?

Joe handled the machine with precision and caution, being more careful than earlier. He always took care when he had a passenger on board. He'd had a spill once and it had made him realise the vulnerability of the motorcycle rider. He wanted this pretty girl with the gorgeous legs in one piece. He liked the feel of her so close to him and could feel the heat from her on his back. It excited him and somehow, it comforted him too. She had been afraid, he could sense it but now he felt her soften behind him, relaxing her grip on the bike and on him. Then she leaned her head against his back for a second and he knew she trusted him to take care of her. He smiled at the gesture, moved.

They pulled up to the end of Wilson Avenue that led into the dead end that was Homer Watson Park. It was a patch of isolated woods near the Grand River. It was rough with only some rustic picnic tables and some trails. A couple dressed in matching track suits walked their unleashed Jack Russell along the path, heading out of the park as Chris and Joe rode in. The dog took off at a manic pace, yipping and digging at the base of an old tree.

Joe pulled the bike to a stop and killed the engine. He pulled off his helmet and helped Christianna dismount, then helped her take hers off. They kissed and held hands as they walked. It was lush and slightly cooler in the canopy of trees that overhung the forest path.

"Queers come here." Joe said speaking the thought that popped into his head.

"What the fuck are you talking about?" Christianna laughed at his random statement.

"This is where queers come to meet other queers," he repeated grinning.

"And how do you know this?" She asked. "First hand experience?" She squealed as the flat of his hand connected with her ass.

He laughed and said, "That's what I heard b'y, just sayin', I thought you'd like to know in case we suddenly come across one...or two."

"So we're not the usual couple to be walking here?" She said grinning. "We might get jumped and beat up?"

"Or redecorated," he joked again and then pulled her around to the front of him. He put his arms around her back and kissed her hard. His hands slipped down to the ass he'd just smacked and pulled her even closer until she could feel what he had in mind.

There was a clearing in the distance off the path, just behind a cluster of trees. It was a perfect hiding place. She skipped over to the spot happily pulling him along, eager and excited.

"I'm gonna get lay-ayed," she sang and her words brought that brilliant light into his onyx eyes yet again. It was a deep purple-blue that flashed suddenly from the depths of his brown-black eyes. He delighted in her teasing and flirting and she loved to see the grin, to engage that sparkle in his eyes and to hear the laugh that burst from him like a song, and to gain it, she only had to be her own silly self. It was powerful.

There was heat and intensity and enjoyment and the excitement of being in nature. Chris was wild and wanton and alive. She never wanted it to end. Hands searched and lips parted and it was all rough and desperate and real. The lovers connected in a way that was new for them both and he was more surprised than she was at the magic of it all. She still believed in romance and love, he had less confidence that it existed.

They were two spirits with bodies enjoying themselves without a thought of anything beyond the very moment they were in. It was flawed and it was perfect. This paradox mirrored every moment and every aspect of the love that was growing unacknowledged between Joe Indigo and Christianna Cormack.

She followed him into each moment and spent it with a sense of peace she only later appreciated. She had always had to plan, would eventually have to plan every step again, for her safety, for her future. In the past she couldn't live in the moment because it usually held too much pain. With Joe it held only pleasure and she revelled in it. They rode the motorcycle again back to the apartment building where they had spent the night and parked it in the parking lot. She didn't know where they would go now, he didn't either. They both knew wherever they went it would be perfect.

13

"Let's go for a walk." Joe kissed her on the bruise he'd noticed on her lower lip that wouldn't have worried him if he hadn't seen the other purplish and yellow marks on her tender skin the night before. He felt guilty for adding to that collection, no matter how it came to be.

It was mid-afternoon the following day and their time was growing short. She nodded an affirmative. They walked down the narrowing street that led out of the east end of the city. The apartment was on the edge of town and a short walk, thirty minutes or so, led to lush green farmland. The north side of the road had a row of trees and they walked on that side taking advantage of the shade the large mature maples offered.

About fifteen minutes into their stroll a family of ducks crossed the road in front of them and Christianna and Joe watched quietly. Mommy duck was leading her babies safely to the brook that trickled in a haphazard way perpendicular to the street at first and then parallel until it ran towards a culvert and out the other side. The traffic lulled and Chris and Joe then crossed to walk on the same side as the creek, looking at the farm in the distance. They followed the railway tracks along and the hot sun shone on them again then. Joe took his shirt off and tucked it in his pocket.

"Wish I could do that," Christianna stared at his bare chest.

"Do it!" Joe teased pulling at her shirt. She tried to push his hands away, laughing.

"Hey, wait, what's that?" Joe pointed across the field suddenly distracted.

"What? I don't see anything," she pulled off her sunglasses to squint. Perhaps she was looking the wrong way. Her blue eyes watered in the sun and she popped her glasses back on.

"Come on!" Joe said pulling her hand and laughing. "I see something!" And she was pulled along towards something tempting him in the distance.

The creek bubbled and flowed between them and their destination and they found a narrow spot and jumped it landing on the mucky opposite side of the creek. Chris felt wetness seep through her Adidas sneakers and grimaced.

Mama duck and her babies looked at them and continued with the swimming lesson, the baby ducks diving until just their tail feathers stuck out of the water in a comical way. Then they bobbed back up, one after another showing off their talent at this new skill.

Christianna followed Joe across a field towards a bush area. She still couldn't see what they were heading towards but she followed anyway. Mosquitoes buzzed in the tall grass, birds chirped their summer songs and crickets sang harmony, as they walked quickly toward a vision only he held.

Then she saw it. And he saw her see it. He had known immediately what it was. He'd built one as a boy. He was as excited as if he *was* ten again and thrilled at the delight in her eyes when she spotted it high in the grove of trees.

The faded structure sat in the branches of one particularly impressive Maple. A canopy of leaves hung over the tree house protecting it from the elements. It was constructed of a faded greying lumber but the shingles on the roof were intact and the little two by four steps leading up one side of the tree to the tree house were firmly attached. The windows were round, like portholes and the builders were obviously trying to build themselves a ship in the sky.

"Whoa, cool!" The little girl smile that always hovered near the surface was brilliant. Her unfulfilled dreams of secret clubhouses and hidden forts tickled at her subconscious. Joe's face was soft and bright. He'd had the same response as she did when he had first seen it. He climbed up the steps and turned to look out of the opening reaching his hand out to help her. He pulled her up and in on top of him, landing them both hard on the floor of this ship in the trees with a thud. Their laughter rang through the small building and up through the rustling leaves of the trees where it was contained in the denseness of the leaves and branches. She playfully smacked his chest, feeling his hard body underneath her as she lay on top of him on the floor.

The tone of the laugh changed as they sobered a bit and she reached down to kiss him. One hand came up behind her head and held her there, kissing her back with a force that left her breathless with sudden and surprising need. She pulled at the belt of his tight jeans, desperate for him. He moved her shirt up and looked at her for a long moment and then his mouth followed the path of his eyes.

She pulled away briefly and pulled off her tank top and bra in one movement. She giggled at the look on his face. Pleasure and happiness and fun lay in those eyes as they moved towards their goal, taking their time, no desperation, playful, hot and excited yet unhurried. The ship rocked in the trees and withstood the voyage they were on. Then they held each other after hot, sweaty and happy.

"Nice place you got here," she joked stroking one finger down the middle of his chest.

"Our place," he said."This is our place."

He caressed her breasts, his eyes watching the movement of his hands, studying what they were doing and her body's response to it.

"Where did you come from?" He was baffled yet again by his attachment to her.

"Me mudder," she joked.

"Thank her for me," he responded leaning his head down. "You're the best." Joe said a moment later.

"Flattery will get you very lucky," Chris marvled at how comfortable she was with him.

His eyes often laughed before his lips.

"You're a lot of fun, I like fun."

"Up until you came along I thought I didn't like sex much."

"Well I can't say that exactly," he replied looking deep into her eyes. "But I certainly am enjoying this."

The heat, the hard wooden boards underneath her back and then her knees, the sexy hard man with the sparkling eyes and evil grin, the smell of nature, the sounds of the orchestra of birds that sang their love song that day as they made love in the tree house that he called "their place" was the memory she most went to when she thought of him in later years. It was for him as well.

Joe pulled on his jeans and went back to sit next to her. She was ruffled and pretty and he liked how she looked after they finished having sex. She was the prettiest girl he'd ever seen. He looked away and blinked, embarrassed to be so taken with her. The opposite wall was papered with comic book pages. He recognised a few from his childhood. His memories were well hidden and the comics were a reminder of a childhood that had few pleasant ones.

"Hey, what is this?" She grabbed a small book off the floor where it had dropped.

"What?"

"This book," she held it up, waving it before his face.

"It's mine," Joe said grabbing for it but she avoided his grasp and opened the pages.

"You read *poetry*?"

"Kinda," Joe was embarrassed to admit it.

"Kinda? I love poetry, *I* write it."

"My Aunt gave it to me," he admitted reluctantly, watching her leaf through the pages of his most treasured possession. He hated for anyone else to have it. He could see himself as a young boy trying not to cry as the circle of boys tossed his beloved book of poetry back and forth between them. Their shout and taunts haunted him still. He had snatched it back though and he'd ambushed the ring leader alone later on and had his revenge on him.

The words **The Little Book of Poetry** were engraved in the leather cover, the gold of the letters peeling off. It was old, well worn, well loved. The leather cover was softened by time and handling. It was one of those created by book stores, a collection of various poems by the *Great Poets* as they were described on the inside pages. The images painted by the words did not lose their meaning on that cheap paper.

"Your aunt?" Christianna was intrigued.

"Yeah, she was all mushy and stuff," he laughed it off, still embarrassed.

"Why did she give it to *you*?" She recalled a little red copy of the New Testament she'd had as a girl. This book reminded her of that one in its size and shape. She opened it to see its tiny lettering, gently, with reverence, turning the pages.

"My aunt, my father's sister was an English teacher but she got sick, started to go blind so she stayed with us. She read everything she could get her hands on. Then I read to her when she couldn't see. Probably wouldn't have finished high school if she hadn't pushed me to, she wanted me to go on, you know, to University."

He thought of the inscription the same time that Christianna read it. *For you and your grand love.*

"You loved her a lot?" Chris flipped through the yellowing pages, fascinated.

Joe felt a tightening in his throat. No one had ever acknowledged the sense of loss he'd felt as a young man when she'd passed away. He'd acted cool and tough but he'd missed her and their conversations. The family had said it was for the best, she was suffering, but he'd never seen her suffer, she'd read him the words in her books, with no pain in her voice, then later, she'd listen as he read the books.

"Yeah, she was special." His voice caught.

"She died?" Chris couldn't help but wonder what the inscription meant. Who was his grand love?

"Yeah, the summer after I finished school. I was signed up for university but after that..." His voice trailed. Her death had robbed him of all ambition. The grieving was difficult enough, keeping that grieving a secret was excruciating. He'd turned the pain outward becoming Joe "Go", the bad boy.

"Read me one." Chris requested. She waited with expectation on her face. She had never met a man who read poetry, and here was this dark, wild, mysterious, hard-looking man who carried a book of poetry in his back pocket. It was intriguing. She handed his book back to him, her fingers brushing his.

His downcast eyes looked into hers and met her bright and trusting blue ones and saw the eager anticipation that brightened them. If *she* wanted to share this with him he couldn't refuse her. He found a favourite reading it in his deep, masculine voice with its east coast dialect.

She dwelt among the untrodden ways
Beside the springs of Dove,
A Maid whom there were none to praise
And very few to love:

A violet by a mossy stone
Half hidden from the eye!
--Fair as a star, when only one
Is shining in the sky.

She lived unknown, and few could know
When Lucy ceased to be;
But she is in her grave, and, oh,
The difference to me!

"Wow, oh my," her eyes were shining when he looked up from the book. "But so sad."

"I wonder who Lucy was," he said. "It makes me think, once we're gone, who will remember us. If I died now, I'd be like Lucy, and who would it make a difference to?" his accented voice drifted off in the wonder of the question.

"Me," she answered without embarrassment.

He searched her eyes and saw the bold truth in there.

"Girls love poetry," she said breaking the spell, trying to lighten the mood.

"Ya think? Do you think I'd have had as many women as I've had if I wasn't they way I am? They like the bad boy not the poet," his voice was light but he was deeply serious.

"You would have had different women," she argued.

"Women like you?" He asked.

"Nah, I'm one of a kind," she laughed.

"I think you are," he agreed and then after a thought. "Do you think *you're* like most women?"

She hesitated before answering, remembering how different she'd always felt from other girls her age. Some of it had been because of her isolation but much of it was her personality.

"No, I don't think I am but I've spent a lot of time trying to be," she confessed. It had led her to Greg.

"Yeah, well time to stop, time to be who you are," he nodded thinking she was already the most authentic person he'd ever met.

"You too?" She requested. He didn't answer.

"Read me another one?" Chris asked him but he closed the book.

"You said you write poetry? I read you one, you have to write me one to answer it, it's only fair." He declared the laughter back in his voice.

"That's not *fair*," she lamented. "I can't write like that!"

"You don't have to write like that, just write like you write."

"Maybe I'll write one for next time I see you," she said wondering if the words would come to describe what she wanted to say to him.

The wind whistled through the bows of the tree that held their ship and they floated on its waves and she was given the pledge nature makes, that in her arms, the right words would come. Chris didn't know if she would ever see him again but there seemed to be a promise in the air, rocking the trees, rocking the lovers. Christianna didn't know when or how but knew that somehow, they would be together again and she would be given the opportunity to read words to him, if she could find ones that fit her emotions.

14

They left the tree house in the early moments before twilight and walked back to the motorcycle. The ducks no longer swam in the creek as they crossed over it. The darkening afternoon held magic and love and poetry suspended next to the sun in the sky.

They both avoided the fact that she had to go home and he had to leave town. Joe was driving his motorcycle to Newfoundland and catching the ferry to Port aux Basques. It had always been the plan. He also had a girlfriend, though he didn't mention that but she knew.

Joee suggested they go to visit his sister. She was happy to go along if only to delay the inevitable return to the home she shared with Greg and her real life there. Chris was also afraid. She tucked the fear into the back of her mind as casually as she tucked a wild strand of hair behind her ear.

The motorcycle vibrated under her as she sat on the back, behind Joe. They whizzed through streets and around corners, stopping at red lights until they came to a halt in a driveway. Her thoughts were jarred to reality in front of a low, red bungalow. His sister's home was set back from the street in a nice neighbourhood of mature trees and well manicured lawns. A dark haired woman worked in an immaculate brick garden beside a grey concrete porch.

"Dar," Joe called and the woman glanced behind her, having not responded at all to the sound of a motorcycle in her driveway"

"Tom's in the house," she said, going back to her gardening, anxious to finish before dark.

"I have someone for you to meet, Dar." Joe said and this time his sister stopped and turned around.

"Jesus, why didn't you say so," the woman laughed heartily and got up." I wouldn't 'ave let her look at me arse all this time."

Her eyes held the same glint in their dark brown depths as her brother's and she looked like an older, feminine version of him.

She didn't shake hands but said, "nice to meet you," and Chris smiled and responded in kind.

"You don't mind *me* looking at your arse though." Joe joked with his sister.

"*You* can kiss me arse," she retorted with a grin. "You gonna tell me her name?"

"Chris," she volunteered herself. "Nice garden, are you planting roses?"

Dar nodded to the bushes on the lawn. "Yeah, these are supposed to be a real good smell," she said.

"I love roses," was Chris's reply. " That's a great place to plant them because when you sit out on the porch and they bloom you'll be able to smell them."

"See? That's what I was t'inkin', Tom wanted me to put them in the back but I want to smell 'em. You want a drink? I'll finish here, you go inside with Joe and I'll be there in a minute, Joe, go get her a beer or somethin'."

"Yes ma'am," Joe said. "Can I have one too?"

"I s'pose," his sister said. "Seein' who you are an' all."

The beer was cold and Tom flirted openly with her.

"Jesus, wa's you doin' wi' a ugly t'ing like dis?" He asked her with a nod and a wink that made her think of home.

"Got a bit desperate," she said going along with him. "Thought I'd slum it out a bit."

"Hey, I'm a prince and you know it," Joe laughed as he snatched back the beer he'd just given Chris.

"You're Prince friggin' Charming then," she gave up easily and reclaimed the frosty brown bottle from his hand with a grin.

"So how did you meet?" Dar asked coming in the door.

"I stole her." Joe answered with his cheeky grin.

"You gonna put her back after?" Tom asked swigging his beer.

"Yeah, tonight." Joe said, and found his joke wasn't as funny as it had been.

"Well keep her then," Dar said responding to his expression rather than his words.

"Come on m' love, let me show you something," and she pulled Chris into the living room. She pointed to a framed photograph on the wall.

"See this kid? Joe was four 'ere." She pointed to an eight by ten picture. The frame was brass coloured plastic and the boy in the picture was grinning, the eyes alight with a familiar sparkle.

"What are you showing her Dar?" Joe yelled from the kitchen.

"None of your friggin' business," his sister yelled back, "go back to your bullshit and mind your own beeswax."

"You're special," she turned to Chris. Her eyes were sharp, yet warm.

"Why do you say that?" Chris asked, startled by this flattery.

"First time ever since he's been coming here this boy brought a girl. I'm 6 years older than him 'n' he's been staying here with me since he moved up to the mainland. He's had more girls than I can count, hard case this feller." She nodded at the picture of the four year old Joe.

"He's some cute hey," she said as though he were still her 4 year old brother. "Hard case Joe is but best guy in the world and I think a good woman would straighten him up good."

Chris took a large swallow of the cold beer licking her lips with a nervous flick of her tongue.

"I never seen him with a girl before, and he's had a lot. It's nice to see, you're special or he wouldn't have brought you here."

"I've only known him a couple of days," Chris wanted to believe her and it was disturbing.

"I saw Tom at a dance and bam, that was it, two days later I wrote in my diary that I was gonna marry him whether he liked it or not," her eyes twinkled. "He liked it."

"Maybe I am special," she agreed laughing at Dar's story. "I told him I was fantastic so if he believes me I'm in big trouble."

"You fall in love with my brother you're in big trouble anyways, you can't just love him a little bit you know, it's one or the other, hate him or love him, that's how my brother is, I think you love him."

"Well now, I don't know that it's gone that far yet." Chris squirmed a bit.

"Tell me Dar," Christianna said after a moment, still staring at the picture. "If I am how much danger am I in?"

"Lots and lots," Dar's laugh was a hearty feminine version of her brother's. "But I think he's in bigger danger." She nodded again towards the picture of the young Joe. "Because he doesn't know and won't admit it, 'cause he's a man but I t'inks he's already half in love with you because you're here." She said with little doubt of her importance in her brother's life.

"Hey, ready to go?" Joe's head poked around the corner. "You finished fillin' her with lies?" He directed this at Dar.

"Yep, all full," she laughed. "She knows everything now." Dar joked.

"Yeah, I'm ready." Chris answered his first question handing him the empty beer bottle.

"Could stay," his sister offered Chris.`

"Gotta get going, stuff to do," Joe answered. "I'm leaving tonight remember?"

"Tonight? I thought tomorrow." Dar asked glancing at Christianna.

"Tonight, after I drop Christianna off." Her full name sounded like an endearment when he said it and Christianna's belly did a little flip. Dar turned to Chris and smiled at the way she was looking at Joe.

"Nice talking to you m' love," she said and wrapped her arms around Chris in a warm hug.

Tom said, "She's a keeper Joe," and turned to her, not getting up from the table. "You could do much better but I hope you don't." He joked and lifted his newly opened beer bottle up to his lips.

"Fuck off," said Joe, his voice light, the ever-present grin visible. He took her hand and led her out the door to the bike.

"I like your sister." Chris remarked as she put on her helmet.

"What did you two talk about?"

"She said she thinks you're falling in love with me."

His hands stopped doing what they were doing with his helmet strap and he reached out to help her with hers. His eyes were dark and the glints of indigo that appeared in their depths twinkled with delight.

"She do, do she?" He was pleased somehow. "What do you think?"

"I think it's too soon but that you're in grave danger." Chris said with mock seriousness.

He kissed her, smiling as he pulled away and finished with her strap. His sister was romantic and foolish, reading all those trashy novels and fawning over Tom like he was some sort of movie star. He'd often envied their obvious closeness though and sensed what they had was what most people wanted, the grand love that their Aunt Mae had spoken of.

He was suddenly overcome by an unfamiliar wave of affection for the pretty girl he'd spent the last two days with. Love, he wasn't sure, but he certainly liked her and had enjoyed his time with her. This would be their last moments. His heart hurt a little at the thought as he mounted the motorcycle she already sat on. He knew her heart was hurting too as she laid her head on his back and held him around the waist. He pulled her thighs forward insuring there was no gap between their bodies as they navigated the streets of the city, winding and weaving, taking her back to where she was supposed to go but where neither of them wanted her to be.

15

Joe pulled the motorcycle up at the top of the street on the corner and Christianna dismounted. She pulled off the helmet and tried in vain to fix her flattened hair.

"I don't want to leave." She confessed. Before this new love could even begin it was ending. Whether it is real or not is tested in the long run but at the time, while in the middle of it, new love is strong and real and defies reality and reason. Such was her love of Joe Indigo. Such was Joe's love of her. It had snuck up on them and was powerful even after two short days.

"Well I don't want you to leave either, grab your gear and drive home with me. Do you have a lot of gear?"

"Yeah, I do, and I can't just take off like that much as I wish I could." She thought of her papers in the bank vault. She had a plan. She couldn't leave.

"He lays a hand on you I'll kill him." Joe said.

Chris didn't doubt his sincerity and it scared her. It thrilled her too, and she reassured him she'd be ok.

"I'll call someone if he starts in."

"Let me know."

"I will."

"I'm going," she knew prolonging it wouldn't help. She kissed him then and left him with a quick wave. Chris struggled not to cry as she walked slowly down the hill towards the apartment building where she lived with the man she feared and away from the one she was starting to love. It seemed unnatural, against the universe to do so, but she walked on. The motorcycle behind her revved up and she heard it pull away from the curb and her breath caught with the emptiness she felt as the sound of the motor faded. Fate and timing had their own pace and that she was at the mercy of them.

She turned the key in the knob. Opening the door slowly she waited for the sound of movement. Her heart pounded. In her sadness at leaving Joe, she'd forgotten her fear. Now it was back.

The room was dark and empty. She stepped inside and hit the light switch. The apartment was immaculate and exactly as they had left it the previous Friday. She walked through each room. She was alone. Then she heard a sound outside and walked to the window, a smile on her face. She gave him a quick thumbs-up and Joe rode off, satisfied.

Christianna walked into the bedroom she had shared with Greg and began to remove her belongings, carrying them to the spare room and putting them in the closet there. When she had finished moving her things she walked to the kitchen and made herself a sandwich, carefully cleaning up after herself.

Later, she brought the telephone into her room, plugging it into the yellowed jack in the wall. She would be ready to call 9-11 if necessary. She closed the bedroom door behind her and locked it. She was grateful for the privacy but her fear that he would show up any moment kept her from falling asleep easily.

Being smacked around by someone you love while still hard to escape, being abused by someone you really no longer care about makes it a little easier to make the decision to leave. Chris thought of calling around looking for him for her own peace of mind, but decided against it. He might take it as a sign that she cared. She was safe for now. She jumped when the phone she was cuddling rang noisily.

"Hello," her voice was soft.

"It's David." Her cousin was relieved she was finally home.

"Hey," she said and left him to reply. Her relief that it wasn't Greg made her breathless.

"Joe called this morning," he said getting straight to the point. "And again a few minutes ago. He's threatening to kill me if I don't keep an eye on you and keep you safe."

"Oh," she said with a smile in the dark.

"Yeah," he chuckled. "I told Kennedy to be careful of Joe, that he'll kill him and I think he's afraid enough."

"Good, he should be." She resisted the urge to ask more about Greg.

"He's been hitting you?" David asked though he already knew the answer.

"Yeah." She was quiet.

"Why the fuck didn't you tell me?" His anger at the admission surprised him. The thought of that bastard hurting her wounded him deeply. The fact that she hadn't come to him hurt him as well.

"Are you kidding me? Would you have believed me?"

"Well fuck, yeah, but I didn't know," he replied on cue but guilt nudged him. Would he have believed her?

"Well I thought you wouldn't, everybody goes on and on about what a great guy he is all the time." Chris replied.

"Well my buddy Joe is pretty pissed off about the whole thing and I think Kennedy better be careful," he said with another laugh.

"Yeah, well as long as Greg thinks that I'll be fine." Christianna wanted the conversation to end now.

"Joe's not going to have you," Dave said. "He's a hard case, women everywhere, he's just using you, you know?"

"Gee thanks for your support." Chris responded but the likelihood of that truth hurt and tears stung the corner of her eyes. "I just need enough time to get out and save money for a plane ticket and leave." This was the first time she'd told anyone her plan to leave town.

"You'll go home?" He would miss her but she'd be safer in another province.

"Yeah, that's the plan." Her secrets were slipping out, marbles rolling from a jar, one by one. She wanted to take the words back, close the lid, toss it away.

"Joe has a girlfriend, Sheila, down there, did he tell you that? He didn't, did he? They live together. He won't have you." David needed to impress that upon her. He wanted her away from Joe Indigo almost as much as he wanted her away from Greg Kennedy.

"It has nothing to do with Joe, he just showed up the other night at your place and made me realise I need to move on and get out." His words stung.

"Well I'll make sure Greg leaves you alone," he promised. Dave hoped he could. He wasn't sure Kennedy would listen.

"Where is he?" Christianna thought she'd feel safer if she knew.

"With his buddy from work, Rob, Roger, something like that. I told him he'd better get the hell out of your apartment or Joe was going to kill him" But Greg knew Joe was leaving the province and he'd wait and come after her then. Joe had told him how he'd take care of that and David hadn't wanted to know how.

"Thanks." That explained the empty apartment and why Joe had left her there. He had guaranteed her safety for now.

She replaced the phone on its cradle and then, restless, got up and went out to the kitchen. Six beer bottles, all Labatt's Blue sat in the door, labels facing outward like good little soldiers. Chris made a face and pulled one out. She didn't particularly like it but Greg did, so they always had it. She laughed then and turned the remaining five around, labels in all different directions. Things like that had driven Greg nuts. She giggled at the silliness of her revenge.

While she drank the beer she fixed a second sandwich for her lunch the next day at work.

Chris set the alarm and turned out the light. She tossed in her bed and thought of her plans. Rent had been paid and three paycheques would buy her a plane ticket. Freedom was a short six weeks away.

She drifted into a nightmare of missing university registration and weeping in a hallway, her future doomed. Then she dreamt of a Harley Davidson driving away from her, disappearing into a foggy Kitchener night.

The rumblings of thunder woke her up and the winds played havoc with the empty flower pots on the patio. Chris listened to the howling and roaring and watched the light flash through the little spaces between the window blinds.

She blinked away tears in the dark and tried in vain to forget the deep chocolate eyes with their strange blue lights that had looked at her as though she were a masterpiece, rare, precious and beautiful. She couldn't imagine never looking into those eyes again. It had only been a weekend but she had felt more alive, more in touch with herself than she ever had in her life, in those moments with Joe Indigo. She felt love for him and knew it for what it was though her logical mind scoffed at the idea.

She flicked the light on, its glow cancelling out the flashes of light that foreshadowed the drumming of the thunder. She grabbed a notepad and pen from her nightstand. Her hand and her heart combined as one and started to write. Her heart was master as the words sifted like salt from a shaker to the pages in front of her. While the feelings were fresh she needed to write them down, just in case Mother Nature kept the pledge she'd made in that rustic tree house. The promise that they would see each other, be with each other again, perhaps even be together forever. She let go of the doubts planted by her cousin's earlier words and her own common sense and allowed her soul to fill up with the knowing, the absolute certainty, that Joe Indigo was her fate and she was his.

She pulled the page out of her notebook, pulling off the little bits from the top where the wire had pulled through, then folded it carefully into a small rectangle that fit perfectly in an empty compartment of her wallet. She smiled at the silliness of the romantic gesture. When she saw him again, and she knew she would, she would be prepared.

16

The walkway that ran from the park and split the neighbourhood was quiet and dark. Greg needed to be at his own place and his thoughts were consumed with that. She was there, but it was his. He had fixed it all up, made it perfect, a pristine little home for them and now she was messing it all up. He would have so much work to do, and he knew she wouldn't do it right if at all. She was so messy, leaving glasses around, books upside down on the tables. He liked clean surfaces. Would she ever learn what he was trying to teach her?

Greg Kennedy's mind shuffled through the events of the past few days trying to work them into some sort of order. There was an urgent sense of making things right, making them appear right. He had fucked up, pulling a stunt like that in public. He hadn't gotten any sympathy from David. He had been drinking, and had smoked a toke he had tried to reason. He loved her he had pleaded. It hadn't worked and David had threatened to kill him if he touched her again. He wasn't afraid of David but it rankled that he had believed *her*. Hell the slut had taken off with another guy she'd just met, wasn't that proof that he'd had good reason? He was afraid of *that* bastard though. Greg believed he'd kill him or at least beat him senseless. But Indigo was leaving town and tomorrow he'd go to her work. She would have to come out there and talk to him. She wouldn't want a scene. He counted on that.

The jealousy blended with the bile in his throat and the rage in his heart hardened it and reinforced the paranoia that felt normal to him. They were all against him. Nobody understood. She was a *slut*, she didn't deserve him but he would give her one more chance. He just had to keep control of her. He loved her even if she didn't deserve it. She wasn't perfect, *yet*, but she would get there. His mind formed a plan, a logical pattern to him and it settled his heart. If the other guys wanted to be pussies and let their girlfriend's rule then fine, that wasn't him. He'd straighten her out one way or the other. His fist clenched and unclenched at the thought.

At the party, before he threw the bottle, that guy had been hitting on her. If she couldn't see that then she was just stupid. Greg was a guy himself and he knew that lighting a girl's cigarette was one way of hitting on them. He'd seen that but she wouldn't listen to him when he tried to teach her these things. His only mistake had been to react in public and he should have kept his cool. The alcohol had made him impulsive. Next time he'd take care of it in private. He always had before.

The pathway was darkest at the ends where the trees covered the four corners of the park behind the first houses. They stepped in front of him there.

The taller one, with the shaven head, looked him over from head to toe and then held up a cigarette.

"Light buddy?" He asked.

"Oh yeah, sure. " Greg patted himself down. He pulled out a lighter from his pocket and held it out to the guy.

The little guy had a face of woven steel, hard, textured and cold. He peered at Greg as he would look at dog shit squished to the sole of his shoe.

"You look familiar." The big guy handed back the lighter.

"I don't think so." Greg said. He tried to stay calm.

"You Greg Kennedy?" The little guy asked. His voice was steel too.

"Yeah." Greg regretted the word immediately.

The two men looked at each other and grinned.

The first blow took Greg off the ground with a loud wumph as the air exited his lungs. He gasped for breath, flailing like a drowning man seeking the sunny surface of the water. The second blow took him to the ground.

"Wallet is in my pocket." He whispered with his first exhale after he could breathe again. "Take it," he whimpered painfully.

"You like to hurt women do you?" The little guy asked ignoring the offer. He kicked Joe hard in the kidney.

The big guy bent down and picked Greg up, rammed him against the tree trunk and held him there. He hung like a rag doll, his breath coming quickly.

"No." Greg said but he wasn't a stupid man. They were talking about Christianna and he knew it. This wasn't a robbery. These were Joe Indigo's buddies.

The blow shattered his face, sending blood across in a splatter, hitting the other tree. The moon drifted from the clouds, illuminating the night with an ambient glow from behind the grove of trees, peeking at the violent display below. Exposed in the light, the attackers looked around to see if they were visible. Then the moon slipped back behind another cloud, giving them cover again as though it had decided that this guy wasn't worth saving.

"My buddy says you hit women." The little guy said then. "My old man used to hit my mother." That was all the explanation he felt he needed to provide. His motivation was clear.

"Please." Greg whined. It irritated his attackers.

"We are going to kill you." The little guy spoke again, his metallic voice matter of fact. He left no doubt that he meant it.

Greg felt the wetness down his leg and his heart burned with shame. When they found his body, every one would know that he had pissed his pants. His eyes welled up with tears of shame. He tried to hold them back. His embarrassment was greater than his fear for just a moment.

"I won't touch her again." He promised. He would promise everything. He didn't want to die here, alone, in his urine soaked jeans.

"You won't." The big guy stated. He was sure of it. He reached out and gently wiped a tear from Greg's face and smiled. The tears made him happy.

"I won't see her, call her." Greg promised.

"Ask nicely." The little guy smiled and glanced at his partner.

"Please." Greg was beyond degraded. Desperation motivated his every move. Hope determined his answers.

"I will never contact her again." He reaffirmed hoping that this was what these guys wanted to hear.

The big guy let him go. Greg slid to the ground. They each kicked him and then backed off.

"I don't think he'll do it again." The big bald man said to his friend.

"Not even a phone call." The little man warned him, "and we're watching your place. We'll be watching it as long as she's there."

"I won't." Greg promised. He was going to live. He was almost happy.

They backed up, turned and walked slowly towards the park. Greg heard the crunch of their fading footsteps. He heard a songbird chirping overhead in the tree, a happy tune that mocked his pain and misery. When he heard their motorcycles move away and the roar of their engines fade to nothingness in the night, he pulled himself to his feet.

His body was battered and bruised and his lungs burned. But he could stand. He could walk.

His ribs were broken and the pain was excruciating. He straightened up anyway.

He needed to get back to Roger's place before he got home, he had to shower. He didn't want anyone to know about this.

As Greg walked the sodden denim rubbed against his thighs reminding him of his shame with every step. He could smell the piss and he fought to keep his stomach contents down.

It wasn't until he was home, scrubbed clean in the hottest shower his battered body could tolerate that he remembered his impossible promise to the thugs that had beaten him.

His anger and frustration burned like a hot iron in his chest, more painful that the bruises on his body. But as much as he wanted her, as much as he knew she was the one meant for him, the fear that had been lodged in his heart by the two strange men in the woods was stronger than his desire. His instinct for self-preservation, his absolute cowardice tipped the scale in his decision making.

It went against all of his plans for them, for their perfect lives together. His anger blended with his grief as he dried his body and dressed in clean clothes. He still felt dirty but he had other things to do. He walked to the backyard with the jeans in an aluminum bucket. The smell of gasoline drifted into the night. It covered the smell of the urine and that made him happier. He tossed the match and it flared quickly, an indigo flame, dancing for a moment, victorious and triumphant, as though it had won a great victory.

Then the denim burned, a pungent smell, the fumes of burnt piss and shame rose and singed his nostrils reminding him of his pledge. He would keep the promise but someday, he'd make her pay.

17

The shower at the terminal had run hot and firm against Joe's sore back. It had cleared the cobwebs from his mind and brought him down from the buzz of the speed he had taken to keep him awake for the long drive from Kitchener to North Sidney. He should be sleeping but he never did on this trip. The ferry home to Newfoundland was to him, one of the happiest places on earth. He hated to miss a moment of the cruise.

Joe looked at the ocean from his favourite place on the bow of the vessel in the most forward part that passengers were allowed to go. He loved it there and today's voyage promised to be a pleasant one. The waters were calm and rose to greet the ferry in a gentle swell. The sun shone brightly on its surface dusting it with aqua-tinged diamond sparkles.

There is a point between North Sidney, Nova Scotia and Port Aux Basque, Newfoundland where the land from neither province is visible. The S.S. Caribou was within this point as Joe stood looking out over the water at the horizon. He did this every time he crossed the gulf in the daytime. Joe loved to watch the horizon grow wider and wider as though some divine hand was drawing in the grey land mass as it came into view. It was his home, that piece of rock lodged in the north Atlantic and it drew him back year after year. He'd been spending most of his time in Ontario once he had graduated high school and his sister let him stay there with her as much as he wanted. He had buddies there and the money was good in the business dealings he made but always, come June, he headed east, back home to his family, back home to the rock that begged his return.

His eyes scanned the water looking for whales and dolphins and when he didn't see any he looked at the horizon again, shifting his weight against the rail. He stifled a yawn. He was getting tired. He probably should sleep but he hated to miss this view. The expanse of sky, the infinite blue waters that were calm today held a promise that always provided great joy. He waited for it to come as it invariably did in this place and he closed his eyes in anticipation of the feeling.

Much to his surprise it wasn't the thought of the ocean below or the land ahead that gave him joy. It was the vision of large blue eyes and a smile with a little dimple underneath the left side of her lower lip that made his heart skip a happy beat. It was then followed an instant later by cold icicles of regret that danced up and down his vertebrae. He was travelling away from her and the joy of the trip was suddenly marred by the realisation that perhaps leaving her behind had been a mistake.

Joe opened his eyes, the horizon still pencil thin, his heart full. He wasn't excited to be going home again. Not this time, not without her. He had gone because that had been his plan. Now he was a few hours from the place he loved and he suddenly wished he was headed in the opposite direction. He tried to shake the feeling but it persisted. He leaned his head forward on the cold rail and took a deep breath. He closed his eyes and her face came back quickly without bidding. He revelled in it and resented it all at once.

She's your grand love

The realisation came upon him as though the words had been spoken aloud. The cynical side of him wanted to disregard it but the beautiful face behind his eyelids held it fast and etched the idea into his mind, and once carved there it could no more be removed than the ocean could remove the granite rock from the cliffs of the land he was sailing towards. He *was* falling in love with her. It had been easy with others, easy to love them and leave them behind because he hadn't actually loved them.

It was ridiculous, he really didn't know Christianna all that well and they had only been together two days. Still there was no other explanation for the sudden despair in his heart and he accepted it as his truth in that moment. He also wanted to discover more than anything else in the world, why she had affected him so. He needed to see her again, to be with her, to hold her and make love to her and go wherever she led him.

Joe was suddenly angry at himself. What if her old boyfriend didn't heed the warning he'd sent with his buddies. What if that asshole found her alone somewhere and hurt her? Shit, he was an idiot. He should have stayed to protect her. That was what he was supposed to do.

So this was the love his Aunt Mae had told him would come, that came to everybody. He remembered her words to him, the advice she gave. He remembered what she had said the last time they spoke of it, when he was just seventeen and weeks before she died.

"When you find it, you might as well just give in to it. The only cure is to let it run its course. It's like a boomerang m' doll, toss it away, it'll come right back around so you might as well just follow your heart."

"What if she doesn't love me back?" He'd asked, his young heart curious.

"She will and if she doesn't then that isn't it." Her voice had been firm and sure.

"And then you get to live happily ever after?" The idea appealed to his sensitive soul though he'd already started to doubt the existence of such a love.

"No." His aunts eyes had gone sad, her voice lower. *"Sometimes it doesn't last, but a love like that goes beyond this earth and if the timing isn't right this time then next time maybe..."*

"In heaven?" He wasn't sure about heaven and all that religious stuff.

"Something like that." Aunt Mae had smiled then and pulled out the little poetry book she always got him to read to her. She gave it to him and he started to open it but she laid her wilted hand across the page for a moment.

"No, not just to read, to keep this time." She had motioned towards the book, her nearly sightless eyes beckoning him to keep it. *"You will need it to guide you*

when you find your grand love." Her smile was soft, like a pillow you could cuddle up with.

Joe hadn't said thank you. He hadn't known what to say. So he'd tucked the little book into his pocket with a grin and grabbed a nearby mystery book to read to her. She'd leaned back against the pillow and waited for his voice.

He put his hand on his back pocket where the book still rested. He always carried it with him. Joe raised his head slowly his emotions written in the pores of his skin. What should he do?

"She must be sumpin' else then?" The man broke into Joe's thoughts and he looked in the direction of the voice. Joe looked away, embarrassed. The man nudged him with his left arm. "Swally?"

"Yes b'y." Joe said grabbing the rum bottle like a life preserver and taking a swig of the burning liquid.

"She must be sumpin' else." The man repeated. His small blue eyes nestled in folds of leathery brown skin like shiny marbles in burlap.

"What?" Joe looked away from the man still holding the rum bottle.

"Only a woman can put that look on a man's face b'y." The stranger said with a cocky grin.

Joe looked at him and then flashed a matching grin back.

"Yes b'y she's sumpin' else and great tits too," he added cheekily as he swigged the liquor again and this time the regret started to melt from his body and he was warmed.

"Main t'ing b'y,das da main t'ing." The old man laughed and nodded, eyes staring at the rolling ocean in front of them.

The warmth came not from the contents of the liquor bottle. It came instead from the decision that had been made for him in an instant and an impulse. He handed the bottle back to the old man.

"T'anks." Joe said and his gratitude was not for the drink alone.

"Yer welcome b'y." The stranger answered and he knew.

The two men looked at the horizon together and as they did the divine hand that drew the seven natural wonders of the world and placed them exactly where they belonged, the hand that sketched the constellations and the planets, the ocean floor and the blue faces of the arctic glaciers, began to etch the grey coast of Newfoundland shade by brilliant shade. Eventually the unlikely companions could make out the individual rocks and trees and by and by they could see the ferry terminal where they would part ways.

They spoke a little more, small talk, laughter and lies, and shared the rum. The chance meeting that was sketched by that same divine hand was forgotten by each in time. It was however, as profound and as valid as any moment ever was, to the hand that had drawn them in that place, at that time, together.

18

The strong chemical smell from the industrial soap on her hands mixed with the fumes of the exhaust from the buses. The black track pants and long-sleeved cotton shirt, that was required for work, were sticky. She pulled the shirt off revealing a faded pink t-shirt. The picture on it was of Michael Jackson from the Thriller album, a silhouette, tall, thin, and black, the single glove a sequined patch under her left breast. It was old and well-worn and one of her favourites.

Christianna had drifted into a calm rhythm of home and work. She read more, she walked more, and she smiled more though there was no one to see it. Greg had disappeared. He had called David and told them he was staying with his buddy indefinitely. Chris wasn't sure if she was relieved or surprised that he was still alive. David had changed her locks for her peace of mind.

The memory of her terror, when she had come home on Wednesday and some of Greg's things were gone, still weakened her knees. She had called David in a panic, afraid Greg had gotten a key somehow.

"Aww, Jesus, sorry." David had apologised. He'd used the extra key and had picked up some of Greg's clothes for him. He didn't want him near Chris and had agreed when Greg asked him to do so in case he was tempted to go there himself.

A black on blue face confirmed for David that Greg's staying away wasn't voluntary. He figured Joe

Indigo was behind it and was grateful. He left Greg's things, and got out of there before he lost his own temper. He also refused to answer questions about Christianna, his own hands itching to blacken the remaining places on Greg's face that weren't already bruised.

The advantage of working in a factory is that you get time to think. The disadvantage of working in a factory is exactly the same. Chris hated the mindless assembly line work and she looked forward to the weekend when she would be alone. She wanted it that way. If she couldn't be with Joe she didn't want anyone else around. She didn't want to talk, she didn't want to answer the questions, keeping her feelings close and spending most of her time by herself. She liked having friends but was comfortable with her own company particularly since she hadn't been able to enjoy it much in the past few years.

She stared at the little girl on the bench across from her and wished she had been as happy as a child. Was there a time when her parents hadn't been disappointed in her? She couldn't remember one. She smiled as the little girl with the dark braids and bright barrettes held up her Barbie for Chris to see, her mother looking at her proudly as she did so.

"She's beautiful." Christianna commented and the little girl responded by shyly hugging her doll closer. Her mom held her at the same time and Chris flashed a bittersweet smile at them.

The previous weekend slipped into her mind. It had been exciting and unexpected and she would treasure it forever. She had no idea what had come over her. She had always been rebellious but she hadn't been promiscuous. Greg had been her first and she had never thought it possible that she would gleefully fall into a casual affair with a stranger. He hadn't called of course. It would be impossible for him to do so yet she had hoped he would. It had been a fun interlude and she'd let her emotions go crazy. She had thought of him all week and had even missed him, which was ridiculous. They had only known each other for a day. She had concluded that the connection was purely on her side, though it had felt mutual.

She opened her copy of Stephen King's latest offering, *The Dark Half* and began to read. She realised after a moment that she'd already read the paragraph and sighing, she closed it with a slam. It was a traditional King book, complicated, and she wanted to do it justice. The sound of the air brakes on the bus pulling up signalled to a group of passengers and they moved forward towards the opening door. As they boarded the bus it changed her line of vision and she blinked at the light from the now too-bright sun.

The rays flashed over the shoulder of a tall man walking towards her. Her cheeks flushed hot and her hand shook a little as excitement brightened her pretty blue eyes. As he got closer he blocked the sun with his wide shoulders and the grin that was on his face at seeing her sitting there was visible. She jumped from the bench and landed in his arms as they opened for her. She held him as though he would disappear like a mirage and he held her just as tightly. Then her lips found his of their own accord, confirming he was really there.

"What are you doing here?" Chris asked remembering that she smelled like industrial soap and plastic chemicals. The little girl with the Barbie giggled and Christianna's eye caught the smile on the face of another bystander and she smiled back when she noticed that an elderly woman appeared moved by their reunion.

"I went down, flew back. I moved my shit to my mother's house and caught a plane this morning." He said.

"Why?" *He* smelled like spice and cigarettes and shampoo and her hand stroked the long silken pony tail that she'd dreamt of so often during the week.

"Because...this." He struggled for a moment. Her eyes were holding his in a strange trance, the intimacy almost too much, but he only looked away for a second. "This was too good." He said holding her stare.

She nodded and kissed him again.

"I'm filthy, I just got off work." She had planned a long bath and she quickly revised it to a quick shower. "I have to go home, the bus will be here any second."

"Meet me when you can. Call me at Dar's," he said. "I don't have the bike, can you get a cab?"

"Yeah, I'll do that." Then the bus was pulling up, air brakes hissing and she reluctantly moved away. "I need the number and the address." He handed her a piece of paper ready for the request.

"Here."

"How did you know I'd be *here*?" Chria asked him, walking along as the line boarding the bus shortened? He walked beside her.

"I figured you would transfer here, I guessed." He shrugged as she boarded the bus. " I would have found you somewhere."

"A couple of hours," she said from the door as she flashed her bus pass to the driver. The door closed and she found a seat.

Three words floated across her mind like the lyrics on a karaoke machine, *Joe is here*. She fought the smile that hovered in the corner of her lips aware of being surrounded by strangers. She waved at him with the hand that held the paper and when the bus turned and she couldn't see him anymore she opened the folded sheet. It held the address and phone number for his sister's house.

Underneath were words that made her snort a laugh out loud and then glance around to see who had heard. The masculine handwriting was obviously his, neat yet strong and the words he'd written underneath his sister's address and phone number were unexpected and sweet. *You owe me a poem, Joe.*

19

The white Crown Victoria with its little taxicab hat pulled up to the tidy red bungalow. It stopped in front of the driveway and Joe came bouncing down the steps like a child whose Christmas package had just arrived. He handed the driver some bills before she had a chance to protest. He pulled her out of the car and lifted her up and twirled her around. As the cab pulled away, tires groaning over the hot pavement, Joe kissed Christianna. Then he put her down and looked at her, eyes searching her face, drinking her in until he was satisfied and had made up for the days he hadn't seen it except in his memory.

"You sure clean up good," and then, "let's go." He waved the soft plaid blanket in his hand at her. She followed him as dizzy from the joy as from the spinning. She caught a wave from the front porch and yelled hello to Dar who laughed and waved back.

The tree house was welcoming. Its sparse floor was covered quickly with the blanket he spread. The windows to the west let in the light of the evening sun.

They had laughed and played all the way there but then, in a moment of realisation, they were both quiet. Their eyes met and the words they had been about to say to each other abandoned their lips at the same time. Joe reached down and touched her face, looking into the eyes that had haunted him for the past week. She was here in front of him. She reached up and mimicked his movement, her eyes following the path of her hand as it traced his face with her fingertips. His skin was smooth where his beard area ended up the side of his cheek and she moved her hand from where they explored his temples into his dark hair. Then she met his eyes again.

"Take your hair down." She asked him, her voice strong and he reached back with his right hand and pulled it loose, his hair moving in a shiny highway of soft asphalt-coloured silk as it was freed from its band. She smiled at his beauty and ran her hands through its loose strands. It was thick and soft and she held it between her fingertips mesmerized. She pulled a section forward and leaned in to smell it. Joe thought he would melt from the beauty of the gesture. No one had ever adored him that way.

He pulled her face up with his hand under her chin and she reluctantly pulled her eyes away to look into his warm brown ones. There the regret ended as their depths revealed the secrets of his heart. The indigo sparkles in his eyes flashed adoration, wonder and love. She smiled a sweet smile and touched the corner of his upper lip where the familiar grin hid and at her touch it appeared, familiar, teasing, tempting and she moved forward to kiss him where the temptation lay.

The sweetness of the kiss was excruciating and the heat of their physical bodies suddenly matched the desire in their souls. He ran his hands down her back and she ran hers in the opposite direction up his broad muscled one. There was no more sweetness, there was no more waiting, there was no more time.

The sun tipped its hat to the moon as it lowered in the sky, the bright orange beams leaving a heated pattern of light on their bodies. They made love in its rays as it dipped lower and lower into the trees replacing the disappearing heat of the day with a warm blanket of mutual desire.

"You came back." She pulled closer to him stating the obvious. She didn't need the heat from his body as it was a hot, humid evening. She needed the touch, the comfort, the security. She needed him.

"Yeah, it was pretty wild." He'd gotten his things from a very angry girlfriend and taken them to his mother's house. His parents had expected him to stay longer but he disappointed them by booking a plane back almost immediately. Work he'd told them, trying not to acknowledge the worry that had melted his mother's sad features. They knew about his work and were scared for him. He considered telling them about Christianna but didn't. He didn't know how to explain her. Perhaps he should have tried so his mother wouldn't have worried.

For the first time ever he had been glad to leave the place he loved. He didn't expect to return there quickly, though if Christianna would go there with him, he would follow.

They held each other, both of them mystified by the depth of their feelings for each other. Had they really only known each other a few days?

"This is wicked." Joe said as he stroked her arm with one warm finger. He kept waiting for it to stop, for real life to break the spell she'd cast over him but it was a romantic heart that beat in his chest and his days of womanizing seemed frivolous next to the connection he felt with this woman he was falling in love with. He stroked the back of her hand and then pulled it up to kiss it.

You must have a grand love, everybody should have a grand love in their lives, especially someone with such a depth and passion for life as you have Joe.

The words of his aunt flitted though his thoughts. He could see her face as she spoke them. Could hear the soft voice that was his guide, the one he ignored much of the time, but not now. Not this time.

He ran a finger around the outline of Christianna's face repeating the gesture she'd made earlier.

She shuddered with the sweetness of it and stroked his bare chest as he kissed her hair. Now things were different between them. It had been fun and light-hearted and magic from the beginning but his coming back had changed it from a sweet memory to a relationship, from a weekend fling to something real. Now there was an added element, the knowledge that this thing between them was rare. They were free to be sweet, to be gentle and loving and open. For them, knowing this, being romantic wasn't something contrived, it was something felt.

"Hey, where's my poem?"

"Poem, what poem?"

"If you didn't write one then you'd better get to work." He ordered. His grin danced at his lips, light in the darkening room.

"Ok then." She cleared her throat, a mischievous smirk on her lips. "There once was a girl from Port aux Basques, she had pimples on her ass." Chris moved to avoid his playful swat, her laughter bouncing off the rough wooden walls.

"Come on, seriously." He laughed, pulling her close. "Your turn."

"It's not very good." Chris was more sober and her eyes lowered. She had never shared her poetry except with her English teachers. Greg had scoffed at her writing as a waste of time. Her parents had done the same.

"It'll be perfect." His grin disappeared, his face was confident and encouraging.

"I wrote it when I thought you were gone...don't laugh." She begged.

"Trust me?" In spite of the mischievous grin, she did.

"I couldn't believe this was real." She said indicating the two of them with a gesture. "On one hand I didn't think it was possible that I'd ever see you again but somehow, the last time we were here, I knew that I would. I was alone in the apartment and I missed you and I remembered that it seemed like, I don't know how to say this but..."

"But it felt like I was supposed to come back? Joe finished her sentence.

"It felt like *we* really didn't have any choice."

Joe nodded. It wasn't until he was on the ferry that he'd felt that. He handed her back the paper she'd given him as she spoke.

"Read it to me." His dark eyes twinkled a message in a code that only she could decipher. He wanted this moment, he craved this magic. His eyes told her with their symbolic flashing that he *wanted* to fall in love with her.

She reached for her tank top, pulling it on over her wild curls and stretched it down her tight belly. He crossed his arms in front of his chest with a gesture of interest and patience, held spellbound by the picture of her. Her hair was fluffed and wild and her breasts were clearly visible through the pale pink top she wore. His eyes flashed and the image was sealed. He'd never forget it.

She caught her breath and started to read, her voice full of him and her love for him. She'd never felt this vulnerable, he'd never felt so wanted. His desire to fall in love with her was fulfilled with the words she spoke.

"It's called Indigo Sky," she told him.

"I like the name." If his grin was endearing, his full smile was completely engaging. She was overwhelmed by his beauty and looked down at the scribbles on the paper in her hands. She had never felt such pure happiness and she cleared her throat. In the dimming light she began to read.

Love greets the morn with a heart beat
her heart greets the dawn with a sigh
while dreams fill the mind of his yearning
with wishes that wish they could fly

Distance. The world separates them
whispering this time is not yours
separated by life and by land
and the ocean that washes its shores

She leans on a tree with her body
he stares at the clouds that race by
they both feel the love of the ages
as they stare at the indigo sky.

Eternity is a promise it whispers
we'll meet and be one by and by
and the promises made are not broken
when made under the indigo sky

She folded the paper and handed it back to him, not looking at his face immediately.

"Well...do you like it?" She asked when he didn't speak for a few seconds.

"You love me."

His eyes were full of pleasure, moisture lurking just beyond their surface. He looked at the paper and read it to himself again. She had captured exactly how he felt, how he'd felt that moment on the ferry when he knew they were supposed to be together, that he had to return to her and try. They were meant for each other, it was just the way it was.

"Where *did* you come from?" He reached for her wondering what he had done that was so good that God had sent him this treasure. He pulled her in close to him and held her there.

She placed her hand on his heart and felt the tapping of his heartbeat under his skin. She wondered how she had lived before she had felt that rhythm under her palm. He held the paper in his hand and when the room had darkened and the sun had dropped to visit the other side of the earth they left the tree house.

Later, water rinsing the snowy lather from her body, she caught a glimpse of the brilliant diamond ring she still wore on her left hand. She had been meaning to take it off but was unsure of what to do with it. She had also wanted to avoid the questions of her co workers who would notice its absence. Joe had never mentioned it but he had to have noticed it. He noticed everything.

She turned off the faucet and looked at it. The full carat twinkled at her with purpose and a smile lit her already radiant face. Tomorrow she would ask Joe to sell it for her, he knew people who would pay for this perfect stone. The money could be put in the safe and used towards her education. Its value a small ransom for the torment the little flicker of carbon had given her in the last few months. She pulled it easily off her wet finger and walked, naked and dripping to her bedroom where she found the fancy velvet ring box it had come in. She took it and the certificate of authenticity and set them on her nightstand where she would see them in the morning. She wouldn't tell Joe yet about her plans. She would simply tell him to sell it. She walked back over the water-slicked floor, grinning at her mess. Greg would not have approved she thought as a wave of joy swept over her damp body. It was the kind of joy that can only be felt by someone who has just gained her freedom and met the love of her life all at once.

20

The thunder that shook the earth around her and the lightening that brightened her bedroom were insignificant next to the vision of stormy black eyes with gentle sparkles of blue light that appeared in Christianna's mind whenever she closed *her* eyes. The storm cut the humidity though, and Saturday morning dawned bright and temperate.

Her first thought was of Joe and she lay in the bed alone, the afterglow of her dreams of him, reminiscent of the moments after they had made love. She stretched her body feeling the gentle ache of muscles unused to that much physical activity. She touched her hand to her smooth belly and felt what he had felt when he touched her soft smooth skin and gently rounded breasts.

The phone rang interrupting her peace and she reached over to the nightstand and answered with a husky hello and then cleared her throat and repeated the word.

"Get up, I'm on my way, I'll bring coffee." She could hear the laughter in his voice and pictured the grin on his lips. He was already vibrant and awake.

"You could have just stayed here." She grumbled, her voice clearer now.

"Had something to do this morning but hey, Tom said I can have the car." He had refused her plea to spend the night and she hadn't pushed him.

"Do you ever sleep?"

"I slept great, how about you?"

"Really good, nice dreams." Her voice took on a teasing tone.

"You'll have to tell me."

"I'll show you."

"I'm on my way, don't bother getting dressed!" He teased back.

"Hurry-up!" Chris rolled over to look at the clock pulling the phone by the cord with her. It was just after seven and she groaned. It was Saturday.

She puttered around in the bathroom in her robe and went into the kitchen to make the coffee. She knew he was bringing one but she'd set up the machine last night and one cup wouldn't satisfy her habit. She enjoyed the sound of the slurping coffee maker almost as much as the coffee that percolated through. The smell of the steaming grounds wafted through the apartment as Christianna peed and brushed her teeth. She was clean and had finished her first cup of coffee when the firm pounding hit the bottom of her door.

She answered it and kissed him as he held the two coffee cups out on either side of her.

"You got dressed?" He frowned, looking at her robe.

"It's just my robe." It was a pretty silky thing that Greg had given her and it barely covered her thighs.

"Take it off, it's been a long night." He ordered, winking, as he walked past her and put the Tim Horton's cups on the half-wall that separated the kitchen from the little area where she stood. When he turned back to her his eyes brightened at her obedience.

Chris made the step that put them in each others arms and she reached her lips up to his as her hands reached for his belt buckle but before she could make any progress she was swept up as though she were featherweight and carried into the living room couch that lay against the far wall.

Its soft green velvet was as smooth as the skin that ached for him. Joe stepped away making quick work of removing his clothes. His dark body towered over her and she reached up hurrying him, it had been a long night for her too and the dreams that had seemed so satisfying in the realm of her subconscious were mere atoms of pleasure compared to the joy they found in the bright light of day.

"Coffee?" He questioned her, his eyes dripping with memories of their lovemaking.

"Oh Jesus, yeah," Chris nodded sitting up as he moved across the room towards the cups that had cooled while they were busy. Her eyes absorbed his long strong legs, his dark skin, the body hair that made him a man sprinkled up his chest and down his thighs. He was dark with no distinct tan lines, his skin graduating in shades from lighter around his buttocks and thighs to dark on his shoulders, arms and legs. His long black pony tail separated the muscles in his back, defining them. He was naturally muscled, lean and taut. She watched him walk back towards her with the coffee, this time her admiration was for his face. He was beautiful and her eyes said so.

"What?" He asked, unnerved by her stare for a moment. Her bright blue eyes saw into his very soul and it made him wonder what she saw in there.

"You're beautiful," she said reaching her hand out for the coffee cup. It was still warm and it had caffeine.

"You think so?" He preened before her, flexing his muscles.

"Yeah," she giggled as he posed holding the coffee cup as a trophy. "Especially your ass."

He turned around and flexed his muscles at her before sitting on the floor and taking a cautious sip from his coffee, then drank more, grimacing at the taste.

"There's more in the pot." She suggested after tasting the disgusting blend. She wasn't fond of Tim Horton's anyway and she got up and walked over to the cupboard and pulled down two mugs. The coffee had been brewed for a while but it was still hot and strong and she poured them each one. He watched her from the living room, drinking his coffee, less particular over it. He admired her petite form as she'd admired his strong body moments before.

"What do ya wanna do today?" His eyes never made it to hers as she walked back to him.

"No odds to me," she sipped the coffee. "Movie?"

"Yeah, sounds good." He was relieved. Money was short at the moment. A movie and then maybe they could eat back here.

"What's playing?"

"The second Lethal Weapon just came out." He'd noticed it on the marquis on the way there.

"Oh yeah, Mel Gibson!" Her eyes brightened.

"Oh, you like that uh?"

"Love that." She hadn't dared express admiration for any other man around Greg but Joe was laughing.

"But I'm more beautiful right?" And he was teasing. It wasn't the needy reassurance she'd had to give Greg constantly.

"Absolutely, you've got the nicer ass." She meant it.

"Where'd ya see Mel Gibson's ass?" He feigned outrage.

"Gallipoli." She had seen the movie so many times, she'd lost count. She owned the tape.

"*Where*?" Joe kidded.

"Not the place, the movie," she giggled. "We can watch it later."

"Any excuse to see his ass uh?" He touched her leg with a long finger, stroking along her knee.

"Yup," she agreed, sipping her hot coffee, distracted by his touch.

This was how it was supposed to be, easy, fun and sweet. She had hidden her copy of Gallipoli because Greg had decided he didn't like her staring at Mel Gibson. The complete idiocy of that was lost to him in his possessive madness.

The tree house called to them after the matinee. They could have gone to her apartment but there was magic in their little hiding place and the convenience of a warm bed couldn't compete with that.

Just after the light died, she remembered the poetry book and she whispered "I should have made you read me something from your little book." Her disbelief was hidden in the dark when he started to speak.

"The fountains mingle with the river,
And the rivers with the ocean;
The winds of heaven mix forever,
With a sweet emotion;
Nothing in the world is single;
All things by a law divine
In one another's being mingle;--
Why not I with thine?
See! the mountains kiss high heaven,
And the waves clasp one another;
No sister flower would be forgiven,
If it disdained it's brother;
And the sunlight clasps the earth,
And the moonbeams kiss the sea;--
What are all these kissings worth,
If thou kiss not me"

He had recited the poem as an actor would on a stage, his heart in his voice, clear and confident. His soft east-coast dialect perfected the balance between the recitation and the reality of this man of contradictions. He loved these words. They held him, owned him. Somehow his genius had been overlooked by school systems and life and maybe the expectations that a boy does not love such things.

The sweetness of the moment moved her. She took his hand and placed it on her cheek so that he could feel the dampness, keeping nothing from him.

With her, for the first time in his life Joe felt that he was authentic. He hadn't learned how to merge the two selves that made him an entire man so he'd hidden the part that was most real from the hard and cynical world that expected a man to be tough and masculine. How hard it was to live that way, to not be able to be who you genuinely are because of the expectations of a cold world.

"Now you owe me one." He reminded her as he kissed a cool cheek where her tears had dried. She nodded quietly knowing it would be easy. Inspiration was a manifestation of their complete love.

"Next time," she moved her lips to meet his. "Next time, I promise."

21

It folded into his wallet so tightly that it burst out of the top edge like a colourful accordion. Joe had taken his time organising it so that the bills were sorted in denomination order, brown, red, green, purple and blue, a currency rainbow. The weight in his pocket was reassuring. The deal had gone like clock work and he was once again flush. This time instead of the large parties of his past, he was taking Christianna for a weekend that she'd never forget and he was particularly happy to be able to do so. He'd been distracted and tense this week and he'd caught her looking at him occasionally with worry on her face and censor in her eyes.

"Dress up nice." He'd told her holding the receiver between his chin and shoulder as he organised the bills, filling his wallet with enough for the weekend and slipping the rest into a small safe he kept under the bed.

"Don't I always?" She'd asked pretending an insult but the smile in her voice was obvious.

"*Fancy* nice...and yes you always look good." He thought of her short skirts and shorts with sleeveless t-shirts and tank tops that were her uniform most days, he thought of her without her clothes. "*Very* good."

She dressed in a little black dress that she'd worn to a wedding once, it was plain and short, and not particularly dressy so she wore gold earrings and a gold chain to make it a little nicer. She felt dressed up but still herself. She worked in a plastics factory and in the winter she wore jeans and a t-shirt or sweat pants, in the summer she wore short shorts and a tank top, though this year she wore the mini skirts that had suddenly come into style. Greg didn't like them but he wanted her to look like other women so he'd allowed her to wear them if he was with her. She loved them, they were cool and comfortable and vanity demanded she admit they did show off her long legs well.

The 1989 Lincoln Town Car Limo pulled up across the street from her apartment. She watched the driver open the back door of the dark blue car on the far side. Its occupant got out and turned towards her and leaned over the roof of the car facing the apartment.

Chris waved through the window and he motioned her out, the grin never leaving his face. Enjoyment danced in his eyes. She picked up her overnight bag. He'd told her to pack for the weekend. Was the limo the surprise? She locked the door behind her and ran towards him with an excited hug. Some children giggled behind her and she turned to see that many of the neighbours had come out, some casually and some quite obviously looking at the car. Joe gave them a little friendly wave and then focussed on her.

A little extra makeup made her eyes larger and bluer and he couldn't help noticing how her breasts bounced when she ran towards him. He had put his hands around her back when she embraced him and confirmed his suspicions. She wasn't wearing a bra. He groaned in appreciation and, not understanding she pulled back.

"You sure do clean up good." Joe explained. His eyes danced with borealis brightness. He felt proud and lucky. The driver waited by the door quietly and he quickly helped her in to the other side of the car.

His white shirt and black dress pants made him look taller and broader than his usual white t-shirt and jeans. He looked as comfortable in the dressier clothes as he was in his civvies. His hair was combed back into its tidy pony tail and his eyes flashed with enjoyment. His clean-shaven dark face was a perfect contrast to the crisp white dress shirt. His brilliant white teeth flashed in his face briefly in a grin of satisfaction. He had an air of comfort in his rich man costume and he enjoyed having everyone look at him when he played the role.

The stretch limousine had a privacy wall that separated them from the driver. Joe fiddled with the cassette player searching for a song he wanted to play. When the current version of the medley Baby I Love Your Way/Freebird filled the Lincoln, he turned to her, eyebrows raised, eyes seeking her approval. Chris preferred the Peter

Frampton version from her old albums but she smiled an affirmative. The gesture touched her and she knew he'd chosen it carefully. She hugged him close, their bodies covering a large Lincoln Symbol in the middle of the leather seat.

"Did you win the lottery?" Though she didn't really care to know how he came by the money.

"Yeah, when I met you." He flirted with a broad smile not really answering.

She smacked him, but she was pleased that he bothered to try to flatter her.

He'd meant it but laughed as well. It *was* pretty corny.

He turned up the music a little. He'd sat and made the tape the night before and had picked the songs carefully. They were all love songs, all important. His sister had laughed and kissed him on the head when he asked her for her tape recorder. Then she helped him, moved by his love for the girl she had liked so much when they'd met.

Dar had told him it was a sure thing that she would love it. She told him that women loved the deep sexy voice but Joe was doubtful. When the first notes of *Love Making Music* started he watched carefully and thanked Dar in his mind when he saw the look in her beautiful blue eyes.

"Barry White?" She reached up and kissed him. The deep voice sang the sensuous songs that it was famous for. They moved towards each other and made love to the music as much as each other as the rest of the tape played unnoticed. The click of the cassette player brought them back to reality.

"Thank God for tinted windows." She giggled in his arms.

"Thank God for Barry White." Was his opinion as he pulled on his pants and buckled his belt with quick movements.

She freshened up noting the Toronto downtown getting closer out the side window. She fixed her makeup and hair as he poured champagne from the bottle into two delicate flute glasses.

As the limousine manoeuvred along the Gardner Expressway she became excited. She'd never been to Toronto, except for the airport.

The Lincoln drove them towards the CN Tower and she fought the wave of fear that overcame her when she realised that was exactly where they were going.

Chris was transported to a moment the previous summer with Greg. They had been at the Rainbow Bridge in Niagara Falls, when she had leaned over to look curiously into the falls. At that moment he had nudged her on the back as though to push her in. She had been startled into tears and he had admonished her for her foolishness and had stalked back to the hotel room they'd shared. She had followed, feeling ashamed of herself, apologizing for over-reacting. He had scared her but the reason she had become so upset was not so much his gesture but that she was deathly afraid of heights. He had known it though, Joe didn't.

It was easy at the base. She simply followed Joe as he walked them towards the elevators. Then they were at the doors. She hesitated a second and he sensed something was wrong. It dawned on him that she was afraid and cursed himself for not thinking of it. They were standing at the base of the tallest free-standing structure on earth and he hadn't thought to ask if she was afraid of heights.

"We can go somewhere else." His eyes searched hers, offering her a way out.

"No way, you planned this all out. I'll try not to puke on you." She had managed the tree house after all. She could do this.

Chris followed him to the elevator and closed her eyes all the way up. He resisted the temptation to tease her. She was terrified and he looked at her with her eyes closed, gripping his hand, trusting him to keep her safe and vowed to himself that he always would.

When the elevator stopped he led her out and she took a deep breath. She thought maybe she could overcome her fear but the pit of her stomach rolled with it. She didn't look at the windows but she could feel the height.

Seeing the paleness in her face Joe manoeuvred her back into an elevator. He held her close until she was on solid ground again. He didn't move. He didn't want to increase her fear. He also wanted to protect her from the embarrassment he sensed she felt. The only looks they got were those of pity and understanding though and he appreciated it.

"I'm so sorry." She was mortified and shaken.

"No, don't be, I am. I didn't know." His firm arms assured her she was safe. More than that, they cared that she felt safe. She breathed deeply, calming herself. She willed herself to feel peace, closing her eyes and repeating the word in her mind.

"Are you angry?"

"You're kidding? This is the best story ever to tell the grandkids." He could joke now that he could see that she was recovering. "Plan B." He said then and walked to the Limo, The driver did not express any surprised at their quick return. He got out and opened the door for them. Then he drove them to another landmark in downtown Toronto, the Royal York Hotel.

The Fairmont Royal York is the crown jewel in Toronto's hotel collection and the history in her walls seeps into the souls of the travellers who are fortunate to rest in her arms. Couples had come here forever and Christianna felt their ghost-loves in the grand foyer the moment they entered it.

Chris settled on the plush gold settee and looked around, taking in her surroundings. There was no noise, though it wasn't silent. There was a low buzz instead, that somehow felt hushed and reverent, as though the place was holy.

Her eyes were large and childlike in their wonder. Her lips widened in a smile and the little dimple under her lip broke free with it.

Joe watched her, smiling. The tower had been a screw up but this was going well.

"Do you like it? He asked.

"Oh, I love it." Her eyes were a galaxy of happiness.

His happiness was fixed by hers. He kissed her gently on the cheek and went back to the counter to finish checking them in.

She saw her surroundings with her heart and quickly pulled out pen and paper to write. She allowed the opulence and beauty to seep into her soul and then flow from her pen to the page. Inspiration lived in this place and she was its vessel.

He watched her for a moment, checked in but not wanting to interrupt. The look on her face was as beautiful as the face itself. Joe glanced around for other admirers of such beauty, surprised to find that he was the only one. He still did not understand that the view through the lens of love was biased and that what he saw was his and his alone. His love of her overlaid her natural beauty and enhanced it for his eyes only. To the rest of the world she was just a pretty girl writing on a bench.

The room was several stories up. She reassured him they didn't need to change rooms. It was different inside. She would not be afraid in this hotel. So they were escorted to the suite he had reserved for them. They would order room service and enjoy themselves alone this night. Tomorrow they would explore Toronto and each other in the big wide world. Tonight, the world needed to stay away.

22

Humans, even in the clustered hives of apartments and the bustle of city living strive for community. It is the nature of the human to want to be with other humans. Pack animals they shift into cages, living next to one another yet apart, unaware of their own nature, so distracted they are by the city culture.

Eventually true nature dominates and within the confines of self imposed isolation, stubborn hearts reach again for the pack. The school, the church, the market are all hubs that bring those who live in cities back to the fold.

Toronto is a mammoth collection of such neighbourhoods. It is clean and welcoming and warm and cold all at once. The throngs walk, heads down on a mission towards Bay Street or slowly and with laughter towards the market at Kensington. Worlds apart, they live in harmony in the pack, the pecking order decided in the depths of the night when the children sleep and the spirits dance.

Joe woke first in that luxury suite that he had bought for Christianna. It was early afternoon. He stretched and looked at the girl that he loved. His thoughts darted from love to wonder to insecurity. What did she see in him?

Usually he was in charge but Christianna made love with the confidence of an older woman though she was still young in her skin. For the first time he'd looked at a woman's body and wondered what it would look like with his baby growing inside of it. He had kissed her belly at the thought that had flitted quickly through his mind earlier, followed immediately by another as his brain took in a new nuance in her flesh. But the idea was planted, the possibility of a future to come.

Hell he didn't even know how old she was. He guessed she was around eighteen but she might be closer to twenty two or twenty three.

Joe had been blessed with an ultra attractive face and from an early age girls were drawn to its beauty. He'd flash a smile, look at them a certain way and they'd follow him.

The difference was that with Chris he felt like he was following her more than she was following him and although he planned their time together, somehow her presence overwhelmed him. He led because she let him but she led because he loved her.

He picked up a little booklet that had been left in their room. It was a small book of poetry called *Twenty Love Poems* by Pablo Neruda. He flicked through the pages.

In poverty Joe had found books a consolation. He'd learned to love them from his Aunt Mae as she lived in that dull room at the back of the house with her overwhelming collection. She didn't watch television, preferring to listen to the radio for the news, sending little Joe Indigo to the library with a new list of books to pick up every two weeks. Everything he brought home and read to her, he absorbed himself. Tolstoy, Stephen King, Arthur Hailey. He loved them all but particularly the classics and especially the poets.

Aunt Mae's room had also been his escape from the dreary family as much as it was hers. He didn't have to see the defeated mother saddened by her inability to give anything to her family that others had, the father who didn't care that they were poor and smiled, plucking his guitar strings, and let them wear the hand me downs that charity provided, his lack of pride angering a young Joe who was teased often about his family's plight. It instilled a determination to do better and he worked hard to remove the stigma of the grey poverty of his family. He would have money in his life and lots of it. The means didn't matter.

He climbed from the luxury bed unable to ignore the needs of his body any longer and he slipped over to the bathroom. A flash of Christianna leaving him crossed his busy mind. Errant thoughts often flipped through his brain like one of those little books that consists of the flip pages you flick through fast to make a cartoon, creating a moving image from the subtle changes of the drawings.

The pictures made a helter-skelter story, the cartoon characters did not run in a steady motion but instead the pictures thoughts ran through his mind with no connections. His brain was more like a fast moving collage than a cartoon.

He needed a joint but it would have to wait. For some the effects of marijuana brought them into slow motion, made them sluggish, sleepy, ate into their motivation like a chomping Pac Man. For Joe Indigo, it brought him down to normal. It slowed the speed of the thoughts in his brain to a level that helped him function and stay focussed. Reading did that for him too.

He popped the cassette tape into the little player that was in a drawer in the room. He flipped the tape to the B side and fast forwarded past the first few tunes. Barry White was not his kind of music. He fast forwarded further to the music that filled his heart and soul and served as the backdrop for his life.

"What is this music?" Christianna was enthralled by the voice coming from the machine.

Joe jumped, happy she was awake. He dropped the little book in his bag and pulled her from the bed into his arms for a dance. The sweet words of *Something Fine* surrounded them and she was immediately entranced by the voice, the poetry and the melody. She was so sick of the sweetly sad lamentations of country music. This was different. This was beautiful and she closed her eyes as she swayed with him.

When the song finished he left her to get them some food and she listened to the beautiful words of the songs alone. She climbed back into the large comfortable bed with a pen and paper to write down the name of them as they played. Just when she thought this weekend couldn't reveal more treasures she was lulled into the deepest peace by a voice as smooth and pure as the calmest lake, the lyrics as profound as the depths of the hidden treasures underneath the still waters. When Joe returned, he set the food on the table and climbed into the bed with her. She turned and shared her joy and sense of newfound peace with him.

23

The spirit of their love flitted around the room and gently kissed its brilliant furnishings. The ghosts-memories of the evening were pleasant haunts and she welcomed them. They played with her body, teased her heart, their stroking of her soul soothing and sweet. Playfully they tossed happiness in her direction and she caught it with both hands, accepting the gift of bliss.

She pulled the gold coloured Gideon's bible from its drawer in the nightstand and set herself up on the heavy dark hardwood table in front of the lights of Toronto. She only smoked pot at night. It made her sleepy. As spice to a chef, she only used enough of the drug to accentuate the flavour of the experience, not to overwhelm and change it. For her it wasn't an escape from her life, it was an enhancement to it.

Carefully her fingers worked, gently pulling the pungent flakes of herb from the little bag. She was good at this. Christianna flicked and rolled the little cigarette between her fingers and then she licked the edges, rolling one end tight. Then she fashioned a little filter out of a piece of cardboard from the rolling papers package.

When she was done she walked to the bathroom and peed in the little area that held the toilet separate from the rest of the large bathroom. The luxury fascinated her. The area that held the toilet was bigger than the entire bathroom in the house she'd grown up in. There was a sink and with big white fluffy towels stacked large to small beside it. The toilet paper was softer than the fur on the back of the white cat that had been her best friend until it passed away when she was seventeen. She rolled it in her hands enjoying its plush texture. When she owned her own house she would have the toilet in its own room and use super soft toilet paper.

Joe turned at the sound of the door opening and welcomed her into his arms under the waterfall that fell in perfect luxuriant rhythm on their bodies. She nibbled his full bottom lip, enjoying the warm-water taste. Her hands slipped over the slick skin of his back taking in the soft tautness of it over the firm muscles. She loved the little dents behind his shoulder blades and her fingers moved up and down in the groove there and then over a little and down the thin spaces on either side of his spinal cord. His hands came up behind her neck, cupping her head, pulling her with both of his strong hands to her tip-toes. He kissed her with all of the love in his soul. Their bodies were young and hard and made for each other and they celebrated with the elements of the earth, air, water and fire that blessed their bond.

"Joint?" She asked him later after they had dried each other off with large, fluffy bath sheets.

"I'll roll," he answered as he hit play on the cassette player beside the bed.

"Already done," she indicated the joint sitting between chapter 23 and 26 of the Book of Isaiah as she tucked the towel to keep it up. There were robes as soft as the towels but, hot from the steam, they were left hanging on the bathroom hooks.

"You're going to hell." He laughed at the joint in the Bible, shaking his head at her, his eyes full of appreciation for her antics.

"In for a penny...anyway, Jesus wouldn't care, after all, he *was* the first hippie." Chris grinned.

"How'd you figure that?" He raised one eyebrow, eyes darting around, looking for the lighter.

"Sandals, robes, long hair, peace, love, compassion, he was a regular flower child, the first hippie." She laughed raising her hands in a little gesture that indicated proof. When she'd left her parent's home she'd left everything including a reverence for anything Christian.

"*You're* a hippie." Joe observed, the joint in his left hand. He looked impressed at her work as he inspected it.

"Nah, I'm a conformist," then furrowed her brow. "I'm a closet hippie maybe." She'd rebelled against her parents, against their church, against Greg, that would do. Rebelling was too hard. A troubled thought flirted for a moment with her mind. Where did Joe fit?

"I'm only a conformist in prison." The taboo had been broken and the topic they had avoided was now out there.

"What's it like?" Her eyes met his, finding a darkness that disturbed her and compelled her to reach out and touch his hand, stroking the dark hair on the back of it.

"It's prison, just guys like me, bad ones." He flashed a grin to lighten the mood but his eyes remained jet and sombre.

"I can't imagine losing my freedom." She didn't laugh.

"There are a lot of ways to lose your freedom. Spark it up." He needed the joint now.

"Uh?" She let go of his hand and searched for the lighter, finding it under a little poetry book in his bag. She knew the name from somewhere.

"People are tied to jobs they hate, lives they hate, poverty." The last was the worse.

"Or partners who control them," she thought of Greg then added. "But at least in those situations there is a chance. You know, to choose to change." She flicked the lighter triumphantly, making weak little sparks instead of a flame.

"Change is hard. Most people never change." He said quietly, taking the lighter from her. She thought she detected a warning in his words.

"True but at least it's possible if you're outside."

"So you think Jesus was a hippie uh?" He made a second attempt at light heartedness. He really didn't want to talk about prison with *her*.

"Yeah, though I doubt he smoked pot," she handed him the joint. "He was a bootlegger though, made wine. I think this stuff should be legal anyway."

"If it were I'd be out of a job." Shit, they were back to that again. She took the joint, drew on it and the buzz was almost instant.

"If it were you wouldn't be labelled a criminal for selling it." Chris shook her head. "It's the law that makes you a criminal, not the weed."

He pondered her words for a moment then asked.

"What about the other stuff?" He sat on the floor in front of her naked enjoying the mellow the first few drags of the joint provided, enjoying this conversation with her. He was fascinated by this line of thought.

"The hard drugs? They should be legal and controlled, like alcohol." Her voice sounded different to him, musical, enhanced, sweeter.

She moved his wild long hair to one side and rubbed his shoulders, immediately forgetting the question, focussing instead on the little dark hairs at the base of his neck as she stroked them with her fingertips.

"Serious?" Joe shivered, handing her the joint and turned his back to her again, losing himself in her touch. One hand continued to stroke the fine dark hair, the other placed the piece of joint to her lips.

"Serious." Chris repeated, confused, as her mind searched for what they'd been discussing. Her lips twitched. She drew on the joint enjoying its pungent taste in anticipation of furthering the buzz. She giggled.

"Okay, you *are* a hippie." Joe insisted, laughing at her giggle, as he accepted it again from her and pulled the smoke into his lungs.

"I'm a hippie like Jesus." She snickered, remembering now what they'd been talking about, as the pot tickled her funny bone.

Joe leaned back against her legs, wrapped warmly in the deluxe white towel and laughed along with her, the yellow haze of peace falling like a flowing wave of warm caramel from his brow downward. He handed her the joint and she finished it tossing the tiny remains in the clean lead crystal ashtray.

Chris stroked Joe's long jet black hair and relaxed into their twin feeling. Their connection grew in the silence as the sweet mellow sounds of Jackson Browne played. They both became lost in the smooth voice of poetry that filled the luxury suite. They stayed that way for a long while until life and the city and the waning buzz drifted them gently back down. Then later they slept in the large king-sized bed, curled together like happy contented children. Neither of them ever slept as well as they did together.

24

The streets of Toronto revealed its treasures to the couple as they strolled and rode noisy buses. The couple window-visited idyllic gothic comic book stores, quant little dress shops, historic record stores and infinite numbers of restaurants and cafes. The weather was temperate, the humidity low and the lake glistened in the sun.

While he saw the city in pictures, one shifting into another on the movie screen of his mind, hers sifted through the sights and sounds through thoughts formed into words. He was the photographer, she was the poet. Together *they* were complete.

The couple ate at a street vendor, drank beer in a smoky little bar and just after lunch on that second day he stopped her in front of a little tattoo parlour that boasted of artists of high calibre and clean, new needles. It was 1989 and this was now a vital requirement. She followed him in with interest. She'd never visited such a place before.

Joe had several tattoos. She'd first studied them by moonlight, kissing the dragon on his bicep, running her hand over the anchor with the intertwined Newfoundland flag on his pectoral muscle and the homemade pentacle that rested on the pulse of his wrist, dark and uneven, her favourite. She'd undressed him in their first days together to find a surprise on his upper thigh, a mermaid with haunting blue eyes and wild blonde hair embedded in the sweet rare place where his skin was smooth and lighter. Christianna had kissed her gently on her inky lips and made him shiver and felt they were now sisters through this man. He thought that Christianna was the mermaid, manifested into a living breathing creature of mythology and dropped in his arms.

The well-inked artist welcomed them warmly from across the room and Joe nodded his hello as they slipped to a counter that held pictures of the work they offered. Custom art was available too.

"Are you getting one?" Chris asked him.

"We both are." He stated.

"We both certainly are not." Chris recoiled at the thought.

"Heights *and* needles uh? Joe teased her about her fear the previous day.

"No, not afraid," she glanced at the man in the corner. She didn't say what she was thinking. She really didn't like tattoos although on Joe they were perfect.

Joe carried on looking for the perfect one. Chris revolted internally.

"Lots of couples get matching ones." The proprietor said coming up behind them. "Names or pictures."

They both shook their head no. She was more adamant than he was.

"A symbol then, something alike, that means something in your relationship but nowhere else?"

The romance of the idea intrigued Chris but she was still sceptical. What would it be?

"My name is too, um, Christian." Any symbol of that wouldn't do.

"Your middle name?" The artist turned salesman said persistently.

"Rose?" She answered and Joe's eyebrows went up. That was his Aunt Mae's name. She was Rosie Mae but had always been called Mae.

"Yeah, get a rose, not the word, the actual flower."

"Too girly." Joe grumbled though it had appealed for an instant.

"Get a blue one." The proprietor joked but he understood.

"Indigo." Inspiration nudged Chris to suggest. She was considering this and blamed it on the drinks they'd had earlier with lunch.

Joe looked at her. An indigo rose, something his, something hers and a tribute to his Aunt Mae. He's always wanted to do that. He liked the colour of his name. It was in the rainbow, it was in the sky. It was in the depths of the eyes of this girl he was so enamoured with.

Chris saw that he liked it and something whispered that this was right. They should have matching indigo roses, permanent reminders of this love between them that, no matter the outcome, would always be special.

"Where?" She asked falling into the trap they'd laid out for her.

"Our hands " Joe suggested. He wanted to see it on her. He wanted the world to see it just like they'd seen that expensive diamond he'd happily sold for her a few days back. This suited them much better though, for now.

"Right here." The artist touched the area between her finger and her thumb.

"On our left hands." Joe suggested thinking traditionally.

"Hold hands like you usually do," suggested the proprietor whose name was Tim. "How you do when yer walking together."

They did as they were told, curious.

"Right there," he advised. "Yer left, yer right." He showed them how the two roses would be placed so that the stems of the roses would come down over their hands and meet. They would appear to grow from one stem, no beginning, no end, just two roses joined when they held hands.

Her dark blue eyes looked into his, enthralled by the idea. His lips kissed the place where her hand would be inked by the creative master who prepared for them in the back. Then he sketched the tiny roses on each of them. Often people did an outline and came back for colour but this couple would take everything that day, and Tim had time. They held each others opposite hands as the pain turned to pleasure and Chris bore up well, only flinching at the beginning but getting into a zone as the artist worked.

She had gone first, a leap of faith that he would do the same after. He did. No sign of pain showed on his face but he held her hand anyway. They chatted sometimes but mostly they were quiet and still. The music of Deep Purple played in the background as the dye became a permanent symbol of their sudden and deep love.

The finished product was bright and bleeding. They put the flowers together, barely touching. It was a sweet impulsive gesture and as their blood mingled the proprietor gave one nod of his head in approval. Blood brothers with a twist! He liked that! He would suggest that to his other couples!

They finished by sharing a joint with Tim the tattoo artist and Joe took his business card when they left.

The hot wind that had begun weaving its way through the Toronto streets, tapped against the sting in Christianna's hand. It reminded her that this pain was nothing, that life would hold greater pain and that great love can only be bought at the price of suffering. She braced against the wind, holding Joe's hand tighter.

The wind warned her that the stem of that rose was delicate and that with time the hurricane would come, the roses would be blown apart and once separated, their connection might never be reclaimed.

But that day the wind lost its battle and the hands that canvassed the roses walked together, new, bleeding, painful, and connected by a strong love that sustained and carried them along the streets of Toronto back to the hotel.

It is likely that the wind *let* them win knowing that on another day, it would blow stronger and that they would lose their grip on each other, breaking the ink-stem that joined their hands and their hearts, with a cruel and painful snap.

25

The humidity was returned by the mesmerizing storm that shook and rattled over Lake Ontario that Saturday evening in July. They played music, watched some porn, smoked some pot and made love as nature performed a light show choreographed by divine splendour and set to the music of a universal love song.

They danced naked together to the music of Jackson Browne then the soothing voice of Joni Mitchell filled in the gaps of time and legitimized their love and sweetened their night.

Then they bathed together in the luxurious bath that occupied the massive marble bathroom that was a part of their suite. They played and kissed and loved each other.

"Tell me one Joe." She asked him, as she often did, and he took the little brown book from his pants that he had discarded on the floor.

How do I love, thee let me count the ways. He read her the sweetest love sonnet ever written. His voice carried history and promise, mystery and hope and she watched his lips move gently with the words he read. He looked up at her when he finished and smiled.

The twinkle in his eye held a different flame, a new flame, ignited by the vulnerability he felt when he read beautiful poetry to her, the poetry that reflected his soul. The flame was slowly burning off the residue of self-doubt he'd always carried, that voice that whispered *men don't love like women* was getting quieter and quieter as he realised his own truth. The truth was that he loved as large as anyone and he loved this woman most of all.

While he showered she sat with pen in hand and wrote a sonnet for him of Indigo roses and Toronto love and he kissed the paper that held her writing and touched it to his heart as though to imprint the words there for all eternity.

The gesture caught in her throat and touched her soul and she looked up into his face and whispered, "I love you."

And he whispered back. "I love you."

And all the words that ever mattered had been spoken.

The heat and humidity of the day decided the activity. The limo was due to pick them up at five so they took a taxi and walked through the soft sand, holding hands.

The boardwalk of The Beaches was busy. The crowds had brought their dogs along this hot weekend in

July. The couple marvelled at the number of different breeds.

Poodles with their curls defined and set at a posh spa strolled proudly. Labradors frolicked, ready for fun while bull dogs, looking ready for a rumble seethed with desire for the pretty poodles.

A jazz festival set the rhythm of the day. The musicians providing a theme song, the view of the Toronto skyline in the distance the backdrop of a day made for lovers.

They dropped their gear in a pile near a place where sand was piled in a little sofa-back. They could lean against it and watch the water and the people as though reclining in Mother Nature's living room.

Cash was tucked in a little waterproof purse that snapped to her bathing suit bra. Joe told her it was clever as he stroked the skin above her bathing suit top with one mischievous finger.

They swam and played and leaned on the beach together, her body turning a soft golden brown, his darkening to a the deep bronze that his native blood promoted.

It was the hardest day. This would end the weekend of magic. They wondered if they'd ever be together this way again. New love has a magic, a romance that dissolves when the reality of life overlaps with the joy of the new love.

"It's nice." He whispered. "Just being here, not doing anything."

"We're supposed to just *be*, we're human *beings* not human *doings*." She joked and he groaned and swatted her ass for her silliness.

She admired his body in the swim trunks that hugged him. His skin was bronzed by the day's sun. His physique was perfect, muscled and lean and at six feet exactly he was imposing. She had not dated a tall man before and liked feeling protected in his shadow. At five foot five, she was not short. Beside him she felt small. His eyes told her though, that to him, she was quite significant.

She watched him petting a golden retriever held by an elderly man as he walked back with a drink for her. The man looked at Chris and said something that made Joe laugh and nod in agreement.

"I wish we could just stay in love forever, I wish it wouldn't change." She whispered to the wind.

The wind whispered back its honest words. It is not the love that changes. It is the life that moves and flows and separates. It is the human animal that places conditions on love and it is those conditions that alter the emotions gifted to them by the Gods. Love doesn't change, the spirit always loves, always knows who it loves. Life is the great interferer.

The words of the wind made her shiver.

26

Originally built by the pioneers that settled the area, the streets of Kitchener, Ontario are completely illogical. They were built along the Grand River and evolved from trails, to paths, to roads to streets where they eventually became a confusing mess of irrelevant direction. King Street, the main artery through Kitchener and Waterloo runs east and west in the first city and north and south in the other though there is no discernable change of direction. Likewise Victoria Street is signed North and South but runs east and west.

Shaking their heads in wonder at these irregularities, Chris and Joe explored that city hand in hand in search of things to do. One early August day Christianna told him the mystery of the Kaiser, the bust that had been tossed into the Victoria river by young soldiers on the day world war one broke out in Kitchener, and its subsequent disappearance during an outbreak of violence between English and German residents when the decision to change the city's name from Berlin to Kitchener was being voted on. The rumour was that it had been melted down to make napkin rings and Joe joked that surely they would find these rings at the Castle then.

White stone walls with green trim on the turrets of the *Castle on King Street* greeted the visitors. Chris had always wanted to go and he wanted to take her where she dreamt of being.

It was a bit nicer than what they were used to and the service was fast. She ate a club house sandwich and he laughed as she picked off the bacon and tossed it on his plate.

"It's the best part." He joked as he ate it.

The day was a bit cooler, the humidity had broken. The restaurant was dark and not castle-like inside at all. The beer was cold and the service slow which suited them well. They had nowhere to be.

"What are we going to do Joe"? She asked him, her voice low. The hidden thoughts of the past weeks suddenly spilled onto the dark table in front of them. She didn't meet his eyes. They didn't do serious very much but this was going to be that kind of conversation.

"With what?" Joe caught the tone in her voice and it put him on guard. Fear knotted in his stomach and he took a breath.

"I'm going to University in September." Chris blurted the words that she'd left out of their conversations for weeks. "I leave in two weeks for Newfoundland."

The moments after those words were spoken were torture for Christianna. The waitress, as though sensing something had changed, paused on her way to their table, then backed up and returned to the kitchen.

Why didn't you tell me this before?"She looked up in time to see the pain cross his face.

"What did you think I was going to do? Follow you around forever?" Chris became defensive in being wrong.

"I came back to be with you," he said, "and now you're leaving?" He needed her to clarify this for him.

"I *have* to go, I can't work in a factory forever, I put in my notice already and I bought my plane ticket back home."

"So where does that leave me?" He was angry at her for the first time since she had known him. He was also shaken. She hadn't expected the latter to affect her so.

"I have to go, I don't want to leave you but I have to go" Her heart hurt with her words.

He pulled money from his pocket and laid it on the table in front of them. He picked up the beer and drained the last half from the bottle. She watched his movements, breath held, waiting.

"I gotta get out of here." The darkened restaurant was closing in on him. His body shook from his anger and his attempt to control it. He had never felt such betrayal. The urge to hit her was strong and he was ashamed of it.

The flash of the sunlight blinded him as he quickly walked up the sidewalk towards the west, squinting. He heard her behind him calling, and then running.

"Stop." Chris said and she halted.

Joe made several more steps. Then he stopped also and turned to look at her.

"Why didn't you tell me?" His voice carried down the sidewalk to her. Chris walked closer to meet him, afraid. She blinked then, at the pain on his face. His anger was from his hurt and wasn't dangerous. She drew closer.

"I don't know. It just never seemed to be the right time." Their love had been so perfect and she hadn't wanted to wreck it.

"So one day you would have just been gone?" He asked her, his voice lower now as she moved toward him.

"I'm telling you now."

"Is this a done deal?" But he knew. It was. And she was right about one part, she was supposed to do this. He'd been thinking she was too good for him and now she was proving him right.

"I thought you wanted to be a writer." This she could have done anywhere. She could have written in Kitchener. She could have stayed with him.

"I want a more secure job. I may never make it as a writer, who knows if I'm good enough. And I'd still need an education for that anyway." Her voice was stronger now in her determination that this was the right decision.

"You're good enough." She could take courses at the local college, Joe thought. There was no reason for her to go away.

"I need the security, I need to know I can earn an income for myself and that I can have things I never had as a kid." She explained wanting him to understand. She had missed out on what she was entitled to in her hurry to escape her parent's house. Now she was ready to reclaim it.

He understood all too well the need to dig out of that soul stealing poverty they both had known as children. He admired her for it because her path was nobler than his. His heart hurt for himself, but knew this was right for her.

He started to walk again but stayed at a pace that was comfortable for her. A few minutes later he reached out and took her hand. They continued walking in silence for a long while, the only sound a sob that broke in her throat at his touch. He led her to the edge of the stone retaining wall next to a church.

Out of sight from passersby they walked between the stones to an alcove of trees. On the cold ground, on that hot day, their spirits danced in love and anger and desperation. Out of their despair they came together, each clinging to the moments they had left together, each needing to know that this thing they had between them would last through a separation.

The couple looked around the wooded area that overlooked the tombstones that lay in rows lined up like dominoes in some crazy giant game. These were not all fancy markers. Everyone was the same in death, plain, round edged marble or tall impressive monuments. This is where my bones lie they all announced to the world. This is all that is left of me though I lived and loved and danced and cried. The blood in their veins merged with the dirt that covered them. Death, the great equalizer lived here.

"This is a first." Joe looked around at their surroundings, a grin threatening around his lips.

"At least they were a quiet audience." Chris whispered, attempting to be solemn but her giggles were determined and escaped. She pressed her fingers to her lips to hush the sound.

"We're sick." The grin became a laugh and he shook his head as though to deny it.

"Yeah, we are." Chris nodded and laughed again, meeting his dark eyes with her blue laughing ones.

He looked at her and tugged a curl, his anger at her gone to play with the spirits that surrounded them. He loved her. The anger couldn't kill that. The hurt couldn't either.

"What will we do?" Chris asked the question again that she'd asked at the restaurant.

"I'll figure it out," he said. He was already forming a plan in his highly accelerated mind.

Satisfied she leaned against him and he held her in his arms looking out over the sea of stones. He kissed her temple and she cuddled closer.

He *would* figure it out. She chose to believe those words.

His lilted voice filled their surroundings with a solemn air again, the mirth of the moments before forgotten in the sanctuary of the poetry.

"This quiet dust was gentlemen and ladies
And lads and girls;
Was laughter and ability and sighing,
And frocks and curls;

This passive place a summer's nimble mansion,
Where bloom and bees
Fulfilled their oriental circuit,
Then ceased like these"

She shivered at the words of Emily Dickinson. Joe kissed the top of her curly head in reply even as his mind worked on a plan that would keep them together.

27

Joe was now uncomfortable in the place she had shared with Greg. It wasn't just because some of his stuff remained behind, forgotten. Neither was it entirely because he could feel the remnants of her terror here. And although the apartment wasn't as painfully tidy as she'd told him it had been when Kennedy lived with her, he still felt the sickness about it. But that wasn't it. It wasn't even because its walls were too white, its decor too trendy.

He paced, then paused and Chris went over to where he stood at the window, shifting from one foot to another.

"What?" She had tidied and bought steak for the little barbeque that was kept on the balcony.

"I want you to stay." The signs of her packing had jarred him and that was the reason he was uncomfortable. He was also running low on cash. If it hadn't been for the rain that dropped from heavenly buckets he would have insisted on the tree house but it was too wet for that today. And they had to be together every night and weekend now, until next Wednesday.

"I want to stay," she admitted. "But I have to go."

"I know, but I still don't like it." He wondered if he told her what he was going to do, if she would stay to stop him from going through with it.

"Let's not talk about it now." Chris moved towards the kitchen. "Can you light the barbeque?" She handed him a lighter from on top of the package of cigarettes that lay on the counter top.

The flame flickered and grew and Joe squirted more of the fuel on to the charcoal rectangles that were lined in perfect rows at the bottom of the pan.

Who the hell lines up the charcoal like that? Joe moved them around, mixing them up. The coals started to turn white at the edges as they heated up and he stared at them, his eyes brooding, his hands grasping the fuel can in a tight grip.

He sat on the edge of the patio, one leg dangling over the grey cement edge of the wall in the corner of the building, the other inside it. He leaned against the wrought iron pillar that folded at a right angle at the corner of the balcony.

Joe's eyes drifted to the street where some children played nearby. The youngest child was crying, big tears of anger and shame as the older boys moved closer and Joe's sense of justice flared. The little blonde haired boy cried out for them to stop, the pain in his voice familiar. Joe slipped off the patio, landing with a quick thud that Chris heard from inside. She slid open the doors and watched as he approached the kids. His long pony tail quickly became drenched in the rain.

The bedraggled boy looked up at him in wonder, the bigger kids unaware that Joe was behind them until he walked past them and picked up the younger child, slipping him up high on his shoulders, away from their cruelty. Then he turned towards the older boys who backed up, one step, then another with an uncertainty on their faces. The rain ran off the hoods of their rain jackets into their eyes as they glanced at each other and then back at Joe. Christianna smiled from the porch.

"Are you ok?" Joe asked the boy on his shoulders. The little boy, who couldn't have been more than five nodded yes, and then whispered it. He felt like a king up this high. He shivered, but it was from the cold of the rain that had seeped through his rain gear. He didn't feel afraid at all though his mom had warned him about strangers. He knew that this stranger was safe.

Joe's eyes darkened as he spoke to the two older boys with a quiet, cold voice.

"If you ever pick on a kid younger than you again I will kill you." The boys gulped quietly and nodded.

"Where do you live"? He asked the sodden little guy who pointed to a building on the opposite side of the road, a twin to the building Chris lived in. Joe walked across and knocked on the door. He spoke to the lady who answered and pointed to the boys who had been picking on her son. He slipped the child off his wet shoulders and into her arms. She held him close and Chris, even from across the street could see the fear, guilt and gratitude on the mother's face. He'd just wanted to splash in the puddles and she would watch him more closely from now on.

The older boys were unsure of what they should do. They stayed exactly where he'd left them.

Joe walked back to them and he went down to their level. Their eyes widened with fear again. Chris felt sorry for them. Joe looked crazed with his long wet, jet-black hair and wild eyes.

"You can be a bully if you want but someone is always going to be watching, remember that. Perhaps you should be protecting little kids instead of picking on them. Like I just did." Then he smiled at them and they smiled back, slowly.

He tousled their hair then walked to her patio and reached up, grabbing the wrought iron post that stood in the corner and hoisted his body back up on the cement wall. The two boys watched him for a moment and then walked quickly to a building down the road.

"My hero!" Chris joked to him and he was grateful. She softened the anger he'd felt moments before. He regretted being so harsh to the older boys. They were just kids too. He shouldn't have threatened to kill them but he wanted them to understand the gravity of their actions. He had been the smallest boy and knew the pain of being bullied. It was the reason he had stopped them, it was the reason he hated the man who had shared this apartment with Chris. He could feel her pain in this place and wanted her out of here. He just didn't want her to leave him.

Joe picked up the lid of the barbeque and felt the heat on his face. Water droplets fell from his face into the coals and sizzled and silenced. Christianna brought the steaks out and sat beside him as he set them beside the grill.

"Rare?" He asked her.

"Yeah," she answered, and then she added. "Yes you are."

She stood to kiss his handsome cheek. He caught her lips with his and held them for a moment, savouring them, loving them.

He smiled then at her corniness and his mood softened further.

"Rare it is then" he answered and threw her steak on the barbeque.

28

Clothes were strewn in surprised piles. The counter contained dirty dishes and there was stale water in the sink with traces of soap bubbles that were disappearing as the water cooled to a tepid, grey pond. The greasy algae stuck to the sides of the stainless steel sink in a slubby white ring. The beds were unmade and boxes were scattered all over the apartment, as though they had been distributed randomly by some selective tornado. Christianna revelled in the mess. Her nose wrinkled at the smell, tempting her to clean it up, put it back the way it was but she resisted the urge, smiling to herself. She would clean it up in her own good time. It was her secret revenge for the days of living in what she called her sanitary confinement.

Christianna had packed everything that wasn't hers into boxes to be delivered to Greg by David. He had not tried to make contact. She hadn't thought a piece of paper such as a restraining order would keep him away. She was still fearful and jumped when the shirring ring of the phone broke the silence.

"Hey, where ya been?" David asked with cousinly concern and curiosity.

"Picked up a second job," she told the lie she'd planned. "I needed extra money."

"Oh, I was worried." He had been afraid the warning Greg had received hadn't worked when he tried over the weekend to reach her to no avail. She'd disappeared several times now with no explanation and had cut contact with all their friends. He worried about her.

"Yeah, I have some cleaning work evenings and weekends and I've been turning the phone down to sleep."

He accepted her explanation. It made perfect sense.

"What's new?" She asked in case he pressed for more details.

"Not much, I heard Kennedy got beat up." This was old news. He was fishing to see if she knew.

"What?"

"Mugged a while back." He didn't know for sure that Joe was behind it but if so, David was he was grateful to him for making sure she was safe. He hadn't heard from Joe since the night of the party. Until today.

"My buddy Joe is in jail," he said waiting for a response.

"What?" Her heart was a bongo drum resonating in her temples. A band tightened around her and she couldn't inhale.

"Yeah, last night, big drug bust. He'll be away for a long time this time."

"Oh," Chris felt the darkness climbing her body like a tarantula, creeping and crawling and she struggled to remove herself from its grasp, to remain calm, quiet, to keep the secret and most of all to remain lucid.

"Have you talked to him?" David questioned her. He had to know if she was tangled up in this. He'd had his suspicions. His mother had told him she'd heard Joe had left Newfoundland for Ontario weeks ago.

"No, not since that weekend." Her voice was clear and strong as her hands shook. She calmed herself with quiet breaths keeping the despair at bay for another moment.

The only part of her body that could feel anything was the blue rose on her right hand. It throbbed suddenly with a million little needles, more painful than the moments it had been imprinted on her skin in that little parlour in Toronto. It kept her from passing out.

"Can you come by and pick up the last bit of Greg's stuff and bring it to him," she asked hoping that changing the subject might mute the scream that bubbled in her throat.

"Yeah, sure tomorrow after work?"

"See you then, I gotta go finish packing it up."

Chris sat the receiver on its cradle with a deliberate and mindful motion. Her hand was steady now. She looked at the rose where it throbbed. She waited.

The pain, when it came, seared her like a red-hot brand, her heart ripped in her chest with the reality of it all and in a heap on the floor she curled, realisation setting in with a cruel vengeance. Her tears burst in a torrent soaking the rug as she sobbed her pain to the indigo flower on her flesh.

He was gone. He was in prison. The words circled through her mind on a loop, repeating the mantra until every shred of disbelief was driven from her thoughts. There was no denial left, he had been involved in a drug deal and he was gone.

Chris had known of this possibility, had known what he did and somehow convinced herself that it was ok. She had seen a different side of him and led herself to believe that what she was seeing was true.

Eventually her heart accepted the truth and the throbbing in her hand ceased. Her limp body lifted itself off the floor and made its way to the shower and, undressing, Chris turned on the water. The sharp hot shards soothed her body and helped her in her despair, washing the edges off so that it was now bearable, so that she could move forward with her plans, so that she could cope.

She would leave Ontario on Wednesday and there was no chance now that he would be following her she'd hoped. It was simply and completely over.

If Christianna knew one thing about herself it was that just because she loved someone, she wouldn't sacrifice her life for them again. An hour later, after she dried more of her tears, she confirmed her reservation for the flight to St. John's.

She would not be held back by this interlude. She threw herself into mind numbing work for the remainder of her time in Ontario, but occasionally, she awoke at night, picturing Joe laying in a cell somewhere, alone, cold and miserable and the tears would come and she cursed her weakness while she wallowed in her misery.

But during the cold light of day she vowed that never again would she be tempted to sacrifice her heart to another. Not that anyone would want it anyway now that it had been shattered like purple glass in a million little pieces. She feared that only a dark eyed man with a grin constantly threatening the corner of his lips could pick them up and reassemble them anyway.

29

The concrete walls of the cell held a cold energy that sucked the spirit out a man and made him a shell of anger and despair. The peeling paint only attempted to hide the reality of the starkness. The window, with its stainless steel frame and bars, held more cruelty than a darkened room would have. It teased him with the flickers of sunshine that taunted and whispered of the life he was missing.

Incarceration was a fact of life for Joe. He'd joked about it to his buddies, made light of it. He'd done time before for possession. The last time he'd been busted he'd been fortunate. He'd been guilty of trafficking, he'd actually only been caught with the tiniest bit of weed. He was good at hiding things in places where dogs couldn't find them.

This time was different. This was a harder drug and he had known the stakes were higher at the outset. The bust had been planned for months though he'd only decided to get in on the deal the last few weeks, the temptation of the money and how it would free him up to follow Christianna to St. John's his only motivation. It had been a stupid idea.

Joe had decided this would be his last deal. He would get out now. In a fit of self-confidence borne of the love he was feeling for Christianna he decided that he was worthy of following her along on her ambitions and adventures. He'd come up with his own as well. Perhaps he'd go to University himself next year.

The lack of activity was torture. He played different scenes over and over in his mind. He craved books. He craved stimulation, hell a cell mate, no matter how much of a bastard, would be better than this mind numbing aloneness.

And the pictures that flipped through his brain were interspersed with one beautiful face that haunted him and whispered to his brain "You fucked up Joe Indigo. You had *me* and you fucked it all up."

The cement walls crept closer as though on spider legs, whispering again. "You fucked up Joe Indigo, you fucked up." Now he had nothing.

He jumped up from the bunk and started to pace. The first few days he'd expected her to show up. His heart tore exactly in two, divided by his desire to see her beautiful face and the dread of seeing his new reflection in those beautiful eyes. Then the agonizing reality came upon him. She wasn't coming at all.

It had been two weeks and by now she'd be in St. John's, attending classes, he wasn't sure exactly when they started but she'd be there, making new friends, meeting professors, meeting new men. His heart ripped like rotten fabric, torn by the force of his pain.

They'd removed the instruments from the prison system decades before however Joe was still tortured, with time. His busy brain kept returning to her and he craved something, a drug, a drink, anything to dull the pain. Most of all he craved Christianna.

He would be released on bail soon. It could be up to two years, with a good lawyer and continuances before he was actually sentenced for his crimes. He could just plead guilty and do his time and hope for a few months but his lawyer advised against it. He could wait and play the game, and possibly never serve another day.

That was what he had decided because it was the reasonable thing to do. But with this decision came the reality that he couldn't go look for her. That he couldn't go and ask her to live with him in limbo while he waited for his trial. He also knew that if he asked the answer would be no.

After the torture of prison was over he would do his best to free his mind of her memory. He knew how to redirect his busy mind when he was in the hustling real world but for the time being, this tiny cell held no distractions and his mind lathered, rinsed and repeated his memories of their time together.

The corrections department couldn't have imagined their penitentiaries held such torture instruments as a man's own mind, left alone with its pain.

And in the depths of his pain, in his heart of hearts he hoped that maybe she would come one day, her love leading to the low grey buildings that was the Milton Jail. He had put her name on the visitor list just in case. He hoped in vain. She never came.

PART TWO

30

The minister was a boring little man with a rumpled collar and a monotone voice. Every time he mentioned Jesus, Joe pictured him-Jesus-smoking a joint and had to stifle a laugh. It likely had a little to do with the fact that he'd smoked one himself before the ceremony. The large brown leather Bible covered the entire podium and atop it the minister held the book from which he read the ceremony. Joe's red-rimmed eyes tried to focus on the words the minister spoke but he was distracted by the cleavage of the second bridesmaid from the right. She had nice tits and they were much more interesting than the wrinkled face of the preacher or even the blissful face of his bride.

It was 1992 and Joe was 28 years old. He was standing besides a young girl who looked at him as though *he* were the saviour. Her hair was piled in a large mass of curls surrounded by a white cloud of some sort of fluffy fabric. Tiffany's dress fell in layers of satin and lace to the floor and the high collar and long sleeves fitted her body tightly, hiding the little bulge below her waistline so that only those that knew could tell. He looked back at the bridesmaid's breasts.

One night when he'd been stoned out of his mind he'd met Tiffany and saw a superficial resemblance to Chris. It was sordid and stupid, she was only 16, but the girl had worshipped him. He was much older, handsome and exciting and he wanted her. He'd taken her virginity one night as she babysat for her sister and their fate was set. Perhaps what was more surprising, particularly to Joe Indigo, was that he'd stayed with her. Part of it was to prove her parents wrong, and some of it was because of the similarity to Christianna. Mostly it was because it was just nice to be loved. Either way, here he was, saying vows and taking adult responsibility.

As the minister spoke his standard drone, asking them to hold hands Joe reached out and took her soft cool one in his. Just then his eye caught sight of the little blue rose. He was holding a hand that didn't quite match and tears threatened behind his eyelids at the realisation that there was more than one thing that didn't match on this day including the bride and groom. Don't do this, the spirits whispered. It's not right. He looked around for his escape.

His young bride misunderstood his emotion and her eyes filled with tears as well, thinking he was as moved as she was by the ceremony. Tiffany hadn't ever seen such a display of emotion from him before. It gave her hope that he loved her too, though she was sure she loved him enough for both of them.

Guilt at her tears pushed him to say, "I do," and to hush the voices and marry this young girl who could never be who he wanted her to be. Christianna was no longer relevant and his determination to prove that to himself grew stronger as he repeated his vows. Besides that, there was a baby coming, he had no choice.

The bar was smoky and the buzz of the alcohol relaxed his overactive mind. He had smoked a joint and the room floated around him. A dark haired woman shifted close to him and he forgot about his wife and his earlier determined decision to be a good husband. He liked the way this woman smelled and he found she was almost immediately open to a rendezvous in her room.

Her scent was pleasant. His drug mashed brain didn't know why it was familiar until the sweet-candied tones of Jackson Browne drifted from the radio on the night stand. Suddenly he recognised the perfume. She was wearing Christianna's scent, something unidentified and unnamed, yet etched in his mind as the music they'd loved sent him back to that room at the Royal York in a blur of heart wrenching *déjà vu.*

The face of the woman he'd lost slammed into his cannabis-baked grey matter bringing him down with a thud. He jumped from the bed and dressed, haunted and hurt. He left the woman confused and deserted under the covers. He made his way back through the maze of hallways desperately trying to locate the honeymoon suite where his wife slept.

When he finally found it he hit the shower, to remove the evidence of where he'd been. Joe allowed himself then to think of Chris, a rare luxury. He thought that perhaps the pain was lifting and that maybe, bit by bit he could think of her now with some objectivity.

Someday he might even be able to give up the alcohol and drugs he used to keep her away when he was alone. Perhaps if he let himself think of her occasionally the memories wouldn't slam into him with such a force when he didn't expect it. But not on that night.

As his tears joined the water that flowed down the shower disappearing into the drain he whispered to the spirits that surrounded him always, the guides who beckoned him daily to return to the place he should be. "Help me, it's time, please help me forget her."

But the spirit guides, knowing his destiny and knowing that his destiny was eternally connected to hers whispered back to him a dark cruel truth, "You never will Joe, you never will."

Christianna Cormack
Rare Moon Tickle, NL
1995

31

The wind howled around outside battering at the frost-painted windows. But still the classroom was too hot. Chris was tired. She had been up late reading some essays she'd assigned the class. Some were barely passable, most were average and a couple would need some remediation. Two were brilliant. She would sit with the troubled ones and help them write a passable paper. She believed in mastery learning and never failed a student if she could help them in some way.

The noise level rose in tiny degrees, slowly stepping up until suddenly she was unable to ignore it any longer. It was Stephen Miles again. His voice became louder and he moved his hands in a furtive gesture as he told his story to a friend in the next seat. She walked to his desk and stood there. He looked up at her with a guilty grin. Then he looked back at the red-haired boy beside him and pretended to be interested suddenly in Hamlet. Then he looked back up at her.

"Sorry Miss," he said sheepishly, a grin lurking behind the fake guilt.

"Can you read the scene," she asked him. She found getting him involved usually calmed him down.

"Ok miss- *I am but mad north-north-west: when the wind is southerly I know a hawk from a handsaw*," Stephen read when he found the page, over-dramatising to the amusement of the class. Chris held back her own smile. He looked at her, his blue eyes flashing, flirting with her. She might be in her mid-twenties now but she knew that look. She glanced away for a moment, something in his face familiar and disturbing. It crossed her mind that he was an incredibly attractive young man. Chris chided herself for a moment, shocked at the thought. Gathering her senses about her again she looked back at him.

"How was that?" *She wasn't even paying attention* he thought, more annoyed than he should have been by her distraction that he interpreted as rejection.

"Good, now tell me what it means?" She was all *teacher* again now, recovering from her highly inappropriate thoughts.

He looked at the page, reading it over. He *could* participate. He was a good solid student.

"He's crazy." Stephen said.

"And?" Chris prompted. He could do better. His was one of the brilliant papers.

"He's going crazy." Stephen revised still reading under his breathe.

"For real or is he just pretending to be crazy?" Chris had become mesmerized by his long finger running under the words on the page and her voice was sharper than she intended when she spoke.

"Why would he pretend?" His blue eyes flashed angrily. It hurt that she was always so short with him.

"Good question. What do you think?" She pushed him a little more, gentler this time. God, she needed a man, this boy, while he looked grown up at already six feet tall, was a child. She smiled then, forgiving herself. It was just a thought, it meant nothing.

He looked at the book again and a familiar spark of mischief crossed his face.

"You may be right, he may be crazy," he sang and the immediate laughter from the class spurred him on. He hopped up and grabbed a pencil case of the blond girl in the seat ahead beside his for a microphone and began gyrating and singing to the amusement of his classmates.

"But it just may be a lunatic you're looking for, turn out the light..." Chris shook her head. She was so bad at this discipline stuff. She walked to the front of the class hiding her smile. She let him finish his tune and had to admit that he was talented. The kids were out of control now and she wrote the next day's reading on the board as the singing continued.

Billy Joel would have been proud. She was proud. She liked the kid in spite of herself. The bell rang and they sprang to the door. Stephen led the way, still singing and he winked boldly at her. She rewarded him with a large dimpled smile that made his stomach crumple with desire and he turned away, embarrassed at how much he liked her and hoping she hadn't noticed it in his eyes. He flicked his binder at the pretty girl, whose pencil case had been his microphone. He attempted to distract himself from thoughts of Miss Cormack by paying attention to a girl his own age.

"Got a minute?" The principal, George Powers popped his head around Christianna's class door a short while later.

"Sure." His tone was serious and caused Chris to wonder what she'd done now. She was wearing a longer skirt, with pantyhose, no cleavage, hair up, minimal makeup, all of the requests that had come down from various parents over the past few months since she'd been teaching there, had been met. It had concerned some of them that she wasn't properly dressed for her profession and she'd accommodated them to the best of her abilities. She waited quietly.

"We've got a problem." Great, here it comes, she thought. She didn't understand why everybody thought she was such a loose woman, if only they knew how celibate she actually was.

"Uh-oh." Perhaps it was the noise in the classroom, other teachers had complained before.

"Stephen Miles."

"What did he do?" That was it then, they'd heard his impromptu performance. She was busted.

"He's been accused of stealing." George's face was glum.

"What?" Christianna looked up, her mouth formed a dismayed no expression, shock lightened her eyes and she shook her head in disbelief.

"One of the other kid's money," George took in her expression and added with his own nod, "I know, I don't believe it either."

"He isn't a thief though he's a bit wild," It surprised her how strong her conviction was.

"We have no evidence but we're just asking the teachers to keep an eye out, you know, see if he lingers behind."

"He's a good kid deep down." There was a glimmer of something special in him, hidden underneath his cocky attitude. She knew she pushed him a little and she sensed he didn't like her much for it but there was something that endeared him to her and she wished there was a way to help him.

"Yeah, he's got so much energy he needs sports or something to occupy his time and his brain but his mother can't afford it and the school has nothing he's interested in." The principal seemed as troubled as she was.

"Tough break but now I have to do the dirty work. I've got to ask him about it." George shrugged his shoulders and then let them droop, his dark brown eyes sad.

She gathered things together, glancing out the window at the blowing snow. Her mind distracted, she struggled to put on the sweater that hung on the back of her chair, sweat beading on her forehead with the effort. She furrowed her brow and forced herself to forget about this situation for the moment. She had to concentrate on getting home in the storm.

A thought was already gathering in her subconscious as she drove home, though it had yet to break through and make itself known. The snow swirled and demanded attention and she gripped the steering wheel tightly and concentrated fully on the road as her tires crunched slowly along the seaside road and up the driveway of the little bungalow she rented. She fought her way to the door and into the warmth and dropped her things, grateful to be alive after the experience, forgetting all about Stephen Miles and classes and school. But it would only be for a little while.

32

The Atlantic Ocean ranted and roared outside the window of the room she'd chosen as her office. Between grading papers or the odd hours of writing she felt compelled to do by her soul, she looked over the suddenly indigo shaded waters, a gift and a trick of the evening sky and the setting sun, and was reminded of Joe. It was the colour, not the place that tapped at the inner walls of her hardened heart because they'd never seen the ocean together.

The town was called Rare Moon Tickle and she loved it. It was tiny place situated against a backdrop of the Atlantic. The little bay was dotted with rich green islands and one larger island, called Rare Moon Island, created a tiny water way called a tickle. It was this area of water, where ships and boats would carefully navigate into the town that became its namesake.

She had rented the small house near the school and settled in. The house was huge compared to her dorm room. She rattled around in it alone, unsettled by the amount of space at first then overjoyed at it. Her dorm room had been big by dorm room standards but a thousand square feet was positively luxurious. She chose the larger bedroom as an office, preferring the view it offered. She set her bed up in the smaller room across the hallway and spent her evenings grading tests as the waters took turns raging or seducing her, depending on its mood.

A shiver of sweet nostalgia trickled through her as the familiar voice of Jackson Browne drifted through the speakers when she hit play on the cassette player. It was a copy of the tape that Joe had made for her so many years before, the original tucked in a box with copies of the poetry she'd written for him and a few other souvenirs. She rubbed her forefinger over the tattoo on her hand. The parents had judged her on that one but unlike the short skirts, big curly hair and tank tops of that time, the rose would stay forever as a reminder.

She pulled the stack of papers from the desk and the name on the paper at the top of the pile distracted her from her memories. She was going to try to do something for Stephen Miles and the glimmer of an idea that had been tickling at the back of her mind shifted into her consciousness as a flash of brilliant inspiration.

Chris glanced at the clock checking it to see if it was too late and reached for the phone book. She found Harry Callum's number and his wife quickly got him on the phone. Harry was a local music teacher. He sometimes helped out at the school and she'd met him when they were planning the annual Christmas concert.

"I'm taking students later in the spring." Harry informed her. He needed students. He was about to lose a few as they grew out of the lessons their parents had forced on them.

"He wouldn't be just starting," Harry also told her. He had taken lessons before, when he was younger but when his mother and her husband split up there was no more money for them.

"The thing is...." This was the tricky part. "We'd have to keep it quiet. It wouldn't look good and I've had a few problems since I've been here." She hoped he'd help her out and tried not to think of the ramifications if it leaked out. That sort of favouritism would be questioned, it was a lot of money from a young female teacher to a young, handsome male student and her motives would be suspect.

"I see." Harry listened to her reasons and reassured her that she could trust him. He needed the student, and besides, this was an amazing thing for her to do for the young man. He believed her motives genuine and wouldn't betray her.

"He'd need a guitar too, for practice." Stephen had been using his mom's boyfriend's guitar before which had left with him.

By the time Harry had space for Stephen, Christianna had found a guitar in a little pawn shop during one of her trips to St. John's. She brought it to Harry after dark one evening telling him that she hoped it would do. She knew next to nothing about guitars but Harry laughed and was shocked when she told him the price she'd paid.

"You've got a horseshoe up yer arse!" Harry joked as he admired the instrument. Or perhaps it was her beneficiary that was the lucky one. He couldn't wait to give it to the boy.

Stephen skipped stones into the water with skill, one, two, three, four, five, they skidded perfectly every time. His brain was bored. His heart was angry. The water was perfectly calm belying the fact that it was a running brook. It flowed slowly. He saw the mallard swim from beneath an overhang of alders that met at the narrow part of the brook just before it turned and widened. He watched the water ripple around the duck in perfect little peaceful circles, completely idyllic in its innocence. He picked up a perfectly round and flat stone and held it between his thumb and forefinger as though to skip it. He stood sideways to the stream and raised his arm to his hip. He aimed for the bird.

"Stephen!" The shout frightened the duck. It took off in a fluster of feathers and water, flying low and close near him so that he pulled back although there was no danger of the bird hitting him.

Harry Callum? Stephen tossed the stone into the water. What the hell did he want?

"Yeah?" He started up the bank towards the road.

"Been looking for you." Harry sounded breathless. His car idled on the curb and he leaned on it as though he needed it to hold him up. Harry was an old man already. His weathered face was gentle, tanned from being outside and his cheeks encased his kind grey eyes like waxed paper, crepe and folded. He waited for Stephen to get to the car.

"What?" He didn't waste much time on social graces.

"Yeah I wanted to talk to you about music lessons. I called your house and it said the phone was disconnected."

"Yeah?" The shame rumbled in his heart, squeezing it closer, oozing out the anger and frustration that was held there by a young man whose life was held in uncaring hands.

"Was thinking you should start the guitar lessons back up." He had to do this just right. He and Chris had come up with the story between them.

"Not interested." There was no way they could afford guitar lessons, hell, they had no fuckin' phone but he wasn't telling this old geezer that.

"Well, it's kind of like a scholarship. You were a good student and I'm offering free guitar lessons and voice lessons. I have a real nice guitar someone gave me that they got cheap and thought maybe you'd be able to have it to practice."

"What do you get out of this?" His interest was piqued suddenly. Free?

"One good student?" Harry smiled because this part at least was the truth. "You were really talented. I have a lot of students and you're the best one I've ever had. You were meant to play and sing. I know you didn't have time for a while but I thought maybe you had a few more spare hours on your hands these days."

He glanced at the spot where the boy had been aimlessly skipping stones a moment ago. He wouldn't be able to use lack of time after the idleness of the previous few moments as an excuse any longer.

"Seriously?" Stephen was starting to feel this might be real. His doubts started to leave and his heart started to lighten. He had loved playing guitar. He loved music. It was his escape, his drug of choice, his passion and when he'd been forced to give up the lessons because his mother and his stepfather had split up he'd been lost. As much as he loved to listen to music, he felt drawn to more. He had been born to *make* music. His stepfather said he had talent and had offered to continue to pay but his mother had forbidden all contact with her son when they split.

"So no strings?" Stephen couldn't help being suspicious, there were usually strings. He didn't acknowledge the pun in his words.

"Well maybe one." Harry said with a smile that was kind. "Keep your grades up at school. I don't want to get in trouble with your mother for taking time away from your school work." The request was really for Christianna but he couldn't say that.

His mother wouldn't care Stephen thought but the anger he felt towards her melted as he held out his hand to Harry Callum who took it and shook it warmly.

Harry saw why that pretty young teacher wanted to help this kid. He was angry, he was alone and he was bored. He'd heard about that mother of his and not much of it was good. He didn't like gossip much but the way this kid was behaving told him things weren't right at home.

Harry drove the little white Chevy carefully back to his house to pick up the guitar Chris had bought. His wife nodded at him when she saw the boy in the car and he acknowledged her with raised eyebrows and took the instrument she handed him. He smiled with wonder and shook his head. The teacher hadn't even known what a treasure it was. He strummed it as he walked out of the house. He'd have to see about getting a case for it. It was too valuable to be carried like this. He opened the front passenger door and handed it in to Stephen, carefully maneuvering it so that it didn't scratch against anything.

Stephen's eyes bulged and he wondered if he should pinch himself. He closed them then and listened as he absorbed the simple notes that filled the car. He strummed the instrument he held reverently between his knees like a cello. He hadn't been expecting this. It was almost exactly his dream guitar, the one on the picture pinned over his desk with a white tack.

He looked over at Harry as he climbed in the driver's side of the car. He wanted to say thank you but he was afraid to. He was afraid he'd break the magic of the spell. He was also afraid he would cry. Instead he formed another chord on the upright guitar and strummed it again.

Stephen Miles was still a kid. But his dream had just been handed to him and he made a choice in the moment he heard those first melodic chords out of that pawn shop Gibson Hummingbird guitar that was dropped in his lap that day. He made the choice even older people often fail to make. He would follow his dream with his entire heart.

His marks dipped a bit. He couldn't put the damned thing down. He spent hours in the shed with it because his mother hated the noise when he practiced.

When Chris kept him behind one day to talk about a paper he'd not done so well on he admitted he spent his time practicing guitar. She'd smiled and told him that was ok then as long as he redid it. She took a red pen and showed him where he'd gone wrong. Instead of the anger he usually expressed at being shown his mistakes he listened carefully and agreed with her, later re-writing the paper to get the A he was capable of.

Then she asked him if he'd play for the Christmas concert. He wasn't ready he insisted but she saw he wanted to. Harry encouraged him as well and he sang a version of Silent Night on a dark December evening that warmed her heart and set him up with a new reputation.

Chris watched silently knowing that his life had been changed by her secret gift. If it was the only reward she would receive for her generosity, it was enough. The universe had different ideas though.

Roxanne Armstrong
Rare Moon Tickle, NL.

33

It came from an unknown place and mingled with the cigarette smoke that filled the kitchen. She couldn't quite pin down the source. The house was quiet, the television was off and the kid should still be at his graduation ceremony.

There it was again. It stopped and started and now there was a different tone to it. It must be a car radio, someone playing with the station button. Roxanne was intrigued. She snuffed her cigarette in the ashtray and went to the door.

She looked out into the dark night. Her house was at the end of the road. She hit the switch for the outdoor light but nothing happened. The bulb was blown. Shit, she'd get him to fix that tomorrow.

She listened. She could still hear it, but it was quieter. It was coming from the back of the house, not from the street. The house was built with the kitchen at the back and that was where the music was loudest.

She slid the window open over the sink and the music was suddenly present and finally discernable. The smooth voice delivered the lyrics of the soulful ballad perfectly, lilting gently over nuanced rhythms. The guitar accompanied rather than over-powered the voice. It had a familiar ring to it and her heart ached in her chest when she heard the similarities.

He sounded so much like his father.

Pulling a chair out from the end of the table closest to the open window Roxanne eased herself into it. She was just over a hundred pounds but she was weighted down with the emotional obesity that life had dealt her.

This song she knew. So many years ago, when she was in love, when she was happy, he had sung this song to her and she had believed him. She closed her eyes and listened.

"Oh My Love, for the first time in my life, my eyes are wide open, oh my love for the first time in my life, my eyes can see."

She opened them quickly. There was no pain.

Had her heart finally mended after all this time? She listened again and felt the onset of another set of feelings, then like a cyst it burst, sending its poison into her system. She gasped as the realisation spread. She felt weak as the regrets came upon her one after another slapping her from the inside.

God, she had fought this. Roxanne had banished every thought of Stephen's father from her mind. She'd married a second musician because of a faint resemblance to her lost love and then spent their entire marriage hating him for not being the man she really wanted. She had fought with Arnold over the guitar lessons and well, pretty much everything that involved her son, and when she'd driven him away she took the beloved guitar lessons from Stephen so she didn't have to listen to the music.

Roxanne had tried with her entire being to prevent Stephen from becoming a musician. She had convinced herself it was for his own good, there was no money in it, and he should concentrate on school, but with the words of the song drifting in through the kitchen window she realised it had been for *her* own good, not his. She had been trying to protect herself from the memories, from the reminders of that betrayal.

And it had happened anyway. He *was* a musician. It had been born into him and it was as certain as the inevitability of the rainfall that he would eventually find it. It was his nature and wouldn't be subdued.

She had held her own hurt selfishly inside, using it as an excuse for her lot in life. The worse part was she'd taken a little boy down with her. She had punished her son, *his* little boy that she'd wanted completely as he'd grown inside her, but whom she had pushed away with cruel regularity when any resemblance to his father became apparent.

Remorse filled Roxanne's heart and spilled out with the tears that flowed. With them came a cleansing. Now, without the pain, she could see things more clearly. She had worked so hard to make him different, to destroy the memories that haunted her when he looked at her with his father's face. She had tried to destroy the essence of who he was.

She considered her emotions for a moment and realised one other thing. That finally, after all these years, she loved her son more than she loved his father and probably always had. She just hadn't known it because she just hadn't been strong enough to compare the two side by side.

She wiped her face with the back of her hand and cleared her throat. The decision followed in a quantum moment. Clarity, its defining impetus, moved her forward. It might be too late but she would try. Maybe he would forgive her, maybe in time she would explain. For now she would start with something small.

She went to the cupboard and pulled down a package of Purity Ginger Snap biscuits and a plate. They were Stephen's favourite. She opened the cellophane on the top of the box and dumped out a handful. Then she pulled down a glass and went to the refrigerator for the milk jug.

Glass and plate in hand she backed through the screen door and let it swing shut behind her. The guitar music stopped with the bang and she hesitated for a moment. She headed towards the shed with the simple gift in her hand, her goal definite.

Roxanne knew it was time and now that she knew, she couldn't go back. She moved forward towards it, then she pushed the door open with her foot and entered.

Stephen's eyes snapped with anger. Then he saw the plate and glass in her hand and looked confused. She understood the look. It was better than the hatred she'd seen the moment before.

With a shy smile she set it on the little Stanley workbench beside the door. The spice-coloured discs slipped around on the plate as her hand shook. She straightened up and met his eyes.

"Just thought you might want a snack," she said with a nervous smile. "Oh and that song was real nice." Then, losing her nerve, she left the shed quickly. He hadn't spoken and she was afraid of what he would say when he did.

Roxanne walked back to the house hoping she had done it right. She wasn't even sure what she was supposed to be doing. He had looked so handsome in his suit.

She only knew that after all this time, she finally, more than she had ever wanted anything, even his father, wanted to be his mother. Roxanne had taken the first of many steps towards that end. She would make that her life goal now and hopefully, with time he'd understand and be her son again. She picked up the half full glass of vodka from the table and poured it down the sink. She then took the ashtray off the table and decided against another. Instead Roxanne Armstrong walked to the telephone and opened the thick phone book that she normally didn't need, she knew all of her regular numbers in the tickle. She hesitated only a moment before she dialled.

The friendly hello came after only two rings and she cleared her throat and responded.

"Hi father Doyle," she said in a shaky voice. "I needs to make a confession and ..." Her voice broke but she cleared her throat again. "And I needs some advice, this is Roxanne Armstrong."

"That's what I'm here for m' love" The priest replied and Roxanne knew by the gentle tone of his voice that she had made the right decision. Father Doyle smiled at the other end of the line.

34

The crimson sunset danced over the calm cerulean ocean, tickling and teasing it, just a moment away from a sweet kiss before it whispered goodnight and dropped behind the horizon. It pulled her in, capturing her imagination and her heart all at once. It was more than oil and canvas, it breathed with her and she was drawn to it, unable to decide if the red or blue enticed her more.

A teacher by profession, Christianna's hostess painted as a hobby and the walls of the home were her gallery. It was one of these paintings Chris was admiring when a gentleman she'd never met before came up behind her.

"Beautiful work isn't it?" He said, his voice was soft and there was a hint of a dialect that was unfamiliar.

"Yeah, she's very talented." Chris turned to the man and smiled.

"I'm Michael Carlisle." He held out his hand to her.

"Chris Cormack," she turned to him and shook it. It was cool and soft, but firm.

His blonde hair was cut short, a few freckles sprinkled over his straight nose and his eyes were blue, lighter than hers and might have appeared grey if he wore a different colour than the bright blue polo-styled shirt he had on.

"How long have you known the Andrews?" His eyes crinkled at the corners and he had some lines around his mouth. He was older than he first appeared.

"Just a short time really, I met Ada at the school when I started teaching there, just met her husband at the Christmas party in December. You?"

"They're patients of mine." He was surprised they hadn't met before. Perhaps she had a doctor in town.

"Ah, yes, I don't get sick, that's why we haven't met." She'd heard about the local doctor. The most eligible bachelor in town was discussed frequently by the available teachers and jokingly by the married ones as well. She could see what the fuss was all about now. He was attractive.

They fell into a comfortable conversation that didn't go unobserved by the other guests. The town had been speculating about his love life and his sexual orientation since he'd moved to Rare Moon Tickle five years before. Chris sensed their curiosity and ignored it. He was nice. At the end of the night he walked her to her car.

"Can I call you sometime?" She was the first woman who'd interested him since he'd moved here. The lilt of her voice as she spoke passionately about her students, her writing, the art on the walls of their hosts' home was refreshing. She was very pretty and highly intelligent. He was surprised she was just a teacher as he suspected she was capable of much more. Her dialect was a little different than the folks here in this town, perhaps partly from her time in Ontario and perhaps because she simply grew up in a different cove. One thing he'd learned was that these Newfoundlanders were as varied in their speech from one harbour to the next as the landscape was.

The call came in the middle of grading papers. She refused his first invitation because it was exam and then report card time. She asked him to call back at the end of June when school was officially out, and she made him promise. She didn't want him to think she wasn't interested. He called again on the last day of school.

"You're determined."

"No flies on me." He repeated a saying she was familiar with and Chris smiled.

They chatted comfortably over dinner and wine at the Avalon Mall's famed restaurant-bar, The Strand and then went to see a movie.

"I like all kinds of movies," he chatted, "thought this might be good for a date night," He referred to the Hugh Grant movie that was advertised on the marquis.

"Sounds good to me." She agreed that a light comedy might be perfect for a first date as well.

They drove up to Signal Hill after the movie and parked in front of the grey stone barricade wall that surrounded Cabot tower. It was clear and the city was brightly lit, the Basilica of St. John the Baptist the overwhelming centre piece of the landscape. She remarked on its beauty, trying to make out the statue of Mary that she'd always loved to visit when she was a student in downtown. The area in front of the basilica and the war memorial were her favourite outdoor study spots and now she sometimes wrote there.

He remarked on her beauty, wondering at the wild mess of her hair. He preferred her subdued, neat style that she'd worn when they'd met.

She laughed at his attempt at flattery and was still smiling when he bent to kiss her, a gentle kiss that barely touched her lips. It was sweet and tender like the man himself. She liked him and he liked her.

The stars dotted the sky, the near-constant fog absent that night and the same constellations that the great navigators had followed to discovered this great island offered her a new direction. She looked into the night and wondered if this nice man would want to come along with her on the rest of her journey. It was too early to say but she felt that he might. His eyes were gentle and kind and she knew he might be open to the invitation.

This time she would go slowly. This time she would make sure it was steady and secure and real before she jumped. She would resist the urge to follow the call of her impulsive and romantic heart. Christianna never once wondered why it was so easy to make that decision, *this* time.

It slipped into romance and Chris was grateful that it held none of the intense emotion of her time with Joe. She felt as though this man was a perfect companion with which to live out her life.

They dated sensibly, getting to know each other well and then one perfect summer day, on a beach where the ocean calmed for them and lapped on grey ancient stones, he got down on one knee and gave her a large diamond set in white gold. She flinched and accepted it because he didn't know she hated diamonds and at least this one was a family heirloom and completely different from her previous one.

He was delighted. He had been nervous to ask. He sometimes wondered if she actually felt as deeply about him as he did about her. Her acceptance confirmed for him that she was just reserved in expressing her emotions, but it didn't mean she didn't feel them. He didn't see the contradiction in his conclusion, that this girl who was exuberant and passionate in all other areas of her life would be reserved in love.

35

The property stretched in a little arch at the end of a long lane. Surrounded by a grove of trees on either side, it opened to the Atlantic Ocean in a sheltered little oyster-shaped cove that held its own special pearl. Rare Moon Island, the owner had told them, was so named because at times the full moon settled over the centre of it lighting it up, sometimes with a bright red-orange glow and at other times it almost appeared blue. It hung low in the sky on those nights as though it actually sat on the island instead of above it. It was an odd little quirk of nature and it was this view of the lot that convinced a romantic Christianna that this was where they should build their home.

Then he explained the legend of the island to an interested and enthralled Christianna while Michael furiously punched the keys on his calculator.

"If you take your lover to the island when the moon is full, the story is the spirits will tell you if it's meant to be in this life." The realtor-slash-local boat-builder told her with twinkling eyes. He was nicknamed Chief though his real name was Glen Francis.

A more practical Michael was concerned at the price but her blue eyes begged him and he surrendered easily, unable to deny her when she asked for so little.

This was how it was supposed to be, a sensible doctor, a nice teacher, a new home about to be built in a perfect little corner of nature. There was also money. She had more than she'd ever dreamed of and Michael was completely open and generous. She'd lived very frugally and was now debt free after only three years out of university. She graded papers in her little office and he made plans for their home.

Her parents were devastated that she didn't have a church wedding and they didn't attend the ceremony but nonetheless, they were relieved that at least she was married this time and to a doctor. Perhaps in time she'd find her way back to the church. They prayed earnestly for this, the card with the cheque for a hundred dollars said. Chris never cashed it.

One day, about a month after they were married, as she sat by her desk and wrote thank you cards, Michael came up to her and kissed her neck from behind. He held the plans for the house they were building and they had to discuss some things.

He rolled them out on her little kitchen table and pointed to an area at the end of the sheet. She didn't quite understand how to read the plans. It appeared there was an addition.

"I decided I don't want to have an office in the basement." He said and she understood that. They each needed their own home office and they had designed it so that hers was upstairs, his down.

"So you added on an office?" She asked.

"Actually I added on another bedroom."

"Why?" Christianna was confused.

"Because if I take this bedroom for the office then when we have children they will be too far away so I thought we could build this as a bedroom on this side and then take the closer one for another child's room and the two further bedrooms could each be our offices." He pointed to the blurred paper in front of her. Her silence was mistaken for thoughtfulness. He didn't catch the gasp of shock.

Christianna felt herself swing back into reality. They'd *never* discussed children. She wasn't even sure why. She had thought if he wanted children he would have brought it up before. He was so driven in his career he would have no time for them and between her teaching and the writing she had started doing at night and on weekends again, she had no time either.

But time wasn't the issue, Chris wasn't sure she ever wanted any. Currently she was completely positive that she didn't have room in her life for them. She didn't say a word and nodded instead and said, "I wouldn't want an office in a dreary basement either."

Michael was happy with her reply. They had never brought up the issue of kids but he assumed she'd want at least two. She could stop teaching and take care of them. He sensed she was getting close to that point anyway. She had expressed some boredom with it and she'd started writing more, a hobby he fully supported. If she didn't want children now, at least the little hint had let her know he was open to the possibility. He called the builder and informed him that the change was a go.

Christianna grabbed her jacket shortly after and went for a walk. The wind was blowing straight in from the ocean across the little breakwater in the distance. It was cold and grey and the evening was closing in on her. The days were getting shorter already and summer had barely started. She'd be back to school in a few weeks and for the first time she wasn't looking forward to it. She had made a lot of progress in her book and she was hoping the first draft would be done before school started. She wanted to quit teaching eventually, but she was thinking of giving it up to write full time, not to raise children.

Her husband wanted children. The thought repeated like the compact disc in her Sony Walkman when she hit replay to hear *Something Fine* over and over. She pulled her collar higher as the wind tugged and pulled and tried to distract her from her thoughts. She was oblivious to the biting sting against her cheeks as she realised something. Of course her husband wanted children. Most married couples eventually had them. She wasn't entirely sure *she* wanted them though. She couldn't picture *their* kids. She couldn't see perfect little Christiannas and Michaels in her arms.

When she could conjure up the image of a child at all it had dark, deep eyes with disturbing flecks of indigo in the depths. She could picture a child with an impish grin and the energy of a million little fireflies dancing on a summer breeze. She could picture Joe's children but she couldn't picture Michael's. She chewed the inside of her cheek as she wondered at her silly heart, still wanting him, still dreaming of him. Would he ever really be gone from her mind? The wild wind again spoke the words that she avoided in the reality of her life.

It told Christianna with harsh certainty that no, she would never ever get over him and for the first time in years she cried bitter tears for the loss of her love, her heart longing as much as it ever did, to be held in the arms of Joe Indigo. And when the tears dried and the hurt subsided she walked home to her husband, knowing she'd never love him that way, knowing she had been horribly unfair to let him think she would and vowing even more fervently to never let him know.

36

Christianna re-read the paragraph again trying to make sense of the words the student had written. Hamlet was getting tiresome after several years of repeating the same work. She should have switched plays but hadn't had a chance to prepare for a new one and now she regretted it. She wasn't sure if the student wasn't making sense or if her brain was just resisting and reading it all wrong. She sighed and closed the folder. How she resented it all, glancing with longing at the computer that she was determined to avoid until her work was done.

She loved the kids. She wished she could go to the school, spend time with them, teach them and then never assign them any work or force them to do any tests. She was starting to doubt the value of it all. She saw children who were not academically inclined fall behind. She saw incredibly gifted students bored and unchallenged. She worked diligently to keep the kids on either end of the spectrum in class. She challenged the gifted, refusing to let them slide by, but the authority knocked her back and the parents weren't much better. So their kid got A's easily, he was smart. *That was good*, they argued. Christianna was frustrated that they couldn't see that they were making kids lazy and that an easy A was not going to build esteem. It would build a kid who was good at writing tests and papers and passing with minimal effort.

They were losing the best and the brightest almost every year when one or two of the smartest graduates dropped out of the first year of university. They were not used to work, to challenging themselves, while the average student who had learned effort got a degree and moved into success. She felt frustrated at the lack of support for any student who didn't fall down the centre and her disillusionment showed in her unhappiness at night as she graded the papers.

Chris found both solace and temptation in her writing. She had recently been successful with some publications and was becoming confident in her talent. She'd neglected her true passion for so long and was anxious to parlay it into a career. She didn't come out and talk about writing to Michael but he seemed to support her efforts, encouraging her to write and submit her work.

Candles flickered tall and graceful from the wedding gift crystal candle holders and the wedding china was set out with the pinwheel crystal wine glasses that didn't quite match the candle holders. She didn't notice, distracted by the smell of something delicious cooking in the oven. She dropped her bags and sniffed appreciatively. Excited, she struggled with the zipper on her boot and he came around the corner with a smile.

"Sit, let me get it." Michael offered and she agreed and kissed him. His lips were nice and warm, gentle as always. She sat on the bench beside the door and he unzipped the boot, pulled it off and reached for the other one.

"Surprise?" She asked with a grin.

"Surprise!" He laughed. "I made a special dinner."

"Yay, starving!" It was already 5pm. "How was the trip?" He'd been in St. John's working at the hospital. He did occasional work at the Health Sciences Centre when doctors were on vacation. He stayed in town as the shifts were long and demanding.

"Good." He was excited but his expression remained calm. He was a man of level emotions, difficult to read. He always kept his emotions in check. Chris could tell he was excited though this was as exuberant as he could bring himself to be

"What?" Chris lit up with excitement. Her excitement made him happy. He would be embarrassed to show such emotional excitement but she'd dance around crazily when a poem was published or an article accepted to a magazine. He smiled at her when she did this as though he indulged a child. If there was little or no monetary reward, he wondered how excited she'd be if she got paid for her writing! He understood she was proud of herself. He was proud of her too. He didn't say anything though, just looked at her with an amused smile. It was a pretty good hobby, this writing she did. It would keep her satisfied at home when they had the kids. He knew she wasn't the type to give up everything to raise a family so this writing thing would be perfect until she was ready to go back to work.

"Later," he smiled, with the soft New England R drifting away at the end of the word.

"This must be big." She had never known him to surprise her with something and to look so mischievous. She liked it, perhaps because it was rare. She liked the way he was grinning to himself as he worked in the kitchen, insisting she watch from the table with a glass of wine while he finished their meal.

He pulled the cake out of the box carefully.

"I baked it myself," he joked. The candles flickered and sputtered as she laughed, their flame dancing with her glee as the air from her delighted breath moved them forward and then back. They were expensive taper candles she'd purchased for just such dinners. This was the first time they'd been used. They didn't do romantic dinners much, they were too busy.

"Okay, I've waited long enough." She held the cheese cake laden fork in front of her lips, completely stuffed from the meal. "What is this all about?" The cheesecake was heavenly, not too sweet with a hazelnut crust. She savoured its flavour and pointed the fork at him.

"Well?" She waited.

"It's big." He warned her.

"What, come on?" Chris had no idea what it could be. Maybe they'd won the lottery, perhaps he had a hangnail. He was so damned hard to read!

"I've gotten a job offer." He smiled, a satisfied expression filled his face and he almost grinned.

"What? Where?" She hadn't expected *that*.

"St. John's, at the hospital, full-time in emergency." His first love was the emergency room but he'd taken this job because it was available and he wanted to move from the States and because he wanted to be near the ocean. He was a city boy at heart though and this small town had never held an appeal for him.

"And you are taking it I assume?" She knew he would. It was a long commute but they'd adjust.

"Wow." Her voice held concern behind the veil of happiness.

"Congratulations honey, that's great." She got up then and went over to kiss him.

"You're happy for me, for us?" He'd worried for nothing, though his worry over her was secondary to his excitement. This job *was* perfect. He loved his time in the emergency room. Some doctors craved their own practice but he was made for emergency medicine.

"Yeah, why wouldn't I be?" She returned to her cheesecake and after a quick bite raised her wine glass in a cheer. "Congratulations!"

"Great! You should put in your notice right away and we'll have to start looking for a new place. You're going to have to do all of that I'm afraid, I won't have time to help, once this job starts I'll be gone." She dropped her fork.

"Sell the house?" She hadn't seen that coming at all. He blinked as the cheesecake flicked on to the table cloth. She picked up the fork quickly, plucking at the crumbs with her thumb and forefinger.

"Won't you just commute?" Her mind sifted over the quit your job part. She wanted to quit her job but she knew that had to be on her terms.

"No, I mean yeah." He pulled at the bottom of his shirt. She hadn't realised the entire deal. Shit. He breathed in quietly, trying to be patient. He crossed his arms and spoke.

"The shifts are too long, there is no way to commute, weekends, evenings, on call, it'll be too demanding but I was thinking," he paused and then decided to forge ahead, "I was thinking it might be time, this might be a good time to start a family."

Anger flared and she tossed her fork on the table again, hitting the plate with a loud ping. She saw him flinch and wondered if he was worried about her anger or the expensive plate.

"Let's see, you want me to give up my job, sell our home by myself, move to St. John's with you to have babies while you work ungodly hours and then I get to raise these babies alone, take care of a house, work at a job?" She caught her breath. She needed to calm down but hell this was a bit big to spring on her all of a sudden.

Her mind frosted over then with the cold realisation that there was no way this was just a new offer. Michael would have been interviewed, had meetings. He would have met with the administrators of the hospital. Hiring a doctor was a complicated procedure.

"How long have you known?" She asked in a quiet voice. Her anger came full circle and it led her to calmness.

"For a while." Michael admitted. He shifted a bit against the counter. He should have told her. He just hadn't wanted to get his hopes up. There was no need for her to be so emotional but he didn't dare say that.

"It didn't dawn on you that perhaps I wouldn't want to sell my home or that I need my job? That I want to have time for my writing and that maybe I don't ever want any children?" Her voice was calm as she laid it all out for him.

"You don't?" It was the last part that bothered him now. Still he was calm. One of them had to be reasonable.

"No, Michael, I don't ever plan on having children, I don't plan on moving and I don't plan on following you anywhere."

"I'm going to take the job, I'm going." He was defiant now and finally his emotions were affecting his tone and he sounded petulant. This job was all he'd ever dreamed of and he couldn't say no.

"And I'm going to stay," the tears on her cheeks were hot and stung as though she were allergic to them. She swiped them away.

"I'll commute then, maybe stay in town a couple nights a week," he said, defeated by her crying. Perhaps she'd come around once she saw how hard it was and she'd want children eventually too. He thought perhaps she'd just said that in anger, women always wanted children. He walked around to the table and pulled her close.

"I'm sorry, you're right, I should have talked to you about all of this. I never considered...I'm sorry." He repeated holding her. He didn't understand. She was sweet and smart and a perfect wife for him. She would make a great mother too if she gave herself a chance. *She's afraid of the idea*, he thought. She didn't have much of a relationship with her own mother, but as she got older that biological clock would start ticking and she'd change her mind.

She wept against the soft fabric of his shirt and was glad he understood. As long as they could stay here, they could make it work. Maybe eventually they could get a second place in town, a small one and she could visit him. She knew she would have to continue teaching for another year at least. She was feeling disconnected from him, and self-preservation had always been her priority. She would keep her job, if things went bad in the marriage, she'd need it.

She kissed his soft lips and felt nothing. Her heart was desperate for connection, for something magical and she closed her eyes and tried to find it. When the image of Joe Indigo's face filled her mind for the first time in months, she groaned in relief. She'd thought she'd forgotten him.

Michael mistook her groan for desire and was delighted to have her respond to him that way, often it didn't feel like she was into it. Christianna felt his kisses change and held on to the indigo eyes that stared back at her from the dream world behind her eyelids. Would the memories ever go away? Would she ever lose the magic of them? And then in her fantasy world the mischievous grin appeared and she fell into a universe of black-eyed lust that sprayed her heart with an imaginary indigo mist. Those memories were all she had left and she hoped with all her heart they stayed with her forever.

37

The fabric of Christianna's life developed a new texture. It was an inconsistent pattern woven with threads of discontent and confusion. It was a time of living alone and visiting or being visited by her husband. The predictable routine that had defined their lives changed to one of phone calls and overnight bags. It unsettled both of them and resentment grew. Hers because he appeared not to try to make it work, his because she wouldn't admit that it wasn't working and follow him as he wanted.

The advantage for her was that she found more time to balance work and her writing. She had written and rewritten the book she'd been working on for almost two years and sent it to some agents. She also sent it to every publisher in the province.

When the phone call came in April of that year from an Ontario company showing interest in her work the real chore began. In order to make it "marketable" the agent wanted her to revise yet again and she resisted. She saved an original copy because she didn't think the new version would be as good as the original.

They would start with Canadian publishers. Somehow she was enjoying teaching again, now that it wasn't interfering with her writing. She walked regularly and was fit and healthier than she'd ever been. She gained a few pounds but she liked the feeling of it. She had always been very thin and suddenly she had fuller breasts and a rounder bum and she liked her body for the first time in her life.

She came back from her walk and hurried to hit the button on the electric kettle. It was freezing outside, the wind blowing off the harbour. The phone shrilled loudly and she ran for it. It was new and the unusual ringer still made her start. She picked it up breathlessly, pulling at the sweater that she still wore.

"Sold it!" The voice at the other end declared proudly!

"Barry?" Christianna dared not hope.

"Your book is going to be published! Aren't you excited?" Her agent sounded like he was on some incredible drug. His normally firm voice was high pitched and excited!

"You said it could take a while." Her heart beat an excited rhythm in her ears.

"I was wrong." His voice was smug. He named a familiar publishing company.

"Oh my God, are you serious?" She sat down hard in the chair, the cordless phone shaking in her hand.

"It'll take a while for the release and we'll have to get a contract signed but yeah, this thing is sold!" They chatted briefly and agreed to talk again soon about the details. She called her parents with the exciting news and they would tell her brother. They were in Florida and were ecstatic. She then called Lisa, her best friend from her University days. Lisa and her partner Carrie screamed at the other end of the phone and they made plans for a girls' night downtown to celebrate the next time she was in town. Michael would call later in the evening if he could. He always called her because she couldn't reach him at work. It was frustrating not to be able to share this news with him right away.

She climbed into bed later alone. Michael still hadn't called. He missed the occasional night but she had really wanted to call him tonight. Then the thrill hit her again. She would be published. She could officially call herself an author, a novelist, a writer.

She was holding her dream in her hands and it felt warm and right. She turned over and looked at the empty pillow beside hers and wondered though, if she would have anyone to share it with.

It was the following morning when she found it. The note had been sitting on the dresser for several weeks. Christianna picked it up to toss it in the recycling. Obviously it wasn't important to Michael if he hadn't read it yet. Then she wondered, had he even been home since she discovered the note in his pocket.

It was written on a prescription pad which was why she had kept it for him in the first place, thinking it might be important. Chris turned it over, realising the message was actually written on the back. It was not his handwriting.

The message itself was innocent enough, *2pm in the cafeteria.* Not a big deal. It was the signature that caused the pressure in her veins to increase ever so slightly and her heart to increase its speed as well.

Luv, me it said.

She stared at the words with a positivity that she never questioned. There was no suspicion, no wondering. She knew. This was all the evidence she had but she knew. She backed up and sat on the edge of the bed she slept in alone almost every night. He had blamed her for their distance, her refusal to move, to live the life he wanted to live. Was this his punishment? The hollowness entered her heart and prevented her from screaming and crying in frustration.

The pain of the knowledge was excruciating. Yet somehow, beyond the pain, there was a sense of relief too. It was *finally* over.

The marriage had strained. He had caused it with his lack of effort to make it work. He had known she would never follow him if it did. She had caused it with her refusal to compromise and move away. They were both to blame.

But they hadn't talked about ending it. Christianna hadn't considered that step although she was lonely most of the time. She had considered her reputation and his as well. She liked being one of a couple even if it wasn't ideal. He loved her, he still said he did and she thought it was true. It simply wasn't enough for either of them.

Luv, me. Only a lover signed a note that way and one who was confident in her place. He was seeing another woman and had been for a while. Things had shifted for them a few months before. He hadn't been as excited about the book deal as he should have been. It meant she definitely wouldn't want a family and he was angry about that. She felt unsupported in her life choices.

Was that when it had started? He was an attractive man and female company would come easy to him. She picked up the phone and flipped through the pages of her little plaid patterned phone directory. She dialed the number she'd called a few weeks ago to review the contract she had signed with the publishing company for her first novel. She would need an attorney.

38

The gravel crunched under the wheel of the tires of her car as Chris drove carefully along the road, for once not paying attention to the azure waters and the emerald landscape that was the backdrop for her home. She was distracted by her passenger. She drove exactly the speed limit all the way from Clarenville and was at wrinkle-speed as she made her way up the laneway to the house.

Her hand reached out and stroked the ears of the little black bundle curled contentedly in the seat beside her. He stretched and licked her hand and went back into his ball. She had made the right choice. Or perhaps he had. Either way she was no longer alone.

Michael had been allergic to dogs. Chris had made the decision to get one almost the moment she knew they were separating. She had placed the order with the breeder when she became sure she would be getting the house in the divorce. Now he was here, cuddly, soft, warm and all hers. She had always loved dogs but she'd not had one since she was a child. She had been too transient to consider it until she'd married. Michael had been allergic to cats too and she thought she might get a cat to keep the puppy company in a few months once the training had been done. The breeder had cats and they all got along fine.

She pulled into the driveway and parked. Sailor's head lifted and he made a quizzical expression with his eyebrows and looked around. Picking up his leash she nudged him to follow her. He jumped up, trailing along behind, following her with complete trust. He didn't seem to miss his mommy or his siblings at all, content to go along wherever she led.

He relieved himself on the grass beside her house and Chris fussed over him and gave him a treat. It was May and a great time to bring a puppy home. Writing was a solitary work and she missed her coworkers terribly and she'd cried when they asked her to come to their Christmas party. She'd gone, alone, desperate for company. Now she had a companion.

"Come on Sailor, let's take a tour." Chris walked him around the outside letting him sniff and pee. She had prepared the floors of the house for his accidents and had piles of cleaning rags in every room. She'd readied a crate for him in a spare room as well. He would be a big guy, Newfoundland dogs grew to be over one hundred pounds.

She decided to let him have a bit of a run. He seemed pretty mellow and attached to her and she unsnapped the leash from his collar. Christianna followed him wherever he went. Then without warning he took off! She chased after him calling him but it was useless, he didn't know his name yet.

He headed for the road and her heart plummeted? She flew behind him but he was faster. She was ready to cry as he headed up the road into town and winded, Christianna stopped for a moment. As he disappeared over the hill in front of her Christianna broke into a frantic pace again, terrified to have him out of sight.

She heard the laughter just before she reached the top. Sailor was being held by a woman who crouched low, holding the collar of the runaway puppy. He was trying to break free, twisting and flailing but to no avail.

"Looks like you got yourself a runner," the lady spoke with a laugh, glancing up at Christianna, her dark eyes twinkling in her attractive face. She was known to Chris, her unmistakeable white smile, perfectly dimpled cheeks and chocolate brown hair memorable. She was likely the most beautiful woman in town.

"Yeah, maybe I'm in over my head, thank you!" Chris laughed at the dog's desperate twisting for freedom and snapped the leash on his collar so the woman could let him go. The dog immediately ran again, bringing up short and in the distance the sound of another dog barking explained why he'd run away in the first place.

"Well I know lots about dog training, if you're interested that is." Roxanne took a deep breath. She had nothing to lose. She needed the money so she might as well go for it. She had taken some courses a few years before but hadn't really had a lot of customers. She did "babysit" dogs a bit for neighbours for money. Perhaps this would be another customer.

"Roxanne right?" They had never met though Chris remembered that she had taught her son.

"Yeah, you're Mrs, oh, Miss, Carlysle?" She stumbled over the name, remembering the divorce a second too late. She swallowed her embarrassment.

"Chris Cormack." She had reverted to her maiden name after the divorce.

"Good to meetchya," Roxanne Armstrong's dialect was like other Rare Moon natives', warm, friendly and distinct.

"Nice to meet you too and this is Sailor, my new baby." Chris looked at the little black ball of mischief fondly. He was sniffing with an innocent air no longer interested in running.

At Christianna's invitation, Roxanne walked with her back to her house where they had a cup of tea and chatted about dog training.

"So you got the house, good for you." Roxanne grinned.

"Yeah, well I paid him off for it, nearly broke me." Christianna replied.

"I heard he had a girl? Can't understand men, pretty wife like you and he goes off."

"More to it than that," Chris didn't go into details.

"Figgered their wuz." Roxanne smiled. "Always is. I'm surprised there wasn't *more* talk." Other than the divorce she rarely heard a word about Christianna.

"No secrets in Rare Moon uh?" Chris repeated the adage she'd heard multiple times since she'd moved here. She believed it. The gossip mill was a powerful engine and she knew that word of her divorce circulated within hours of her meeting with the lawyer.

"Not many." Roxanne cleared her throat and looked uncomfortable and then Chris remembered that Roxanne had been shredded by that machine many times herself.

Well maybe Stephen hadn't liked Miss Cormack much when she taught him but she was a real nice lady Roxanne thought as she headed home. She'd always figured she would be stuck up although she hadn't known first hand. Guilt and embarrassment snuck up on her as she remembered she hadn't gone to any of his parent teacher meetings and that that was the reason she didn't know. It was one of many moments of regret Roxanne had about her son's childhood.

She shook the thought from her mind. She had made her peace with all of that and her relationship with her son improved with every change she made in her life. She looked across the churning waters of the little cove and pulled her collar closer. The cross on the steeple of the tall white building that sat on that side of the cove was visible from wherever you walked in the town. Roxanne's eyes were drawn to it as they had frequently been over the past few years since she'd returned to her faith. She drew strength from it now, breathing in the divinity in the air and the peace that distant tarnished symbol provided and she touched its twin hanging from the silver chain around her neck. Something told her that another prayer had been answered and she exhaled her gratitude into the moist twilight air. It would seem that, after alienating every woman she'd ever met in her life, Roxanne Armstrong had finally found a friend.

39

The gift of solitude in the wake of her divorce offered up opportunities that Chris had never been given. She spent life at extremes, hiking the rocky terrain of the Newfoundland coast, testing her physical limits to see sights that made her tremble with awe at their beauty. Sailor went everywhere with her.

In the spring icebergs, still impressive after a lengthy drift from a distant glacier, enhanced her insignificance and teased her sense of the magnitude of her world. Following close behind the playful humpbacks entertained her with their child-like romps over caplin breeches and around guided visits from bobbing tour boats. Chris climbed the hills around the cove and from different angles she hiked and watched with wonder as the universe unfolded before her in Rare Moon Tickle.

She then turned those experiences inward, working on her writing at every opportunity, submitting, being rejected and then improving and being accepted. Short stories were published in literary journals and poetry was published in anthologies. Her life was bared on pages, her pain laid out for a world of cynics to read and they felt moved at her heartache.

When she wrote Christianna was transformed. Just as she watched from a safe distance above the rocky shores, absorbing the beauty of the rugged Newfoundland shoreline, so she wrote. She hovered over the scene in her mind like some omniscient being, the scene on the page unfolding as though she viewed it from above, her mind's-eye capable of seeing a blade of grass as no one had seen one before.

On a damp Tuesday morning the phone rang a happy sing-song ring that Christianna answered as a bouncing Sailor jumped excitedly. He was starting to slow down but for some canine reason he loved the sound of the phone. Roxanne had guessed it was because she was usually the caller and she often followed with a quick visit. Chris was forced to agree. Her puppy loved her friend almost as much as he loved her.

"Two things." Barry always got right to the point. "You won the Aylward award and I've set up a television appearance for you for next week to talk about it."

"What?" Chris was floored. She had known the publisher had nominated her but she hadn't thought she'd win. It was a prestigious award, highly respected and best of all it was from the University and voted upon by her old faculty there.

"Congratulations." Barry was happy but unsurprised. She was his prized author and completely deserving.

"Now about the television gig." He was all business again.

Chris was used to a certain amount of recognition and she was popular at speaking engagements and worked hard to help promote other authors. She also taught writing classes to supplement her income. She was happy though, for a free trip to the west coast to visit her brother and accept her prize, because money was still tight and she had wanted to go for a long time.

Corner Brook is on Newfoundland's west coast, a sheltered wooded harbour. It is surrounded by mountains including the famous Marble Mountain, a popular ski resort. The awards ceremony had been a bittersweet night attended by her entire family.

"I can't believe they did it again," Eddie was as sad as he was angry. He had warned them.

"I can." His wife, Leah, looked glum.

"It's ok guys, don't worry," Chris consoled them and the truth was the insults had been hurled at them, not at Chris, she had just been the collateral damage. Their speeches and insinuations about hell and damnation and their children's likely descent into both had destroyed the hope that Eddie's and Leah's announcement of a baby coming into the family would get them to lighten up on their proselytising a little, particularly to Leah, a practicing Catholic.

Chris and Eddie were used to it, they'd lived it their whole lives and had heard of their impending doom all of their adult years. Leah was as steadfast in her beliefs as they were, though without the need to convert others, but she'd taken it well until their judgment had extended to her unborn child. When their fear that they would raise the child Catholic had been confirmed it had turned into a nasty fight.

"We shouldn't have told them today, we should have let Chris have her night."

"It's not your fault." She was grateful that they'd been there to watch her get the award. Her parents leaving in an angry flap over their son's putting his foot down about preaching in the house had done a great deal of damage to the already tested relationship between children and parents.

"It's done now," Eddie's voice was defeated, "I'll never contact them again. I can't have that around my kid." Chris believed him. Unlike previous declarations made in heat and anger, this time the lack of emotion convinced Chris he was serious. This time he had a family to protect.

"I hate to say it, but if I had kids I think I'd do the same," Chris was ashamed of her parent's, embarrassed for her brother and she felt sorry for her sister in law who she loved very much.

Roxanne came over when Chris returned to Rare Moon to see the award and her friend and the drama of the previous night was discussed as they sipped their wine and chatted.

"Why can't they just love us? They ignored us our entire lives except for trying to convert us. They fed us and went to church. That was it." Her heart ached for her young self who had craved acceptance from those that were entrusted with her care. It's ok to love God, *you* go to church, you're pretty religious, but how can someone love God or anyone for that matter, more than their children?"

Roxanne sipped her wine, memories of her own failures as a mother causing her to hesitate a moment. She wasn't one to judge parenting. Then something told her that maybe she should speak. Perhaps her mistakes were what did qualify her to do so.

"Parents are just human. Life screws 'em over sometimes and makes it hard to be a good one. I messed up somethin' fierce with Stephen and now I spends me time trying to straighten it all out. But they loves you, underneath it all. They just don't know is all, they don't know that the best way to love God is to love the people he made, especially the ones he gave you to raise. They just don't know honey, they just haven't learned it yet." Then

she reached out and stroked her friend's hair pretending to
ignore the tear that slipped from the corner of one eye and
skidded down her cheek and underneath Christianna's chin.

40

Joe's movements were quick and manic as he
worked quickly, washing down the huge heavy yellow
machine. It had gotten stuck in the mud and he had
sweated the entire morning to get it all out of the tracks.
He aimed the power washer low and waved to one of the
crew who was going by with a tray of Tim Horton's coffee.

Joe wasn't unhappy exactly yet always a little
tremble of dissatisfaction rumbled in his soul. He had
moved to Newfoundland from Ontario, bringing his family
with him years before. The business was doing well and it
was a miracle he was here doing this, it could so easily
have gone the other way. When he thought of what would
have happened if he had been caught, if they had seen him,
hanging there, arms aching, hands burning, where they
grasped the rough bark, as the lights flashed blue and white
below.

It was his daughter's face that had done it. He had
never considered giving up his lifestyle until he had come
home from that night, adrenaline coursing in his veins and
his daughter had looked into his eyes with her large black
ones, happiness lighting her entire face when she saw him
standing there. He had seen that look a hundred times but
that night something stirred in him, an awakening, a
moment of enlightenment that told him that it was time.
Suddenly he understood, what would have happened if,

instead of greeting him happily, she had learned that her daddy was in jail. As he held her tight, smelling her fruity clean scent he understood that this little girl that he adored also worshipped him and that this lifestyle that supported them financially, endangered her.

Without the numbness of the drugs that he'd used to dull the pain, he realised that there was something he loved as much as he'd once loved Christianna. He also realised that he no longer winced when he thought of Chris and because of it he was able to resist the urge to reach for a chemical escape. He quit it all beyond his social drinking, cold turkey.

It had been a risky decision but now their bank account looked good and Joe found great satisfaction in the fact that he'd earned this money honestly. He had never realised that such a feeling existed, that of pride in a job well done. He was not only well-to-do financially but he was becoming well-respected and he liked it.

When he had packed them up and settled them with his parents until their home was built Tiffany had been happy. But the house had taken a long time what with being so busy saving his uncle's business from going under. He had settled her and their daughter in the new house just in time for Christmas of 2002. They had awaited the beginning of the year at a large party and that night their second daughter was conceived, the fulfillment of his commitment to her that they would have another child if she agreed to move to Newfoundland, to his tiny home town with him, and help him care for his aging mother. His sister had moved in with them after their father had passed, but she couldn't cut the wood or do the outdoor work that was required and Tom had severe arthritis. He'd also promised Tiffany he'd go straight.

He had made changes that would have made most wives dizzy with happiness but Tiffany expressed her resentment of their life on a regular basis. She missed her parents, hated her in-laws and despised Angell's Cove. She wasn't a Newfoundlander and found it hard to fit into the tiny community. She loved Joe though, so she followed him when he asked.

Though life for Joe Indigo was more peaceful than it had been in years, there were no police investigations, no hanging in trees, no hiding and though he smoked a bit of pot, life was relatively boring and it was easier somehow in this little town. He walked his daughter to school and threatened bodily harm to any boy who looked in her direction, though she was just a child.

The morning's argument still burned bitter in his throat. Tiffany was expecting their second child in a month and though he was excited, he wasn't a hands-on type of dad, he was the buy them whatever they wanted kind of dad. Tiffany had been upset over something he'd done or didn't do and he'd been harsh and had slammed out the door in anger. He loved his daughter and would love the baby but Tiffany mostly annoyed him and as far as he could tell he annoyed her as well.

He was hungry. He shut off the power nozzle and decided to stop by his mother's house. She always had something good cooked and he didn't want to go home. Tiffany would expect more of him than he had to give.

"What's for dinner?" He walked into her house, the habit of calling the midday meal dinner instead of lunch, flowing easily from his lips as though he'd never left Newfoundland.

"Shhhh," Dar said and then. "Come see this, your old girlfriend."

Joe hesitated for only a moment. He moved closer, mesmerised by the familiar face on the screen. This was not like the memories, this was Christianna, alive and oh so beautiful and her reality pounced on him like a rabid mountain lion, chewing into his flesh with sudden and sharp teeth. Her beautiful face looked at him. Her eyes, large and bright, stared at him with the soul-piercing searching of the past. Her voice, reading a love sonnet, one that she'd written for him, was exactly the same and transported him to the only time in his life when he was truly happy. He had been so close then, to being what he was now but with *her*. He'd ended up here anyway but it was impossible not to wonder about the missed possibility.

She spoke with passion and honest emotion. He caught his breath and sat slowly on the chair. How could she read those words, that she written for him so long ago and not think of him. His sister watched his reaction and saw the shadow of pain followed by love and then back to the pain again. *Poor Joe* she thought, kicking herself internally for doing this to him. *My poor Joe, he still loves her*. She watched the end of the segment with him and when it was done she flicked off the television. Laying the remote control on the chair she walked over to her beloved brother and hugged him from behind as he remained sitting. He sobbed, just once, then she felt him trying to control himself.

She stepped back giving him the moment and left the room. She returned a few minutes later with a book and handed it to Joe who smiled a sheepish grin.

"I already have this one." He confessed, fully recovered except for a quiet embarrassment at his show of emotion.

"Good." Dar said grinning back.

Dar had watched her brother fall in love all those years ago. Then later she had watched him fall apart. The look in his eyes when she'd brought books to the jail for him to read told her he was close to disaster and that it wasn't from the incarceration. It was because he'd loss Christianna. She'd left the volumes of Oscar Wilde for him with a heavy heart.

The true tragedy was he'd never served another moment after the first few weeks. The evidence had been lost somehow through the two years of continuances that followed. He had left his little brown poetry book with Dar after he had retrieved it from the personal belongings he'd claimed on his release. He had asked her to guard it with her life as a memorial of their Aunt Mae but Dar had guessed that it now had become a sad symbol of two women he'd loved and lost. Along with it, folded, carefully were the wrinkled pages of prose and poetry that Christianna had either written for him or found for him to read.

"Do you still have that little brown book of poetry I gave you a long time ago." The pain on his face a shadow now and he spoke as though he read her thoughts.

Taking the novel back, she brought out the box that held his things. He sat with it and re-read the words he'd read to Christianna all those years ago. He slowly unfolded the papers inside, written by Christianna, words of love meant for him. The sonnet she had just read on television, there in her handwriting, he passed to Dar. The paper said *For Joe* and was dated *July 19, 1989*.

He tucked the little brown book of poetry back into his pocket. Dar smiled as he did so. She knew his intentions before he knew them himself. If he ran into her ever, he wanted to let her know that he remembered. He wanted her to know that it was real and that he was sorry he'd let her down back then.

Why did she love me? Joe sometimes wondered. It was obvious she had back then from the words she had written. Dar passed the paper back, moved to tears. She knew what there was to love. Any man who could love with the depth of her brother was worthy of being loved that way in return. He remembered the day she'd read it to him in that tree house they called *their place.*

Serendipity danced a pretty jig on his heart when the phone rang later that evening.

"David here." The familiar voice said.

"Hey buddy." Joe hadn't heard from him since he'd gone down to help him work on their new house for a week the year before.

The conversation filled with small talk and memories until David got around to the reason for his call.

A house warming party at his place, bring the wife, stay the night. David and his wife had built a beautiful new home and it was time to show it off. He'd invited everybody he could think of and since Joe had helped so much perhaps he'd come by.

"You remember Christianna, my cousin, don't you? She's divorced now, doing well, on television, famous author type now." They'd had a thing David remembered then, yeah, Joe would remember.

"Yeah I think I do." Joe admitted and wondered how he could convince Tiffany not to go with him. In the next moment he had his solution, he'd bike in, she was pregnant and wouldn't go on the motorcycle. He'd tell her it was a guy thing. She would fuss as she always did, but he'd go anyway. His heart leapt at the plan. It was wrong to go seeking Christianna out this way but he had to see her just one more time. If only to finish what had never been ended. He didn't want to think about his true intention, pretending he simply needed to know if he still had the same feelings for her and even more importantly if she returned them. He never considered what he would do with the answers he found.

41

Newfoundlanders leave the rock out of a desperate need to find work and almost without exception spend their time away conspiring and planning to return home. Christiannna's entirely fanciful theory was that there is an undiscovered and completely native to Newfoundland chemical element found in the water and air and that when people breathe it or consume it creates a magnetic force that draws the people back for renewal on a regular basis.

David and his wife had succumbed to that pull. They had a beautiful new home overlooking the small town they lived in. The A-frame front overlooked the ocean. They had cleared the land and built on it themselves, living in an old home on the back of the property until they were ready to move in. That home would soon be converted into their garage.

Christianna drove up the driveway admiring the breathtaking landscaping that had been added since her last visit a few years before. David had been lucky. His business was successful, Yvonne had a good job as a custodian at the local school and their children were bright and happy. The kids were both at camp and this was a party weekend for the adults. They needed it. They had precious little social time in the past few years, building the house, little kids sucked up time and work had been steady and hours had been long. But things were settling. The house was all but finished, the kids were older and the couple had been able to carve out this time for themselves and their friends.

The large kitchen was beautiful. Hardwood cabinets surrounded a centre island where Yvonne worked. The dark rich granite countertop was strewn with cooking supplies and foods of all kind. She was assaulted by Yvonne and the smell of the delicious food cooking at the same time. She was hugged and fussed and fawned over.

Yvonne was a short, pretty woman, a few years younger than Chris. She bounced when she talked, her face animated and bright. She almost *smelled* of joy and happiness and the scent of her vivacious nature was welcoming. She made people happy just by being herself. Chris liked her. Everybody did.

"They're all in the backyard, all of the old crowd and a few more, just checkin' on stuff in here." She flicked a few buttons off on the stove before she led Chris out the door.

David stood at the barbeque with his back to her. She spotted several people she knew from back in the day and they came forward to say hello. A beer appeared in her hand as people asked her about her books and television appearance until it began to embarrass her.

David turned around and with a happy grin at her protests, dropped the barbeque utensil. He came over to pick her up and spin her around.

"How are you cuz?" He asked as he ducked her smacking hands and kissed her soundly on the lips.

She caught her breath and clung to him, dizzy from being spun. Piercing dark eyes met hers. She grabbed David to steady herself and was grateful for the excuse to be off-balance when he put her back down on the ground. She glanced across the yard behind David's shoulders as he laughed at her reaction.

The trees of David's backyard were mature and full. The lush greenness surrounded the entire back fence, completely keeping it private from the neighbours, though the ocean was visible through the end. Several trellises held roses that climbed and broke the solid green blanket with red, pink and yellow blooms. It was a beautiful garden and several couples had used it as a backdrop for their wedding photos.

Against this brilliant backdrop, completely at ease in khaki shorts and a black t-shirt, was Joe Indigo. His laughing eyes and silent grin were still as familiar as her heartbeat.

She looked away. But it was too late. He'd seen her expression. He stared. She was unaltered, her hair longer, lighter, but beautiful, with curls tumbling down past her middle back. He thought it would be easier, casual and with shock he realised nothing had changed. He rubbed the little brown book of poetry in his pocket.

Chris faked calm and no one noticed a thing as far as she could tell. Her brain felt blended as though it were being mixed in the processor Yvonne was using to violently whirl pina coladas for the crowd. She swigged some beer while eyeing the rum bottle.

She gratefully accepted the frothy sweet coconut drink Yvonne handed her and tried to be calm and sip it. Her heart had been scattered like confetti on the breeze in that moment. Now those tiny fragments had started to drift and shift back into position as though her heart's pounding was tapping the little pieces back into place.

"It was a long drive, think I need the facilities," she said to Yvonne. Her calm under pressure was astounding. Years of practice teaching high school kids and never expressing shock at their antics had trained her well.

"It's all finished, remember where it is?"

"Yeah, I got it."

She went inside, double-fisted, beer and cocktail in hand.

Holy shit.

Holy fucking shit.

The walls closed in as the cloud of disbelief descended upon her. She looked in the mirror. It was as though disbelief and belief were battling under her skin. She breathed again slowly and deeply and let the truth set in. He was here. And he was still incredible.

The bathroom was large. It had a chair. She sat in it to compose herself, swigging her pretty white frothy beverage until it was gone. She set the glass down and started to work on the beer, grimacing after the cloying sweetness of the creamy Colada.

She was close to being ready to face the backyard again when the knock came on the door.

"Just a sec, almost done," Chris said in what she hoped was a calm voice. She ran the water over her already washed hands and dried them quickly.

She opened the door and stepped back. Joe stepped into the room, back into her life and closed the door behind them.

The large spacious baby-blue bathroom was suddenly much smaller and her heart pounded out the rhythm it always played for him.

"I didn't know you would be here," she said.

"I knew you would be," he replied. His lips formed a familiar expression, wreaking havoc on the emotions she had tried so hard to get under control moments before.

He hadn't changed at all. Joe was a little older but still handsome with brilliant dark eyes and their flecks that matched his name. Their fire was blue though their colour was as black as his hair. The pony tail was gone. He looked respectable. He looked incredible.

Her lips parted in a little surprised gesture when he said he'd known she would be here and his eyes caught their movement. His dark hand came up and touched them and she looked down at it and up again at his face.

Time dissolved like salt in hot water. No longer linear, suddenly all time was now, all that had been in the past, all that was to come was with them in this moment. They met as though they had never parted. They never had. It was an illusion and there was only the present, this moment, now. With them there was only ever now.

"I wish...."

The knock made them jump.

Joe responded. "Need another few minutes, another bathroom downstairs." The footsteps faded over the landing.

"I'll go out first." She slipped reluctantly away from him.

"Play it cool, maybe we'll connect later."

"Cool?" She was seared inside, cool was impossible. Chris took a deep breath, nodded, and left the bathroom with him inside.

She needed time so she slipped out of the house and went to the car for her bags. She took the house phone with her to make a call. She stood in the driveway listening to the machine answer, completely lost in her own thoughts. She forgot to leave the message.

"Where were you?" Yvonne called from the driveway as she pulled her bag out of the trunk.

"Called Lisa," she held up the cordless phone. It was the truth although the call had only taken a minute because the machine had answered. "She thought she might come out this weekend."

Just like that the secrets were back. Old friends that she'd left behind with the memory of Joe Indigo. With his return they came, following him and attaching to her by mutual agreement. Christianna couldn't have one without the other. She decided then that if he was open to it she wanted them both, the man, and the secrets that came with him. It was vital and important to have whatever he offered. She had to learn for herself if the love that she'd given up had been as real as her memory told her it was. She had to know if it was still worth hanging on to. Only then would she know if her secrets were a gift or a burden.

42

The evening passed slowly, Joe and Chris avoiding each other except in the most casual way. Then, just as things were winding down she found Joe beside her in a chair. He spoke to her as though he was finally getting around to saying hi. His eyes held the familiar, devilish twinkle she knew so well and that inspired one of the most beautiful smiles she had ever smiled.

"I've been well." She answered his inquiry going along with the ruse that this was the first time they'd talked. Her stomach did a little flip flop that it hadn't done since she was a twenty year old falling in love with this man.

"I hear you're a big shot now, another book coming out and all." He looked impressed and something else, proud. It warmed Chris's heart to see that in his eyes,

"And you're this big shot businessman?" She was proud of him too. David had filled her in on the details. He looked pleased with himself as she said it.

"I want a copy, would you sign it?" Joe asked, just wanting a little more, the best and biggest part of her. He'd sounded too eager and he looked around to find no one was paying attention. He realised that this was not an odd request anyway, that people asked all the time.

"I'll send it to you." Christianna wondered at the logistics of that.

"You're still really hot." She looked at him appreciatively, a mischievous smile tugging her lips.

"So are you." Their voices had lowered.

"Where did you come from?" He asked, mystified as always by her and even more by his feelings for her.

"Hocus-pocus magic." She said laughing with a flick of her hand still avoiding the serious look on his face and trying to break the spell. They both recalled the first time they'd had this conversation.

"Is that a disappearing spell?" He asked.

"Nope, that was an invisibility spell so that no one could see us and I could just jump you right in that chair." She winked suggestively at him, half drunk.

"I've always loved the way you think. I'm sleeping in the old house," It was out there now. The invitation. He hadn't cheated on Tiffany since they'd moved back to Newfoundland and he'd changed his life. He felt a twinge of guilt well-hidden behind his need to go back, to experience once again how it felt to love Christianna. "Just to the side, the back door, across from the room you're in."

"How do you know which room I'm in?"

"I'm a crazed stalker, I know everything," he said with his best evil grin. He had seen her there earlier.

His eyes closed softly, pausing as though he were in pain. The words that came into his mind begged to be whispered so he breathed them. *"Room after room, I hunt the house through, We inhabit together.Heart, fear nothing, for, heart, thou shalt find her…"*

"What the hell are you whispering about Go?" David interrupted.

"Just charming your cousin." Joe recovered. He reached for his beer.

As they picked up their drinks with their hands, her right, his left, David saw them. His eyes narrowed. The twin purple-blue roses, bright and vivid on her paler skin, his, deep and dark though more faded than hers, were disconnected now, but, if the couple held hands, they would join at the stem perfectly. The roses were not only identical they were made for each other. He understood everything. He said nothing.

"Yeah I was telling him he'd make a fascinating character for a story." Chris lied. He would. The words he'd quoted still rustled in her mind like the crisp leaves underfoot in the brightest autumn.

"What about me?" David asked, shaking off his discovery.

"Boring as hell," she kidded. "Want my readers to stay awake." Joe's familiar laugh thrilled her.

"Smart ass." David returned, good-naturedly threatening to punch Joe for laughing with her at him but it was a lying laugh and he drank his beer, staring at Chris as Joe got up and slipped over to talk to someone else.

43

The kitchen was empty. David had sent his protesting wife into the backyard with instructions to keep everyone away. He glanced out the kitchen window and was happy to see her sitting with Christianna. That was perfect. She was the main person to keep from coming in and disturbing him.

Joe came through the kitchen from the bathroom and smiled at his friend.

"Hey." He picked up his bottle of beer from the granite covered island and pointed it at David. "You waitin' for the can?"

"Waiting for you, Go" David's eyes were direct and Joe was suddenly on guard at the tone, "What are you thinking?"

"What?" Joe's eyes narrowed. David was serious about something and he had no idea what it was.

"Christianna?" David said.

"What about her?" Joe lifted the beer to his lips in what he hoped was a casual gesture.

"Come on buddy, I'm not an idiot, I know there's something up, you had a thing years ago, I'm not stupid." His eyes never left Joe's and he could see the truth in them. He was right. It had been more than a one night stand. He didn't know how much more but enough that he was here now and he sensed it wasn't a coincidence.

"So, what if I am? She's a big girl. Or am I still not good enough for your cousin?" Joe's tone was defensive.

"No, that's not it." It was the truth. "You're a good guy and Chris could do a lot worse." He hesitated, "If you were single."

Joe looked out the kitchen window where Christianna stood. He could see her back, her tanned arms gesturing as she talked, he could hear her laughter, distant and familiar through the open window. His heart was so full of her that he couldn't imagine not being with her again now. David took note of the expression on his friends face. In a quieter voice he decided to try a different tact.

"You could lose it all buddy." David said, his voice carrying a truth Joe hadn't wanted to consider.

Joe didn't answer and he didn't look away from Christianna even when she turned and caught his eye through the window and looked quickly back at Yvonne.

"You've built up a good business, you have a gorgeous house, a great wife and family and you pulled yourself away from a bad path Go and you'll lose it all. Tiffany will take half of everything, she'll get the kids."

"I know all that." Joe drained his beer.

"Don't do it, you've come too far to mess it up now."

"Thanks." Joe slammed the bottle on the counter and it made a clink against the granite surface. David winced and Joe walked away wrenching the door and it swung back with a mournful rhythm behind him. David made a mental note to fix it later as he followed Joe into the backyard. Joe grabbed another from a cooler and opened it with an angry twist. David hoped he'd been heard.

The cold wind blew against Joe, whipping at his bare legs, taking his measure. His eyes shot towards Christianna and she glanced up at him and smiled a secret smile that crept inside his heart and seemed to still the errant wind. He glanced away from her but not before he saw a moment of confusion in her eyes and guilt mixed with his need for her, confusing him.

The breeze tapped at his skin again and he braced against it walking towards the old house. He couldn't have just one night with Christianna and to have more than that meant he could lose everything he'd worked so hard for. He shoved the door in, grateful for the escape. It would be easier to make his decision away from her intuitive gaze.

44

Joe looked up at Christianna as she approached and she could see by the light of the lamp that shone over the barbeque area of the backyard, that he was serious now. She moved closer and then sat next to him on the bench. He looked straight ahead and they were both silent for a moment.

Joe stood, walking away from her, his shoulders hunched, his hands jammed into his pocket. He had changed into a pair of jeans and wore a plaid hooded jacket that kept him warm in the cool night. Christianna had changed into jeans and a knee length cardigan of a burnt orange colour that she pulled tight. She felt the change in the air and knew it wasn't a temperature drop that was making her shiver.

"I'm married." Joe said the words, his voice flat, as though he were reading a number from the phone book.

"I know." Christianna stood up and walked to where he stood, standing directly behind him.

"It was a long time ago, we were kids and I think I was just caught up in the romantic idea of it all." Joe said the words that were so opposed to the feelings that drummed in his chest and in every cell of his body.

"Turn around Joe." His name on her lips made him catch his breath. But he turned hoping the dark would disguise the truth in his eyes.

"I thought maybe there was something left between us but it was all just romantic silliness, all that poetry, it was fun but it was all just foolishness." Joe's voice had drifted back into a comfortable lilt since he'd moved back to Newfoundland and Christianna watched his lips as he said the words, not immediately comprehending.

"Go on?" She whispered.

"We were so young and I think I just thought, you know, remembering it all, but it's all...gone." He stopped. There was nothing to add.

The silence between them filled with the sounds of the night. A loon screeched a comforting coo and the trees rustled a consoling embrace around the couple. Christianna let the words drift through her, filtering through her heart and her brain and they didn't compute with what both organs knew to be the truth.

"Bullshit!" She slapped the word in his face and he stepped back as though she had made physical contact. He had expected sadness, perhaps embarrassment but he hadn't expected the venom in her voice as she spoke that one word.

"I call bullshit Joe Indigo." Her voice shook with her anger and hurt but she continued. "Perhaps all the romance and poetry was silly kid stuff, perhaps we were a little over the top with all of that but you can't tell me that that's all it was. I did not waste all those years still wanting you, thinking of you, wondering why the hell I didn't come and tell you that and then wondering why the hell you didn't call *me* after. Perhaps it faded for you over the years but even if it did, don't dare tell me it wasn't real! It wasn't romance and fluff. It *was* love, so I call fuckin' bullshit!" Then with one deep sob she turned swiftly, embarrassed at her outburst of emotion and walked towards the house.

"*Something Fine*," the words tumbled out behind her, stopping her short. He walked towards her then, drawing closer and closer. His hands by his side he inhaled. The scent that was always his undoing hadn't changed.

"I can't listen to the damned song." Joe confessed. "Every time I hear it I think of you. I bought my wife a bottle of perfume one Christmas and I had to tell her I was allergic to it because it smelled like you." He took one more step bringing up behind her lowering, his head into the side of her neck. He placed his hand on her shoulders and turned her around so that he now looked at her eyes. They sparkled in the twinkling lights that decorated the branches of every tree in the backyard.

His lips moved forward and she brought hers up to meet them and he came undone. He pulled her into his arms, desperation washing over him but he stopped, pulling back from her just long enough to whisper.

"Bullshit is right," and his lips found hers again and their hearts slipped into their old harmony, the song of destiny, composed for them in the ages and played on the strings of their soul.

And so they discovered that there was a third kind of secret. A Secret like a gemstone of untold brilliance and light, locked away like precious jewels should be, to protect them from those that would steal or destroy their beauty. The kind kept in private caverns and safes, or gold-engraved music boxes with ballerinas who only dance for an audience of one. These secrets are too beautiful to share with anyone. That night Christianna and Joe committed to that secret.

They weren't fooling themselves. Their secret had the potential for great destruction as all secrets do. If the secret were discovered and the truth revealed, lives would be shattered. But it was a secret such as this that they would bear quietly and without shame, for this love that they had thought had been lost forever.

45

The hot rays of the summer sun made Sailor uncomfortable and Chris was always grateful for her ex-husband's idea to build the house with the patio sheltered around three sides, facing the pretty little cove that looked out into the Atlantic and the water way that was Rare Moon Tickle's namesake.

Keeping the salt off the windows challenged Chris but was worth it. When it became too hot for Sailor's comfort Chris would walk with him down to the cove and let him swim to his heart's content. She often swam with him, happy to have companionship in the water. Then she would dry off and watch him play and swim and shake dousing her in the spray that would come off his fur as he shook his large body free. She would have to bathe him after but he loved that as well and it kept him cool.

Joe had come in the back service road and parked behind the house after dark and Sailor had alerted her to the stranger on the property. He was very anxious about the arrival until Joe spoke to him and let him sniff his hand. He licked it, then slobbered on his face and went back to Chris to tell her this guy was approved. They laughed as the dog stared at them as they kissed and walked into her home.

"Wow, this is magnificent," Joe admired the house. It had a raised ceiling at the living room area, the great room Michael had called. It looked out into the waters of the ocean and the deck was immediately in front of the windows, over the cement patio below. The kitchen was behind her when she faced the ocean view but was an open concept and the island off the kitchen also looked out into the same dark blue waters. In this room she could sit and watch the rare moon sitting on top of the little island and bask in the magic spell woven in those treasured and uncommon moments.

The following morning sun shone hot and they ate a quick breakfast. Chris showered first and when they had cleaned up the dishes she took the dog out for his walk. She only went as far as the cove. The heat already overwhelmed her and she took off Sailor's collar letting him run into the salt water. She laughed at his antics. A thought tickled her sense of adventure. She slipped out of her clothes and stood naked on the shore for a moment before running and diving into the cold water. She shivered and gave a little squeal and then swam to warm up. No matter what the temperature, the Atlantic Ocean was cold! But her body adjusted as she swam back and forth with Sailor following her as he always did.

Joe came out of the shower wearing only his denim shorts and looked for her. He saw her and the dog playing in the water. He laughed as he watched Sailor follow her back and forth and then in towards shore. He didn't have to worry about her in the ocean, she wasn't alone.

She stood up and his breath caught and then he laughed at her nudity. Her body had changed a little but it was curvy and strong and it was obvious she had been nude in the sun before today.

He looked around and realised that this place was perfectly isolated and that no one could see them. He walked back to the bathroom and grabbed two towels from the outer room linen closet. He admired her bathroom and how the toilet was in its own space at the back, separate from the tub and the sink. He slipped of his denim shorts and walked back out through her house, naked, holding the large soft white towels in his hands.

Chris saw him coming, wearing nothing and smiled. He walked out on the deck and down the steps towards her. She climbed out of the water looking like a mermaid, hair messy, eyes wild with excitement and completely uninhibited. She reached for the towel and draped it over her shoulder pulling him away from the ocean where he intended to swim. She led him to the grass instead.

She tasted of salt and sunshine and nature and he used the white towel to keep her body off the ground as he became acquainted with this woman who had always owned his heart.

As their bodies moved under the hot hazy sky, the large black dog sat guard on a grey slice of granite, looking away as though to give them privacy. Then, after, they swam in the cold waters enjoying each others company and the gifts nature had given them.

"You never talked about your parents." Joe said. Christianna was surprised, she usually initiated conversations.

"No I don't," she admitted. "I don't see them very often." She pulled a long black dog hair off her wet leg flicking it in the grass and leaned back on him again. They rested against a little hillock that protruded from one side of the sandy beach. It was a perfect lounge-back.

"Why not?" He had a strange relationship with his own parents. His father had spent his days strumming his guitar or talking of the glory days while his mother carried on the bulk of the work and ran the family. She had never complained about the balance in the family though and Joe had realised as a man that they'd reached this agreement somehow. His dad had given up his glory days for his family and his mother hadn't nagged him because she knew he'd sacrificed much for them, for her.

"Religion, they are very religious and they don't approve of me." The pain was a low ache in her heart. It was that of a child who had never been good enough because she didn't conform to their ideal of what good was.

"What kind of religion?" Joe tightened his arms around her, sensing her hurt and wanting to absorb it from her, to take it on as his own.

"They are born-again Christians, have been since I was little, I was forced to go to church, until I moved away. Much of the reason I left and moved to Ontario when I did was to escape that."

"You didn't go for that uh?" He kissed her neck. He had only known the impulsive and wild Christianna and couldn't imagine her sitting innocently in a church pew.

"I just didn't believe what they taught. It made no sense to me, the judgement towards those who didn't believe." She shifted against his body, loving his warmth and his touch against her neck. It soothed her heart as she talked to him about things she'd never spoken of to anyone before.

"Well you fell far back." Joe chuckled as she ran his hand over her bare belly.

"Yeah, I've had to step far back or it becomes an argument every time. I cannot be a part of the life they live and they don't approve of mine. They were a little better when I was married but not much, they tried to convert my husband the first time they visited us and they didn't come to the wedding because it wasn't a Church ceremony. We talk once a week, well they talk, I listen. I go home a couple of times a year to visit but I've pretty much left it all behind. My brother too. His wife has had a really hard time with my parents. She's Catholic and the poor woman has been torn apart between her parents and mine."

"So I guess you'll never introduce *me,*" his eyes twinkled at the thought.

"Don't tempt me," Chris laughed at the imagined look of horror on her mother's face. "That's what's odd, it really backfired on 'em. As a young girl the more they nagged me with their bull crap the more nasty I became. I was a terrible teenager but completely behind their backs." The only thing she'd taken from them was their work ethic. And that was all she still wanted.

"What about *your* parents?" She only knew basic information.

The breeze blew Joe's onyx hair a little and he looked at the water. He'd never spoken of his parents to anyone either. Much of the resentment he'd bore them over the years had shifted into understanding.

"Dad was half Mic Kmaq, he's gone now."

"I'm sorry." She stroked the dark hairs on his arms. "I figured you were part native, that's kind of cool, to have that history, that legacy."

"Not to Dad, he never mentioned it. My aunt used to tell me that he was tormented horribly over it. They grew up in a town where they were the only Indians and it was very hard on him. My dad doesn't *look* Indian so it was easier for him once he moved away. She told me that he denied his Indian background and it broke their father's heart and he refused to listen to the stories. I don't know anything about that side of the family except they are all dead now, my grandparents anyway. My mother was an only child so we really have a small family."

"Somehow I pictured you with a big family behind you."

"Well there might be because I just don't know my father's family at all. He even changed our last name legally to Indigo."

"Good choice." Chris twisted to look into his eyes where the little flecks danced with a deep hue, more blue than purple today.

"Do you want to know? About your roots I mean?"

"Yeah, I think someday I'll want to know, my daughter looks like me and she might want to know."

In the centre of the cove in front of them was her little island and they looked towards it together.

"We should go there sometime," Joe said. "It looks amazing."

"Yeah, we should, there's a legend about it." Sailor barked suddenly from where he lay sunning himself.

"You can come too." Christianna laughed.

When the weekend ended they felt they had loved enough to sustain them each for another month when he could come back. It was how it had to be and their sadness at parting was lightened by the knowledge that it would only be a few weeks and they would be together again. It wasn't perfect, but it was all they had and it would have to do.

46

September was always a bittersweet month for Christianna. She missed the start of school. She knew it was silly, she hadn't taught for a few years, but every year in September she wistfully thought of her old life, her old career. She had made the right decision but still, she missed the kids and teaching sometimes.

It was the third week in the month when Joe visited again. Later than they had planned because the baby had come and it was another girl. He was excited and showed her pictures then of both his children. The baby had dark eyes and looked like him. She thought the older girl looked like her mother, though she had Joe's dark complexion. They were both beautiful and for the first time she wondered if she was missing something, not having children, not planning on ever having them. She was fanatic about birth control, even considering permanent methods but her doctor refused to discuss it.

This time they were stuck inside the house but for the lovers, becoming reacquainted, that was not a hardship. The wind and the rain pounded mercilessly on the windows and the ocean provided a show for them, white seas bashing against the rocks, curling and retreating and then bashing again in a never ending persistence that fascinated the couple as they sipped their wine and watched movies in her high-ceilinged living room.

"Why did you quit teaching?" Joe inquired.

"I wanted to write full time." It was something people asked her all the time. "I liked parts of it but I like living this way better. I'm free. If I were a teacher I'd be more petrified that people would see you coming here, these small towns are crazy with gossip. Everybody insists there are no secrets in Rare Moon Tickle. Now I only want to keep it quiet because of you, they don't seem to care much what a writer does, but a teacher has to have a code of behaviour that I find hard to live up to." She looked into his eyes.

"*This* would get you in trouble?"

"Not officially, but within the community yeah."
Her skirt length alone had gotten her in trouble at the
beginning.

"So now you're the wild and free girl who doesn't
care about her reputation and I'm the solid, hard working
respectable family man that has to watch and sneak and be
careful." He laughed with her at the thought.

"Yeah, I guess I'm the bad one now." Each had
kind of ended where the other had started. She'd been the
one seeking respectability and security and then had come
to this place where it was all up in the air most of the time.
He'd been free and uncaring and suddenly had to be careful
and respectable. Life had certainly spun the needle for
them in a strange circle.

"Well I'm not exactly *good*." He looked at their
bodies lying together on the couch, legs around each other,
a little shawl of a coverlet lightly around their lower
bodies.

"And I'm extremely happy about that," she grinned.

"But I'm not free." He said realising that this was
the biggest difference. She was free but he wasn't and
wouldn't be. "It's really not fair to you is it?"

"I'm free to say that it's fair," she said and Chris
leaned back in his arms. He shifted trying to let go of the
thought that had been circulating in his mind. After a long
quiet pause he spoke.

"So you left me for something you ended up
hating?'

"I didn't leave *you*, you went to prison." She turned to look at him, her eyes snapping with colour, the old hurt suddenly present.

"Because I did a dangerous deal so I could follow you."

"You did what?" Christianna sat upright. "So now it's my fault you went to jail?

"No, I thought I could make some quick cash and then follow you." It sounded stupid and it had been, but it had been his life back then.

"And what was I supposed to do, throw away my entire future on a convict?" He winced at her words as though she'd hit him.

"No." The hurt made his voice quiet and he lowered his head, the old shame of what he'd been still a wound in his heart.

"So you eventually straightened up, why couldn't you back then?" Christianna wondered aloud.

"It was a long while after. I was already married, we had the baby" His defeated voice was still low and Christianna realised her words had hurt him more than she'd meant to.

"I'm sorry, I mean, it's just always been so painful, you were there, then you were gone, then you were married and then you were living the perfect life, the life we could have had."

"I know, I felt the same and I feel pretty guilty about it."

"And now you've decided I should feel guilty too?"

"No, I shouldn't have told you that. I just wanted you to know, I don't want to *hurt* you. I love you." The words hadn't been spoken again though they drifted there, ever present between them.

"I know Joe, and I love you too." Christianna found the words easy to say. The anger had gone as suddenly as it had come.

"Why? I've never understood. Sure I read a few poems and it was all romantic but we were kids. Why did you love me then? Why do you love me now?" He was such a regular guy, less than a regular guy. Her love baffled him.

Christianna's smile held the love of an eternity and she took his hands into hers, kissing them one after the other enjoying their heat.

"Oh you silly man." She said. "The poetry stuff was all sweet and romantic but it wasn't what made me fall in love with you. I loved the man who protected that little boy all those years ago, I'm betting that kid never forgot that, and the same man who felt almost as bad for the older kids who were teasing him. I've loved you all these years for that huge heart of yours that drove me away in the fog from a dangerous situation and later made sure I stayed safe. I don't know how you did that but I'm sure you did something. I love you because of the strength you must have had to completely remove yourself from a lifestyle that is almost impossible to leave. I love you because of how you treasured the little book your aunt gave you and how you loved her so much. I loved you because your sister told me I did before I even knew it myself. Hell I think I loved you before I even met you." Her eyes met his, tears pouring over the edges of her lids and down her cheeks.

Joe pulled her towards him their hands still clasped, his heart full of her to such a degree that not having her in his arms left him unbalanced and lonely. He wondered if he'd ever find the words to tell her why *he* loved her. He wasn't even sure himself but he knew that he always had and he always would.

The wind howled and fought with the rain for dominance over the night and neither won the battle. The sunrise that early Sunday morning revealed that the lovers had not slept and they watched it creep up into the sky through the rain-washed windows.

In the scarlet light of the sun's rays, through some magical trick of the atmosphere, the ocean appeared to be a brilliant indigo rug, spread out over a brand new earth, reborn, ready to be walked on by new beginnings, ready to support life, ready to bear the preordained promise of never ending love. They imagined they walked on it, defying science and nature, hovering above the gentle waves, buoyed by this love of the ages.

47

The merlot teased her throat and the gentle buzz relaxed her angry soul. It was Saturday and Joe hadn't shown up last night as promised. She had not heard from him and she hadn't been able to call. She worried, she became angry and then, at around three in the afternoon, after a long walk with Sailor she decided to open the bottle of wine that was intended for dinner. She called Roxanne and asked her to join her. If Joe walked in she'd make up a story. Or she'd confess. They would have to deal with it.

Roxanne was happy to stop by. She had nothing to do that long autumn day, her house had been scrubbed clean, her church duties were completed and a relaxing glass of wine and a good laugh with Christianna would be perfect.

Chris was already on her second glass when Roxanne got there. Sailor greeted her and she rubbed his happy ears and spoke to him as she always did, as though he were human. She helped herself to a glass of the wine and plopped beside Christianna on the floor, leaning up against the couch. She touched the rim of her glass to Chris's and sipped.

"Some good." Roxanne said. "What's up?"

"Stood up," Christianna admitted. She wondered how much she could say without telling the entire secret but she had to say something to someone. As much as she liked to keep her privacy she trusted Roxanne to not judge her.

"Guy was going to come by, old flame, didn't show." That was enough.

"What a jerk." Roxanne was shocked more by the fact that Christianna was seeing someone than that she'd been stood up.

"Yeah, jerk." Chris started to laugh. "Good fuck though." She gulped the glass empty and got up to get the bottle.

"Chris!" Roxanne was shocked at her language. "Who *is* dis guy?"

"Oh, old flame, nothin' special." Chris avoided Roxanne's eyes as she brought the wine bottle with her. "But I'm pissed, I wanted to get laid tonight." She poured her glass full and slammed the bottle down on the coffee table.

Roxanne had never seen Chris drunk and she was enjoying it. She took a sip of her own wine carefully. She no longer drank more than a glass at a sitting.

"Merv Lincoln is free," she said with a mischievous grin.

"I heard he's well hung." Chris answered straight-faced. Merv was the local postmaster, all of five foot two and completely smitten with Chris. He got all flustered when she came into the post office and Roxanne teased her about it endlessly.

"He's probably got special talents." Roxanne said, her eyes narrowing to an evil glint.

"Like what?" Chris poured again, ignoring the numbness in her kneecaps that said she should slow down.

"Well after all those years of lickin' stamps..." Roxanne let the innuendo stand in the air.

Chris fell in a huddle on the floor. She couldn't catch her breath and she drank some more of the pungent wine and wiped her eyes, the alcohol making it funnier to her.

"What about you?" Christianna asked Roxanne when she could speak.

"Me, What about me?"

"Anybody lickin' your stamps lately?" Chris wiggled her eyebrows.

"Nope, and me stamps is gettin' pretty lonely." Roxanne joked.

"How long?" The wine had loosened Christianna's tongue.

"Years," Roxanne answered. "I had some real losers and the one good man I had I lost."

"Who was that?" Chris had heard stories of Roxanne's earlier life but she'd ignored the gossip. It was hard to figure out what was true in a small town.

"Arnold, my second husband, he was a good man but I was in love with Stephen's father still and I drove him away. I was so messed up for a long time, then I brought home everything that walked for a while, I was 'eart broke back then." Her eyes watered a little and she looked away to blink and regain her composure.

"What changed? I mean, women have needs too." Chris had never been prudish about her sexuality. She liked men and didn't believe that it always had to be about love. She preferred it that way but it wasn't necessary.

"I think my needs changed. I wanted a man who was worthy and I haven't found one yet. Otherwise I prefer to be alone." Roxanne confided. "I realised I deserved more than someone else's husband looking for a good time and I realised they deserved more too." She had also gotten tired of all the women in town hating her. Chris was her first woman friend and she sometimes wondered if it was because she had no husband to risk.

Chris drank some more wine and let the words marinate for a few minutes.

"So no more married men?" She waited for the answer in guilty silence.

"For a while I *only* chased the married ones but then I realised I was getting the shitty end of the stick." Roxanne laughed.

"How do you mean?" Christianna poured more wine and drank it back quickly. She wobbled a bit as she leaned forward to hear Roxanne's answer.

"Well, holidays, birthdays, family stuff, they did all of that with the wife and kids. They had all the stuff that mattered and I sat alone over in that house every holiday, every birthday, and then they wouldn't show up because the wife needed something. It wasn't worth it. I realised *I* was worth more."

Chris picked up the bottle and filled her glass again, draining it and shaking the empty bottle.

"Well that sucks." She said.

"What, outta wine?"

"That you haven't gotten laid in years - that really sucks." Chris giggled.

Roxanne's laughter burst and flowed free like a river. "Yeah, it pretty much sucks." She agreed.

"What about you Chris?"

"Oh I get laid pretty regularly," Chris confided slurring the words through her wine- loosened lips.

"Who?" Roxanne furrowed her brow. She hadn't ever heard a whisper.

Chris realised she had said too much and she started talking about her brother's friend in Corner Brook.

"And this guy that was supposed to come this weekend?" Roxanne wouldn't let her change the subject.

"He didn't show up." Chris was drunk but she still knew that she had to keep the secret. She couldn't take the chance for Joe's sake.

"Yeah, I know," Roxanne said with a patient sigh. "But who *is* he?" He must be a one-time thing.

"A big jerk." Chris felt a little sick.

"Ok, don't tell me." Roxanne was dying to know but knew it was futile. Christianna held her secrets close, rarely talking about her family, her marriage, her teaching career. The one exception was her writing. She talked about that all the time.

"He's a really good fuck though." Chris leaned back against the couch and closed her eyes.

"You my friend are very drunk." The conversation was going in circles.

"Yep, intoxicated." Chris nodded, her eyelids drooping.

"Get on the couch." Roxanne pulled at her and Chris felt too tired to protest. She lay there listening to Roxanne pick up the empty wine bottle and glasses and put them in the kitchen.

"I'll take Sailor home with me." He needed to go out and Chris was in no state to disagree or to walk him.

"Kay." Chris felt as though she were sinking into the cushions on the couch, the room was spinning a little and she put one foot on the floor as she'd been told to do as a teenager. She didn't drink often and a full bottle of merlot had knocked her out.

She awakened in the middle of the night, dazed and confused with a blurry memory of Roxanne leaving with Sailor. Her head pounded as she made her way to the bathroom and brushed her teeth. She took off her clothes and put on her robe and turned to go to her bedroom when she heard the motor of a car behind the house. She glanced at the clock in her bedroom, it was nearly two am and Joe was here.

She walked to the back door and opened it, the cold wind blasting her as she watched him climb out of his black Dodge Ram pick up truck.

"I'm sorry." He said and she resisted the urge to slam the door in his face. Her head pounded with the residual of the wine and her increasing anger. She bit her full bottom lip to prevent herself from screaming at him.

He stopped before he got to her and she stepped aside to let him in. She closed the door and waited, the anger in her heart overwhelming her love for him. She was glad to see that he was okay, that had been a great concern to her, but it wasn't enough.

"I can explain."

"I don't want to hear it."

"I want to."

"I don't want you to."

"I couldn't leave, we had unexpected company."

"You couldn't call?"

"I kept thinking I would be able to leave, that they would leave and then it got too late and Tiffany invited them to stay the night, then they stayed for lunch."

"And you couldn't call?"

"I'm sorry." Joe knew she was right. He should have called.

Chris headed towards her bedroom and took off her robe. She slipped in between the warm sheets, her body naked and her mind still fuzzy from the drinks. He followed her and took of his clothes very quietly and joined her under the covers, his arms pulling her close.

And she couldn't resist him then and it wasn't because of the wine. It was because her body needed him and her heart was relieved that he was ok. Tears trickled from the corner of her eyes and down her cheeks as he held her and she couldn't decide if it was from relief or anger.

He thought that her quiet loving was forgiveness but it wasn't. Christianna held resentment in her heart for that long day and night of waiting and it ate at her and made her wonder if it was all worth it. She wondered if Roxanne was right, that she was the loser in this deal. It was the first of many bites that ate into her confidence in their love and their right to be together.

She remembered what Roxanne had said. She wondered if indeed, out there waiting was someone she could love with the fiery passion that felt for Joe, but who could give her the love she was starting to crave. Perhaps her time with Joe was interfering with the possibility of it ever finding space in her life, because it was so filled up with him.

But what if she ended up with nobody like Roxanne? She didn't want to be alone, she wanted to be loved. The inescapable fact was that she loved Joe Indigo and always would. This had to be better than being alone. She was torn by the love she felt for him and the love she deserved to receive. Though she was confident he loved her, he had nothing to offer that would satisfy her longing for every day with him. Could she keep this up long term? It was something she was beginning to wonder.

Joe Indigo

Angell's Cove, NL

48

The checker board sat between them on the low coffee table and the young girl with the eyes that were perfect replicas of Joe's laughed as she jumped his black pieces with her red ones yet again.

"You suck at this dad," she said as her dainty hands clasped the checker pieces and laid them on the pile in front of her.

She was right. He didn't like board games, had never been able to sit still for that long but he'd promised her he'd hang out and play with her today and at her age he knew that this was rare. Most girls didn't want to hang out with their old dad but Merina was different. She worshipped him and Joe loved it and soaked it up. He made a move and she jumped him again putting him out of his misery. It was quiet in their home, peaceful. Tiffany was puttering around somewhere and Morgan played outside. The grey tabby slept in a favourite sunbeam that shone where the curtains parted, leaving a hot pattern of yellow heat on the hardwood floor.

"Another one?" She asked.

"Sure." Joe found it hard to say no to his girls. They'd begged him last weekend to stay home when he was supposed to visit Christianna but he'd told them it was a business association meeting that he couldn't miss. So he'd negotiated a movie date in Gander for the following weekend. This meant that this Saturday he was to drive four girls to the movies and then wait for them. He would then drive them back home for a sleepover at his house. Joe would chaperone because Tiffany had other plans. He enjoyed it, they loved their daddy and he loved them.

"Dad, I have a question." Merina's young face was serious.

"What m' duckie?"

"How do you know when you're in love?" Her dark eyes looked away from his, embarrassed a little.

"Who is the boy? I'll kill him!" Joe looked fierce.

"Dad, no, I was just wondering. Some of my friends think they are already in love," She giggled at his silly protectiveness.

He thought for a moment, remembering back to that day so long ago when he saw Christianna sitting on the back porch in that house in Kitchener. He remembered being compelled to go talk to her, of somehow knowing that she was important. He remembered immediately thinking the very conscious thought, one he hadn't had before or since, that it was different this time.

"You'll just know," he answered. He knew it was inadequate.

"Dad, come on." She said dad as though it had two syllables. Dayad.

"Well, I think it's different for different people but for me, it was instant. It was as though the moon and the stars and the entire universe placed her right there and I kept wondering where she came from and how I got so lucky. I knew right away, from the first second that it was something different from anything else. I knew that this was the person I was supposed to be with right from the start. It was like magic, I can't explain it. All of the girls I liked in my teenage years and early twenties that I thought

I was in love with were nothing like the real thing when it hit, so don't expect it to happen in your teens."

Hell he hoped not, it was hard raising daughters. He saw himself in every boy who looked her way and prayed Karma would skip his neighbourhood.

The hand that touched his shoulder made him jump. Tiffany had walked quietly up behind him as he spoke. He waited. He couldn't believe he'd been so careless. Fear welled in his chest, a physical feeling that caused him to catch his breath. Then she bent down to kiss his cheek and he could feel her complete and utter bliss in the gesture. He sighed in relief as his conscience pulled at his heart.

He had so wronged this woman whose only real flaw had been that she was not Christianna. She had been patient for the most part, stuck by him, given him children. He simply didn't love her. Not the way he loved Christianna. But he felt he owed her something and he squeezed her hand with forced affection, avoiding her eyes.

Tiffany thought his embarrassment sweet and pulled up and walked away from her husband. She hadn't known he'd felt that way. She brushed at a tear, a rare smile on her lips. She was happier than she had ever been before, knowing how he truly felt about her. It was more than she'd ever expected.

"Mom said pretty much the same thing." Merina grinned at her dad. She liked seeing affection between them, she didn't see it often, parents generally didn't do that and that was a good thing. But it was better than seeing them fight which they often did, especially when dad was going away.

"What?" Joe returned to the moment, not understanding what his daughter was saying. He started to set up the checker board again.

"I asked her the same question and she said pretty much what you said except she said it was possible to fall in love like that as a teenager, because she did." Merina informed him as she concentrated on the next move.

The thought that his wife loved him as much as he loved Christianna disturbed him. He wondered if he'd have to make a choice one day, a choice that he'd already made in his heart, one that would break Tiffany's and destroy his family. It would be devastating and he looked at the sweet face of his innocent daughter and grieved for the heartbreak he might eventually have to inflict on her. He decided, for now, not to think about it.

49

Chris sat amidst the sheltered walls of Fort Amherst with her pad and paper in hand. She found inspiration in the depths of the harbour waters, the whipping of the mild winter winds adding to their mystery and beauty. She felt the cold penetrate the cream coloured cabled sweater that came to just below her knees. It was December but a freakish mild day. Her jeans were cold against her legs now though, and as the sun dipped further in the sky she shivered and looked at what she had written. Chris loved to sit outside and write but nature nudged her with the cool breeze to go.

It was Christmas. Chris was spending it with Lisa and Carrie at their place. They had been fussing and getting ready for a nice dinner with some of their friends. Chris had been invited because her parents now went to Florida every year in the winter and her brother and his family had joined them there this year. She had no one else to celebrate with. Joe was, of course with his family. A certain distance had built between them. The last visit had left her frustrated and though she loved him deeply, she was discouraged that they couldn't see each other more.

Chris had made a decision. She would live the life of a single woman when he wasn't with her. She needed to make steps to assert the autonomy she craved. She would not sit and wait for him to show up occasionally. He loved her, she loved him, and she needed him in her life but she would still live when she was without him. Even if that meant being open to other relationship and to other men. Their love was a rare love, a once in a lifetime love, but it wasn't a committed love.

It was a strange place to be, not single, yet not available. Just as Roxanne had said, holidays were for family, not for her. As much as she tried to convince herself that she could handle this and that the relationship with Joe was all she needed, she was becoming more and more aware that she was starting to mind.

The smell of roasting turkey filled the house. She entered to a party already in progress. Dinner would be around six but the friends had all come early. Chris had gotten there the evening before, staking her claim on the spare bedroom. The others would crash in the basement on couches or air mattresses if they lived outside St. John's or cab home if they lived in. There was a bar set up in the corner of the large living room and Keith was designated bar tender. Chris had met him several times at Lisa's house and she headed over, still bundled in her sweater to ward off the chill she still carried in her bones from the cold Atlantic winds. A glass of red wine and she'd warm up quickly she told him.

"I read your book," he told her. His eyes danced with fun and he couldn't help admiring her. Her long blonde hair smelled of apples and fresh air and her cheeks were touched by wind and sun.

"And?" She was curious, Keith hardly seemed the type.

"Not my thing," he admitted. "Romance, blech. I'm more of a mystery kinda guy." He winked.

"Don't be cynical, you're too young, you should still be romantic." He was several years younger than her, a confirmed bachelor with no signs of settling. He was Carrie's younger brother and the only straight man at the party.

"Aren't *you* yet?" He handed her the large goblet half filled with a dark burgundy liquid.

"Cynical? Why would I be?" She asked sipping the wine and nodding appreciatively at him over the glass.

"Well you're still single, biological clock, tick-tick and all that," he joked.

"My marriage broke up partly because *I* didn't want children and he did."

"No tick-tick?" He asked.

"No tick-tick." Sometimes she felt like she was missing something deciding against children but she knew her situation was wrong for it.

"Still single?" He was digging now. He wondered if the chemistry he sensed between them was mutual.

"Yeah." She hesitated just long enough that he caught it but he left it alone. She'd said yes, that was enough.

"Party with me tonight?" Keith said with a large wink.

"Sure," she smiled at him, her eyes letting him know she was up for whatever he had in mind. She was very physically drawn to him, always had been, so why the hell not. He was handsome and fun and there was wine and hell yeah, she *was* single.

The golden brown turkey reined over the table. Heavy crystal bowls of vegetables held perfectly diced, mashed and julienned vegetables. It was a traditional Newfoundland meal complete with salt beef and peas-pudding but it was resplendent and dressed for royalty in the fancy china and silver serving ware. The dinner was a masterpiece, both Lisa and Carrie were fantastic cooks and entertainers and their combined efforts resulted in the generous complaints of overindulgence that accompanies a large, delicious and long anticipated meal. The pumpkin pies and coffee were sampled and put the final seal on the diet failure of the season. They all ate too much, grumbled after, and then ate some more.

"Walk?" Keith suggested?

"If I can move." Chris knew if she didn't do something active she'd feel crappy later. It was still early and there was further partying to be done. She handed the tea towel to another guest, playing the relay game they'd set up for cleaning up after dinner.

They took Sailor with them as they walked around the streets that made up the little neighbourhood of Lisa's home. She lived in Paradise, a little town just outside of St. John's and after a delicious dinner, on a cold winter night, stars twinkling happily in the peaceful evening sky, she could see why it had been named so.

They chit-chatted about this and that and at one point Keith took her hand. It was nice, on this quiet Christmas evening to have a friend, even if it wasn't the person she wished for.

The tenor of the conversation changed and he seemed intent on charming her. She held up her hand.

"Keith, don't work so hard." She advised him with a smile.

"What?" She was smiling so he didn't think he'd done anything wrong though he was being chastised for *something*.

"You're trying to impress me. Like I'm a strange girl you're trying to pick up. It's me, we know each other and you don't have to."

"Guess I forgot." He laughed. He had thought she was interested in a little more and he was embarrassed that he'd been so obvious. He had been attracted to her for a long time but she always seemed older than she was somehow, out of his league. He took her as the kind of girl who would want a relationship and he didn't like to get involved in anything serious.

"Let's keep it fun ok?" She asked and her voice held a suggestive tone. She was out of practice.

"I like fun." He was getting mixed messages.

"Me too." She moved in to kiss him and the dog nuzzled between them interrupting the effort. Now the message was clearer though.

Their laughter fluttered in the night and she reached out and petted her large dog.

"Do you really think we should do this?" Keith asked. He rarely became involved with women he already knew and she was his sister's friend. This was different plus he liked her. It could get complicated.

"Yeah, I really *really* think we should," she smiled, then she faltered. "Unless you don't want to." Perhaps he didn't, she *was* older. She flushed a little, embarrassed.

"Yeah, like I'm *that* stupid?" Surely she knew how beautiful she was. He bent down to kiss her again. She kissed him back and the sweetness of the moment settled it for both of them that this was a great idea.

They found their way back to the house, Sailor walking slowly beside them. They joined their friends and sat together and spent the time in frivolous fun. They each drank too much and eventually, after the party dulled, he left his made-up bed on the couch and joined her in the spare room.

If she thought about it, she would have noticed few parallels between this night and her first night back with

Joe. This night was the same without the love and magic. But she didn't need magic this night. She just needed a friend. She needed to be held and she needed to be close to someone. In the early morning hours, Keith left her with a gentle kiss, and crept back to the couch for the rest of his sleep.

As she laid there alone her heart began to wonder if maybe it didn't need Joe to beat, that it might have its own perfect rhythm. It was a bittersweet feeling and the possibility saddened her.

She wondered, as she drifted off, if love required for two people to actually be together, if it wasn't possible to love and let go, for the sake of making room for other possibilities, for other loves. They had been apart for years and it had been hard but they hadn't concluded their love that time, they had been wrenched apart by circumstance. Maybe this was not the beginning of their time together, but the beginning of the end.

The wine weighted her eyelids and sleep brought a dream that baffled and spoke of promise and hinted at another love. One that was just out of her reach but magical and real, one that provided her with everything, not just a dream of everything. But it wasn't substantial yet, it wasn't fully formed and until it was she would remain in the status quo as Joe Indigo's secret lover. She wondered if perhaps her theory of once in a life time love was as flawed as the notion that a blue moon is in actuality a rare moon.

The snowmobiles whirred past Christianna's home interrupting the picture on her television screen as they buzzed by. Each time they came close the television picked up interference from them creating a blurring streak of snowmobile tracks projected on to the screen. She couldn't be irritated. The show was a repeat of M*A*S*H. Chris ached to be one of the laughing teenagers that rode carefree along the edge of her property. It was her birthday and she was lonely.

Roxanne was at a church conference in St. Johns, but she had come by in the morning with a beautiful pen in a box and a card for her. She knew Christianna didn't want an entire cake so she'd brought her a container of cupcakes and insisted she blow out the candle on one before she left for her weekend trip.

Her parents had called from Florida as had her brother and his family on the West coast taking time to talk to all of them for as long as possible. The kids shared details of their lives and friends and she loved feeling the excitement in their voices. She really couldn't wait to go see them again. She would be there in March she assured them.

She missed talking to Lisa and Carrie who called every year but this year it was impossible. They had flown out that morning to the Dominican Republic. They had needed a vacation. Nursing was hard work and they worked the same hospital and found it difficult to get time off together. They had swung it this year and she couldn't feel regret towards them.

The show was good but Chris was having a hard time focussing. She had assured everybody she would be fine at home alone, that she wasn't hung up on the whole birthday thing and she'd meant it. But now, she was starting to feel lonely. Her thoughts drifted, taking stock of things in her life.

Her writing was going well. She didn't earn as much money as she had teaching, the starving artist thing being a reality in a lot of ways, but she loved what she did and she was successful at it. Her latest book had been nominated for *The Lunor*, a highly respected Canadian Literature award. She hadn't won but it was indeed an honour to be recognised for her efforts. Her agent was reading her latest work and she was between projects now. She had jotted down a few ideas but nothing concrete had come to her yet.

There were huge chunks of her life that were lived without Joe's presence. She lived as a single woman and wondered if her little interlude on Christmas had been a sign of a greater dissatisfaction. She certainly didn't feel guilty. Joe had a wife, he hadn't committed to her nor had she committed to him. Not all relationships were traditional and she was untraditional herself so it worked. Except when she was lonely.

Keith had been a positive experience. They were still friends and he had called her the weekend after just to talk. He had seemed a little too attentive the day after, tip-toeing around her awkwardly but she reassured him she was completely cool with their night together and that she had no regrets. She liked having him for a friend and had gone to a wedding with him at the end of January and they'd spent another night together.

But her heart longed for Joe. All of the promises he couldn't make to her, that he'd made to another, were emphasised in the emptiness of the days after he left and went back home. She didn't know how to reconcile the happiness of them being together with the niggling doubts in her mind. She didn't feel used, she knew he loved her, no one could fake the intensity of his feelings for her, and she loved him, he was her favourite person in the world.

The knock interrupted her thoughts. Her mind went to Joe and pre-emptively disappointed her. She opened the door to a cool clear starlit night and a familiar man who had grown up in Rare Moon Tickle. He was visiting family down the road.

"Hey, heard you were all alone here," he smiled at her. He had told his friends he'd always thought she was hot and they'd dared him to ask her to join them. A few drinks later he took their dare and was at her door.

"Yeah, how ya been?" Chris didn't remember his name. It took her a moment to recall that it was Robert.

"Good, just visiting for a week. Want to go for a ride, get out of the house? His smile was eager. Good-looking in a boyish way, she guessed he was well over six feet tall.

"Yeah, give me a few minutes to get ready." Her mind was racing. What did she know about him? She was grateful for small town gossip. His reputation was that he was a good sort, had done well in school, younger than her but not young enough that she'd taught him. He was perhaps in his late twenties. He stepped inside when she stepped back.

She dressed quickly in her snow gear and they chatted. He was visiting from Calgary. He was on his father's snowmobile. She waved to the other snowmobilers, she knew them all from around town and they seemed excited to see her. Perhaps she should have made more of an effort to get to know the younger set in town. Her friends were mostly married and family people other than Roxanne. She climbed behind Robert and held on. It reminded Chris of riding on a motorcycle.

Chris invited the party back for drinks after and the last of them left in the early hours of the morning after finishing the cupcakes and singing happy birthday for her. Except for Robert who left just before the sun rose again to warm the snow that blanketed them.

Chris snuggled under the covers and chuckled to herself. That wouldn't stay a secret for long. As far as the town knew, he was the first man she'd ever been with since she'd lived here other than her ex- husband. They'd be buzzing about this tomorrow. She drifted off to sleep and for the first time in her adult life she'd spent the night with another man and hadn't given Joe a second thought. Her mind and body were leaving him even if her heart hadn't yet. It wanted other people and was comfortable and happy in the arms of other men. It wasn't the same as having love in her life but it was better than being alone most of the time.

Christianna knew that her true nature craved for more, it craved for a deep, magical connection, with the intensity she felt with Joe when they were together. She was also just starting to realise that she needed it all the time, that she needed a man of her own, a commitment and that it had to be with someone other than Joe.

The realisation scared and excited her at the same time. She still craved to be in his arms and broke at the thought of never being with him again. But she was separating from him as well. As though her heart now understood that it could love him but be with out him. If she listened carefully she could hear the whispers of her soul telling her that this lifetime wasn't theirs, that while their love was eternal, their lives right now were meant to be spent apart. Sadness at the possibility steeped through her veins tempered by the excitement of new possibilities. She just needed to see him again to be sure.

51

The cake, decorated like a little kid's cake, had a motorcycle on it, a replica of the bike he'd been driving when they'd met so long ago, that machine, now replaced by a shiny modern model.

Joe came around the back as usual. Silence followed a quick cut of the familiar motor. Sailor lifted his head and then flopped back down on the floor, disinterested.

"Great goin' buddy, protect your mommy," Christianna spoke to the lazy dog. Then she went to the back door and let Joe in. They'd negotiated more time together so that she felt a little more comfortable in their relationship and Chris decided to be happy with the status quo.

The time between their visits always vanished in the first moments of their reunion. This one had been long.

Several months, family, time, and weather had interfered and she wondered if he had finally given her up. He had missed her more than she could imagine though and he resented every domestic responsibility, every winter storm that kept them apart.

Their connection was like silver elastic, stretching across the distance, growing thinner and more fragile as they spent less time together but eventually the tension reached its limit and with a snap they would come together again, out of necessity, out of love and because the fates had said it must be so. Once the band snapped it retained its original shape, sturdy, strong and bright. When she was with him she wondered how she could have forgotten their connection. How she could have thought she could let him go. When she was in his arms she forgot about her loneliness, she forgot the other men she'd shared her nights with while he was away.

Christianna made their dinner outside on the deck. Joe joined her there and shivered next to her as she tossed the steaks on the grill. He liked to think he was a barbeque pro, he always barbequed at home for his family. He had to admit now she was better and he let her take over. Perfect steak won over pride.

After their dinner they settled in with a couple of Blue Stars and watched the Leafs-Canadiens' game, bantering back and forth and eating popcorn. She liked Montreal and he preferred Toronto. They both threw popcorn at Don Cherry, she because she thought he said something bigoted, and he because he disagreed on his hockey views.

Sailor had managed to lift his body long enough to lie on the floor beside the couch.

The game ended and Joe whispered, "We should get to bed early."

"Why? Don't you want to watch the next game?" Hockey night in Canada always played a western game.

"Well I have to leave first thing in the morning, thought maybe we should get to bed early."

She sat all the way up. "Why?" She asked.

"My family wants me home for a birthday dinner," and though he tried to be casual he couldn't disguise the guilt in his voice. They had made an agreement. When he came to be with her it had to be for the entire weekend, it had to be for them, just them, no family involvement. She didn't mention the agreement and that bothered him even more.

"Ok then," she said. She didn't feel like arguing. He'd broken their arrangement but then, she was getting used to this now. He wasn't showing up, now he was leaving early. Dissatisfaction rolled around with disappointment in the pit of her stomach. She was angry but resigned.

"Are you pissed? Joe didn't know why he was so concerned that she didn't appear to be.

"No, I'm getting used to this now."

"I am sorry." He almost wished she was angry. This acceptance scared him.

He longed to tell her he would stay with her. He wanted that for himself. But his daughters were so excited about his birthday. The little one was finally big enough to get it and they had presents for him. They had made him promise to be home early from his business trip. He couldn't break the promise to his girls. They were too young to understand. But he was torn because he would have preferred to stay with Christianna and although that was selfish of him, it was his wish.

"Perhaps it's time to stop." Her voice broke. Thinking the thought was one thing, saying it out loud was entirely different. Her chest heaved and she felt the tears pressing her eyelids.

"No." The word burst from him, his understanding of what she was suggesting immediate. Oh God no, he couldn't not have her in his life. He knew it was unfair and he knew she deserved more. He promised himself he would make an effort to do better.

His lips found hers. How deeply they loved each other and immediately she felt herself in his arms and then on the bed. Their love was becoming a desperate and endangered creature and both of them knew it. Life was suggesting that they move apart but the despair of the possibility of such a separation drove them to be closer. They inhaled each other, as though they were trying to memorise every moment together, as though it were their last.

Later, after Joe had taken Sailor outside, she spooned against him in a familiar way, loving the feel of his strong arms around her, holding her, protecting her, adoring her. She whispered because she hadn't in a long time, "tell me one Joe Indigo." He smiled and kissed her shoulder.

"I thought you'd never ask." He whispered in her ear, the verse he'd found for her, words not written in his little book. He spoke it in his beautiful lilting voice.

"I crave your mouth, your voice, your hair.
Silent and starving, I prowl through the streets.
Bread does not nourish me, dawn disrupts me, all day
I hunt for the liquid measure of your steps.

I hunger for your sleek laugh,
your hands the colour of a savage harvest,
hunger for the pale stones of your fingernails,
I want to eat your skin like a whole almond.

I want to eat the sunbeam flaring in your lovely body,
the sovereign nose of your arrogant face,
I want to eat the fleeting shade of your lashes,

And I pace around hungry, sniffing the twilight,
hunting for you, for your hot heart,
like a puma in the barrens of Quitratue."

"What is that? She'd never heard it before and it was different, almost of a different time than the classic poetry he'd read to her over the years.

"Remember that time we were at the Royal York?" Joe asked and she could feel his smile in his voice.

"Of course, "She picked up his hand with the rose and kissed it.

"Well there was a little book in the room, a book of poetry by some Spanish guy I think, Pablo Neruda and I took it that day when I left as a souvenir. I went searching for it this week because I thought maybe I should find some new material."

"That was incredible." She remembered it and had read it but when they checked out that day she had forgotten to take it with her. "I remembered picking it up."

"I didn't know if you had seen it or not. I had read the first few pages and they were so sad, all about losing your love that I stopped reading it. But I took it when we left as a keepsake."

"That is the single most romantic thing ever."

"You liked that one uh?"

"I like the fact that you kept the book."

"I never wanted to forget that weekend, it was special." It was that weekend that he'd fallen completely in love with her. It was the time they'd gotten the tattoos. He had kept the book all those years just had he'd gathered everything she'd written that he could find. He was proud of her, proud of their love and it frustrated him that he couldn't share the fact that this amazing woman loved him back.

She turned in his arms and held him close. His heartbeat thumped in her ear and she stayed like that until it was no longer comfortable for either of them. And the rhythmic drumming of his heart was her promise, the heart that beat with the melody of their love and she knew, in this moment, for this time, that it was more than enough.

52

Christianna slammed the notepad on the table, frustration building at the writer's block that had been taunting her for six weeks now. She knew it was a direct reflection of her emotions. *She* was blocked and frustrated. Chris made her way to the freezer and pulled out a container of ice cream grabbing a spoon from the drawer while ignoring the little voice inside her head that said she'd been doing this a little too often. She took the first bite of the creamy goodness, rolling it around in her mouth slowly, the flavours of caramel, chocolate and pralines her best friends in the moment, soothing, comforting and available. She picked up the remote and aimed it at the television, flicking aimlessly through the channels settling on *Survivor*.

The shrill of the phone interrupted and she grabbed at the receiver, excited that the call display showed Joe's cell phone number.

"Hey," She answered. Even their phone conversations were getting shorter now, it had been three months.

"Hey," Joe's voice was familiar, soothing like the ice cream had been moments before.

"I'm on my way in, just gassing up. Is that ok?" He had never asked permission before.

"Yes, of course." She sat up at the words. She plopped the container on the coffee table ignoring the condensation dripping down the sides on to her normally well-loved wooden table.

"Really or is it a bad time?" There was something that made Joe seek reassurance. He'd never doubted her before but he'd been unavailable to her for so long.

"Really." The sob left her lips before she could contain it and the embarrassment brought further emotion to the surface and her tears were obvious, that one word full of them.

"Oh babe I'm sorry, I'll be there in a couple of hours." His eyes filled at his end, and he resented even more the circumstances that had kept them apart so long this time.

"It's ok." Chris reassured him her voice stronger now. "I just missed you." She swiped at her face, tasting the salt on her lips and savouring it for a moment. She hadn't realised she had bottled her emotions so tightly that they had to burst like this. She had been considering the idea that she might not ever see him again and had been learning how to accept it yet living in limbo, unwilling to say the words and cause him further pain.

"I missed you too. I love you too." He waited to hear her response hoping it wasn't the automatic one he'd been getting from her lately at the end of their calls. He'd been in survival mode with Tiffany's illness and two kids to care for and had burnt out from the stress of it all. He knew that Christianna had felt ignored and she had been. It was a fact but he was ready to fix things now.

"I love you too." It came from somewhere inside her deeper than her heart, beyond the physical self. It came from her soul and it relieved Joe's mind and made him smile with relief.

The motorcycle's rumble a few hours later had her running out the back door in anticipation. It was a moonlit night, damp and cool and the house was warm and inviting. But that first kiss heated their bodies and the absence that had tortured them both was forgotten along with the cool temperatures.

"You're here," she looked at him as though she'd discovered an oasis was not a mirage.

"Yeah, I'm here." His eyes were dark and moist and she could see her face in them under the yellow lamp light below her front deck, reflected and reversed. Tiny little Christianna's loving him, needing him and grateful for his presence.

Joe held her close again, hugging her, feeling her body heat under the sweater she wore over her corduroy pants and tank top. He ran his hands over her strong back and down her backside to her legs and back up again. She'd filled in a little in his absence and he liked the roundness of her. He kissed her lips again and then moved to her neck, inhaling the fragrance that was all Christianna's to him, though it was a common Calvin Klein perfume.

Tiffany had kicked up a last minute fuss about his leaving this weekend and it had resulted in a huge fight. He'd hopped on his bike and left in a fit of anger. While she hadn't been able to help getting sick, he still resented every moment and knew she'd used her illness to keep him close. He hadn't wanted to lose his wife, particularly for the sake of his girls, but it had been a stressful three months and he ached for Christianna every moment of it. Finally he was here and it was heaven to feel her, smell her, to just be with her.

Her body huddled against his. She was always surprised by how immediate her need of him was once he was with her. His need was equal to hers and he went to direct her to the house but she said no with her head and eyes and moved him quickly over to the side of the trees.

She wanted to be with him here, outside in nature, where they had spent most of their first time together all those years ago when they had no choice.

They moved as one to the little grove of trees that sat to one side of the road. She pulled at his belt desperately and he kissed her lips and face and breathed her essence as she worked to drive him mad.

They lowered themselves to the ground as one and under the cool clouds of an early July morning they were together again. They brought all of the love and desperation of their time apart. It was intense and sweet and it infused their lives with love again, renewing their faith in a relationship that their time apart had damaged.

Never again Joe thought, would he go this long without her. He was complete in her arms and he couldn't even think of letting this go. He would work towards being with her every day. There had to be a way.

When they went back into the house, giggling from their fumble in the trees, the moon and the night-birds their only witness, unbeknownst to Joe, Christianna acknowledged in her heart that as wonderful as it was to be together, she still felt she could let it go when she was ready. Not quite yet, but when she was ready.

53

The sun glistened on the calm water of her little cove behind her house and the little row boat she'd purchased sat waiting for them as she pointed for Joe to look in its direction. The dock had always been there but had been rotten and unusable. She'd hired a local man to come down and fix it up for her and she'd been rowing to the little island frequently. She loved to row and it had been one of her favourite pastimes as a girl.

She was a little nervous when Sailor decided to come with her, the little boat rocked under his weight but he learned to settle down and be still at the front. The Tickle was deep and she wore her life jacket and only rowed in calm weather. She often dropped anchor and just sat there, in the middle of the ocean outside Rare Moon Island. Although she had never given up meditation as a practice, sitting on the ocean in a little wooden boat under the blue sky was her idea of complete peace.

Joe's eyes danced, the indigo highlights flashing in his black eyes. Usually he only managed during a hunting trip to be outside. His wife hated camping and refused to go even when he tried to convince her that the girls would love it. When he left Tiffany and came to be with Christianna permanently they would do this a lot, perhaps later, when things were settled, the girls could come as well.

She had walked to Roxanne's to get Sailor. She would have felt bad on a camping trip with Joe without her dog because he enjoyed their boat trips so much. She returned to find him ready to go, a grin of excitement on his lips. Roxanne issued warnings to be careful unaware that she wasn't going to be alone this time.

The punt was low in the water but the Chief had built it sturdy and there was plenty of room. They sat beside each other, Sailor in the front, a small tent and some supplies in the back for balance.

Their backs were towards their destination as they rowed in perfect unison, their rhythmic strokes perfectly matched. In this too they seemed to be made for each other.

She directed him to a little shallow spot on the far side of the island where they could tie up the punt. She stepped out into the cold water and pulled it closer. Sailor followed his mistress causing the boat to rock and tip with the jump and Joe laughed and held on as the little boat steadied itself, Sailor doggie-paddling towards the shore.

"Punts aren't meant for big dogs like that, he should just swim to the island." Joe laughed at the dog's antics. He loved this idea of hers and his happiness lit his eyes on fire and his grin grew in to a steady handsome smile, his white teeth flashing with boyish delight reminding her so much of the young man she'd fallen in love with so many years ago.

"He has." Christianna laughed. "But odd enough he prefers the ride."

They set up the tent in a little clearing up against the wooded grove of trees that stood in the centre of the little rocky island. They could see her house in the distance.

"You brought a lot of stuff." She noted as he unpacked. A little square grill-top with some coals, a small cooler, water, glasses, a bottle of wine, sleeping bags all came out of the boat and were set up on the shore.

"Well we can't starve and we have to sleep." He said as she tucked the sleeping bag into the tent. He had packed while she picked up the dog. She'd prepared the basics but he'd added the wine and glasses.

"Is it going to rain?" Joe asked glancing at the sky. It was clear and deep blue dotted with a few shredded-coconut clouds in the distance.

"Nope, not a drop" She'd checked the weather network and the temperature would dip but it would be fine and clear.

"Well in that case let's sleep outside in the sleeping bag."

"Yeah? I've never done that." Her blue eyes sparkled at the idea and she nodded in her excitement.

"Me either." Cuddling in a warm sleeping bag with Christianna would be amazing.

"Ok let's." She smiled and a dimple danced on her right cheek. That would actually work with her plan for the night. It was a full moon and time for the test.

They set up camp and he built a little fire pit in the ground. They cooked and strolled and made love as Sailor guarded their little island. Just before dark Christianna brought out the papers, the research she had done and handed it to him. He read it silently, the legends of the weasel sisters and their star husbands and the beliefs of the creator that were held by the people whose blood ran in his veins.

"Why did you do this?" He asked, moved.

"I knew you were part Mi Kmaq and I decided to explore that for my next book but then I found all this stuff I thought maybe you would like it. To know more about it."

"My father was ashamed of it."

"That's so sad, such a rich heritage." Her research had been fascinating partly because it was Joe's background but mostly because it was just interesting.

"He felt looked down on so he never wanted to claim it and we were to never speak of it."

"I thought that you just might want to know."

The sun dipped lower in the sky and they sat near the small fire reading together, she read him stories and poetry from his history and he said the words of his people's creator slowly *Kisulkw* and it sounded right in his voice, in his heart, in his spirit, more perfect than the name of the Christian God had ever felt. He knew it was his truth and it soothed him.

They lay upon the ground looking at the stars that held the mysteries of the ages, witnesses to all that happened on the earth and he was overwhelmed with this newest gift she had given him.   The first full moon of the month shone directly in front of them and its magic delighted Christianna and Joe as they talked of the history of his people that were his although he had no first hand knowledge of them.

He had always been aware of his Indian blood and now he felt it in his veins strong and proud. He stared at the sky from this sand-grass beach as his ancestors had likely done for generations until their lifestyle was changed by time and settlers and now he felt in tune with them. He heard a loon call and he stared at the round silvery moon that hung there though it was still early and felt that indeed the creator of *his* people had gifted a miracle to the people of the earth.

Then he rolled over and looked at Christianna, and thanked this *Kisulkw* for *her* most of all. It was getting close to that time. Here in nature, without the disturbances of the outside world, his senses were heightened, his sensitivity at its peak. It was time he repaid her for all the gifts she had given him. She had taken all the pieces of him and assembled them. He was becoming whole because of her. He owed her his entire life. Soon this would not be enough for her but he couldn't live without her, she was his anchor and when the time came he would come here one day and stay with her. When the time was right he would come home to her for good. His choice had been made and it was simply a matter of timing.

Christianna felt his eyes on her as she watched the moon in the scarlet sky in the distance appearing as it always did. Steady, reliable, hot and beautiful. It was her favourite individual piece of nature. Mindful of the legend she'd been told of when she'd bought the land where her house had been built, she willed the answers to come, the knowing that the old legend spoke of. She grew slowly mesmerized by the red sky. *Sailor's delight* she thought, as she looked at her large dog sleeping nearby them, laughing to herself at her silly pun. The red sky spoke to her as she lay in perfect contentment but she resisted the message it was giving her. *Not in this life time.*

She loved *this* man. She wanted his happiness and she wanted hers to be with him. As they lay together under the sky, she knew suddenly without a doubt that her happiness could never truly be found with him. The sky pulled her towards its scarlet flame whispering that Indigo was not her colour after all, that the red hot steady orange, red and gold that made up the sunset of miracles, the sunset that foretold of peace and safety, that this was the colour of her heart.

And the red sky whispered also that her dream was close at hand and she would know it soon. She reached her hand out and pulled up the hard strong hand that bore the rose that was theirs. She kissed the purple bloom trying to infuse it with all the love she felt for the man beside her. Willing the legend to speak the answer that she had been sure would come to her through the full moon magic.

When it didn't she wondered if, when another called, she'd have the courage to go, to wander away from the indigo fire that had burned in her heart for almost two decades. Tears fell on the rose and she kissed them away and turned to him and took her heart with her as she kissed his lips, her spirit settling for this moment that was entirely theirs. She ignored the voice that consoled her with a subconscious thought that perhaps she was meant to have both.

54

Chris loved the familiar sign over the Duke pub on Duckworth Street in St. John's and had won the argument easily with Lisa over which was the best place to grab some late lunch on that foggy afternoon. The pub had become a regular stop on her frequent trips to St. John's. Though Lisa lived in St. John's she rarely went inside a pub. She trusted Chris on this as she'd heard good things about the Duke as well. Carrie met them there about five minutes after they'd settled.

The previous night's entertainment had worn the citizens down and only a few patrons were about. There were the already half-drunk regulars holding up the bar on the right, a couple of young men playing pool and some giggling girls, tourists Chris guessed, eating and talking loudly about their previous night's adventures.

The little waitress with the St. John's accent took their order and brought their drinks.

"Little Hair of the dog that bitchya?" Carrie had asked as she ordered a pitcher for her and Lisa. Chris had scotch.

The chit chat progressed to a pool challenge. Chris declined. She sipped her drink as the others walked to the pool table together. The young men had finished and Carrie and Lisa started racking up the little marble balls with severe clanks and firm expression.

Chris sat back, staring without seeing, thinking of the previous day. They had taken in the annual festival to beautiful weather and exceptional music. The local talent was amazing and Chris watched and listened and enjoyed as many performances as she could. She never missed the event and every year it got better with bigger national names coming to play at the popular event. There were several local bands who had impressed her as well.

The venue, an outdoor field, was perfect for such entertainment and when it ended everybody walked downtown to their favourite bars. Lisa and Carrie had taken a cab back to their place but Chris had opted for a room at a local hotel. She wanted to stay downtown. It was one of her favourite places and she intended to walk some St. John's streets to get inspiration for a piece she was writing.

"Excuse me?" One of the young men who had been playing pool earlier was speaking to her.

"Sorry?" Christianna was enjoying her thoughts and was annoyed at the interruption until she looked at him. He was a handsome young man, maybe mid-twenties. His hair was a dusty blonde, long and shaggy and his face was open and friendly, his smile warm. Her heart fluttered a little and the annoyance dissipated.

"Are you Chris Cormack?" He asked his voice sure that she was.

"Yeah," She was occasionally recognised but hadn't been in a while. She straightened up, aware of herself suddenly and put out her hand to shake his, "Yes I am."

"I thought so, you haven't changed at all. You don't remember me do you?" He slipped into the seat beside her, all confidence now that he knew he had the right person.

Some gentle lines had formed around his eyes. His sandy blonde hair hung long and brushed down towards the front in wisps that just met his eyebrows. But his eyes were his best feature. They were a bright blue, darker than hers and rimmed with black that made them appear even bluer. His eyelashes were long and dark and the envy of every woman who cursed the mascara tube in the morning. They were also familiar. They had looked at her from a gaunt, angry young face years before. They had begged for understanding and had hoped for escape from the sadness in their depths. She knew those eyes and in a moment she put a name to them.

"Stephen," she said when the gift of recognition touched her heart. "You're Stephen Miles." He was as thrilled as she was by the fact that she knew him.

"I didn't think you'd remember me," he said. "It's been a long time."

"You graduated what, ten years ago?" He'd grown up well.

"Almost, I'm 26 now." Chris felt old and silly for thinking he was interested in her. Wow, I can't believe you're here." Out of the corner of her eye she noticed Carrie and Lisa finishing up their game and starting over, stopping and then heading to the bar. A chuckle escaped.

"What?" He asked, confused.

"Oh, nothing." She grinned then pointed to her friends who were pretending to casually ignore them, "they think you're hitting on me so they're giving us alone time. So how have you been?" She went back to him. He hadn't mentioned his mother and she knew they had been at odds for a while. She would wait to mention her friendship with Roxanne, it might scare him away. She bragged about him all the time. According to his mother he was intelligent, talented, handsome and pretty much perfect in every way. Perhaps she should have paid attention because it appeared her friend wasn't far off the mark.

"Oh I graduated with a music degree from university and now I'm highly unemployable." The light in his eyes said he was joking. "I'm actually in a band, we're doing well, making a living."

Chris she was suddenly struck with another fact. She'd *just* seen him perform. He was the lead singer of a traditional group with an incredible amount of talent. He played multiple instruments and was the lead singer. She hadn't recognised him from his performance, she was back from the stage too far, but now she put it all together.

"You're in Trinity, I watched you yesterday!"

"What did you think?" The way he asked made it sound as though her answer was important to him.

"You guys are fantastic." She loved their music. "Do you write the original stuff?"

"I write the music, not the lyrics." The waitress brought a new drink and placed it in front of Chris, looking at Stephen but he declined to order anything.

"Well you are really good." Chris became aware of two more young men standing behind her and turned to see. They were his friends from earlier and she knew they were also in the band.

"This is Chris," he'd hesitated over her first name wanting to say Miss Cormack but that was silly. She hadn't been *Miss f*or a long time. "This is Ryan and Reese." He introduced the two brothers who were his band mates.

"Ready to head out?" The taller brother, Ryan asked.

Stephen hesitated. "In a minute." He gave them a look that they seemed to know and they slipped back to the bar to wait with a nod and a wave to Chris.

"How long are you in town? I'd like to see you again, I want to talk about a couple of things with you." He was almost shy in his request. She had been his teacher, he had respected her for a long time, never mind the massive crush he'd had on her back in grade 12. He waited for her answer, his eyes searching hers to see if she was interested.

"I'm here for another night, staying nearby," she said, fascinated by his talent and the fact that he was her best friend's son. He was also very beautiful and she scolded herself a little for those thoughts. He *had* been her student.

"Are you around later this afternoon?" He took a pen out of his pocket and handed it to her with a paper napkin from the table.

She wrote the hotel name there next to her name and he offered to stop by to meet her around four.

"Wear your walking shoes," he suggested with a grin. "I need some exercise." Then he slipped from the table with a wave to his friends who met him at the door.

The sound of the same door clicking was the cue for Carrie and Lisa to come back to the table.

"Was that the singer from Trinity?" Lisa asked.

"Yeah, he's an old student of mine." Chris explained though her bright eyes sparkled as she lifted her drink to her lips.

"Oh." Disappointed Lisa slipped to her chair and picked up the beer. Carrie took the seat next to her.

"Yeah and he's picking me up at four and we're going out." She added with a sly grin, isn't that sordid and scandalous?" Christianna winked sipping again.

"It's about time you did something sordid and scandalous." Carrie joked.

Chris threw a paper napkin at her and lifted the scotch to her lips again. Sordid and scandalous was commonplace for her, but they didn't know. Then a thought crossed her mind, and she caught her breath at the unexpectedness of the realisation. Lisa and Carrie looked concerned and she mumbled something about the drink going down the wrong way. She had realised that had been so taken by Stephen Miles that she had completely and utterly forgotten about Joe.

55

The Blue Rodeo ring tone of her phone pulled Chris from her beauty regime in front of the mirror. She had showered again and spent some time pampering for the day. It was hazy and humid and she let her hair fall into its own natural curl. She was glad she'd fixed up her roots. She liked her hair light and was satisfied with her appearance. She didn't look all that much older than Stephen and the sunglasses would hide the lines that had stealthily crept around her eyes, tiny but visible, the first sign that she was heading swiftly into middle age. She cringed at the thought. She'd never given it too much weight but now, with a younger man coming to visit she was exploring her face for signs of decay.

"I'm in the lobby, should I come up?" Stephen's voice was sweet and gentle, musical like his singing voice.

"I'll be down in a second." The room was messy and she straightened up before running out the door tucking her cell phone into her jean shorts pocket. She'd been ready for a while and had spent the whole time like a nervous teenager. This wasn't even a real date was it? He'd just wanted to talk to her. She went back and forth. Did she want it to be? She finally admitted that, yeah, she did.

The handsome young man in the lobby sprawled in a fake leather chair, making it look way more comfortable than it was, picked at the threads in the seams of the chair's arm. He was the school boy who had a crush on his teacher again. She was still very pretty, beautiful even. She had aged some, but she had aged well. He wanted to get to know her better, as a person, not as the teacher he remembered, the one who had saved him from himself. He wanted to thank her but more than that, he wanted to be with her.

He was an avid reader but he'd bought her books, mainly because she was from back home, a place he rarely visited but still loved. He read the poetry books regularly too, keeping them in the bathroom. His buddy's teased him about that. He'd been musically talented and poetry should have naturally followed but he'd had little luck with writing songs himself, lyrically he was remedial but Reese wrote with him and they made a great team.

The lobby smelled of stale beer and old men. It didn't seem the type of place she would stay. He'd thought she'd be a little fancier in her accommodations and it pleased him that she wasn't. He liked simple things too like music and art and beautiful women. He loved this city he called home, fog included. He wanted to share that with Chris now. Let her get to know the man he'd become. And he needed to ask her about some things. She'd had secrets and he had discovered them. He wanted to know her truth.

"Hi." Her voice was nice.

"Hi, wow!" The look was obvious and any doubt she'd had about this being a date vanished. His eyes were those of a man, not a boy, and that man appreciated the woman in front of him as a woman, not the teacher from his past.

"Where are we going?" Chris questioned him as he stood up from the chair.

"Everywhere." His smile was as pretty as a girl's, yet made him more masculine. He reached down and took her hand with a question in his eyes, as though to ask permission.

She wrapped her hand around his and gave it a little squeeze and he lifted it to his lips kissing the skin. She shivered at the thrill down her spine and didn't even notice the bruise coloured place where his lips had touched.

56

St. John's is the oldest city in North America. The ghosts of the merchants and fishermen, who had bartered over the price of the catch, mingled in the fog with the ethereal voices of the orphans that had once resided underneath the grimy boards that were the first wharves built along the ancient shore.

Stephen told her about these orphans who had lived under the docks in the early days of the city's history. Wharfingers they had been nick-named. They were misery in small packages, forgotten waifs who survived by working for food, selling both their souls and their bodies for their lives. Chris was haunted by their stories as they walked along the harbour front. Times had changed but this city held the past in its fist with a grip so tight that even now she imagined she heard the long extinct urchins laugh with child-like glee from their historic graves and the drunken ghosts singing endless happy sea shanties in dark alleys and corrugated row houses.

"I truly love this city." Chris confessed after they had walked quietly for a while.

"Isn't it amazing?" He agreed. "It feels alive all the time, it's ghostly and present all at once." His words echoed her thoughts.

"It's beautiful too."

"Then there's the rain," he joked.

"And the endless fog," Chris volleyed.

"Don't forget the drizzle," Stephen laughed.

"The best part!" She joked along. "And when they all show up together, it's perfect!"

He smiled at her and then move a little closer. Damn, he wanted to kiss her. The urge was overwhelming but he resisted. It had to be right.

"You wanted to ask me about something." Chris reminded him. She needed to regroup.

"Yeah, let's wait, do some walking, I need some exercise. Is there anywhere you want to go?"

"The Basilica, but we could go later."

"No, let's go now." They headed back up the city heights.

The Basilica of St. John the Baptist sits in the centre of old St. Johns and is overwhelming in its size and its importance to the people of the town. The walk was uphill all the way, a gradual climb that challenged them though they were both fit and able. They came to the front of the church and stopped.

"This was my favourite place to visit when I lived here." She breathed deeply tasting the cool salt mist that lingered always just around the corner, not visible but still there, the damp as much a part of the landscape as the outer battery or the narrows. Chris wasn't Catholic, hell she wasn't religious at all but she was no longer as irreverent as she had been as a young woman who rolled joints in the Bible. And this place was special to her. It held peace and the spirit of contentment in its bricks and mortar. And it also held her favourite view of St. John's after Cabot Tower.

"Yeah, why?" His eyebrows lifted.

"Her," Chris pointed to the large stature of Mary that greeted visitors to the famous cathedral.

"The statue?" It *was* impressive. A gift of gratitude to the people of St. John's from the Portuguese fishermen who had spent so much time being welcomed on these shores.

"Mary, she just looks so peaceful, it always brought *me* peace." Christianna had spent a lot of time here repeating the Bible verse that had comforted her through a tough childhood. *My peace I give to you* she thought.

"She does look peaceful but I wouldn't expect otherwise." He'd never really looked at the white marble face before but now he saw the serenity and aura of surreal acceptance Chris spoke of. When he looked back at Christianna's face he saw the same look and averted his eyes. He felt like an intruder.

"I know it's just a statue but I think it's interesting that they think she should look peaceful when, if I were the artist I would have made her look sad and grieving." Chris spoke again still looking up at the unseeing eyes in the marble searching for some sign of another emotion. "Her son had been tortured and killed and she was at peace, doesn't seem realistic. Yet somehow I believe it. She makes me wonder, is it possible to have that kind of peace? Sorry, perhaps a bit too serious?" She smiled then, shaking herself from her reverie, hoping she hadn't bored him.

"The Beatles." He answered softly.

"What? Random!" She laughed not making the connection.

"No, no, they answered the question." He explained. "In the song."

Then completely oblivious to his surroundings he began to sing quietly as Chris stilled, spellbound by the beauty of his voice.

"*When I find myself in times of trouble, mother Mary comes to me, whisper words of wisdom, let it be...*" He sang softly and she listened with a quiet reverence. Tears tapped like gentle jack hammers at the corners of her eyes. Some tourists discretely slowed their pace to hear the melodic perfection of the beautiful young man singing *Let it be* at the base of the marble statue of Mary.

Moved by his voice, by the profound truth of his words, she felt a break in the barrier and the tears slid down her cheeks as he finished the last notes.

"Hey was it that bad?" He laughed and then they both heard the applause of several people behind them. He looked around and bowed a little and waved and someone whispered, recognising him.

"That was beautiful," she smiled into his eyes with hers. "Thank you for that, it was amazing." She wiped her eyes, unashamed.

"Payment on your investment," he said quietly.

"What?" She stared at him, a baffled expression in her red-rimmed eyes.

He took her hand again and led her to the little retaining wall that held the grass in front of the statue in place. They sat together there and his words when he spoke saddened her.

"Harry Callum passed away last fall." Stephen's eyes lowered as he spoke.

"Oh no, I hadn't heard." Harry hadn't lived in Rare Moon for years. He had moved into a nursing home in St. John's when he became to elderly to live alone. His wife had passed and his family lived in town as well. Her eyes filled until the drops spilled over their edge, down her smooth cheeks again.

"I heard he was sick and thought I'd stop by and thank him for all the music lessons he gave me over the years."

"Oh." She fidgeted a little and looked away.

"You paid for them didn't you?" Stephen held her hand in his, warm and gentle, talented instruments that played with her heartstrings as well as they played his guitar strings.

"Well you had talent and you needed music lessons," she admitted. There was no reason to keep that secret any longer.

"Things were really tough back then," he knew she knew that but still needed to say the words.

"I know," She had heard all of the stories from Roxanne. She knew that Stephen had not had an easy childhood.

"Those guitar lessons saved my life, changed my life."

"I had hoped they would help," she admitted. "A diversion."

"Do you have any idea how much that guitar was worth?" He burst out almost angrily. "Lord Jesus, a Gibson Hummingbird no less." Stephen remembered the thrill of the moment he first held it in his hands. "Why all the secrecy though?"

"You didn't like me much," Chris said. "And I was afraid you would say no just out of pride. And well, it was a bit, tricky. It would have been frowned upon as favouritism, people would have wondered, talked, gossiped. Jesus, in Rare Moon, a handsome male student accepting favours from a young female teacher, frankly, it was too risky. I trusted Harry though. He was a good guy so I knew he would keep it quiet. It would have just... *looked* bad." A drifting sadness lingered around her at the knowledge of Harry's passing.

"Yeah, he kept quiet until his death bed actually, but then he thought he should give credit where it was due, and I'm glad he did." Especially now, that it brought him to this moment with Christianna. Suddenly he was far more than grateful to her. He sensed there was something special between them, something destined and right.

"Wait, you thought I was handsome? Man, I had a crush on you. Wish I had known that!" His eyes twinkled at the thought.

"How inappropriate would that have been? Anyway, you were well worth the investment." Christianna's smile revealed one happy dimple in her right cheek. She loved knowing that she really hadn't wasted all those years when she'd been a teacher. She had done something right. Teaching *was* a noble profession. It just wasn't the one she'd wanted.

His eyes looked into hers and things changed. The fog that had been sitting just outside the harbour waiting for a perfect moment moved into the city, darkening the sky to a beautiful grey mist that cooled their skin and heightened their senses.

"I want to thank you Miss Cormack." Stephen said in a voice that sang even when he was speaking.

"You are welcome." Chris looked into the eyes that were now the colour of the fog, dark grey and gently pleasant and full of her reflection.

"Is it really bad to want to kiss your teacher?" Stephen had wanted to since he was sixteen.

"Not as bad as wanting to kiss your student." She invited. She saw something in his eyes that was as warm and gentle as the crimson sunset she loved so much. He was genuine, he was reliable and she wanted him as much as he wanted her.

Stephen's hand reached out and pushed the hair back from her face. He moved closer and her scent brushed his nostrils and tempted him further. He moved his whole body closer to her. Now it was perfect. Now it was time.

Their lips met as the fog enveloped them, the mist dancing around the newfound lovers, happy, contrasting its regular dark reputation with the blanket of warm love against the cold droplets that hovered magically in the air. Millions of them, together, close, floating, creating a cover of dark beneath the approving marble eyes of the mother of God. They were unaware of anything but each other.

If Chris had taken the time to think at all she would have wondered why, once again, that it was in the thickness of the fog that she saw things with the greatest clarity.

57

"It's a bit *bijou*," she joked as they slid along the wall from the door to her bathroom, along the edge of the bed. It was a small room, her budget only allowed for this kind of accommodation. There was something about the character of the Captain's Quarter's Chris loved though. Sitting in the historical building restored to its original decor appealed to her romantic side. As much as she sometimes wished she still had the nice income of a school teacher, this hotel was her favourite and she was grateful she'd discovered it a few years ago. It felt like home.

Stephen reclined on the green and burgundy floral bedspread and waited for her. He was over six feet tall, lean and limber. His presence was beyond physical. The thing that made the girls scream in the audiences and drew the crowds to the venues where he played was present even one on one with Stephen Miles. And what made him even more attractive was the fact that he was completely oblivious to it. He was often bewildered by his success, he was musically talented and he could sing but so could a million others.

He didn't dwell on it all too much. People liked his music, he was gaining popularity and his band would be even taking things off the island to Nova Scotia next year. They were hoping for a record deal soon. He didn't quite get that he had something special, an aura that was magnetic that showcased his talent and brought to light a brilliance that would be hidden in others.

Chris walked out of the bathroom and smiled at him. *She* saw that something was special about him and her writer's mind searched for the right words to describe it. Too real to be called charisma, too natural to be called presence, a flame of scarlet light that encircled him and set him up as one of the chosen ones. She'd seen it first, back when he was her student. She'd always known he had something special and she was glad she had acted on it. His gifts were too precious not to be shared.

She climbed up beside him and looked at his handsome face. He was incredibly perfect. Damned he was so *young*. Then he pulled her towards his lips and she quickly forgot. She was here in this room with this amazing man and she felt warm and safe and comfortable.

The light and temptation of the city was outside the room but they stayed in. They tasted and sampled each other amazed at each new discovery. She was proving sweeter than the memories of the boyhood crush delivered, he was much more grown up and patient and mature than she imagined a man this young would be. They spent the night discovering and rediscovering each other. Each loved the treasure they uncovered.

Christianna had not been this full of a man, been this enamoured in a long time and she knew it was profound. It wasn't forbidden or secret. This was something to be proud of, this was a man she could count on, this man, Stephen would put her first, be hers alone if she asked him to and even better, he would without the asking. She could tell by the words he spoke and the way he loved her that he was sincere. Joe had been sincere but he'd never been able to give himself fully to her. This man would and she knew it immediately. She just had to decide if she was willing to take it.

When morning came he slipped out and returned a while later and sat in the little chair that accompanied the tiny table in the corner by her window. With no other choice available she sat in her bathrobe on his knee and kissed him on the lips in gratitude for the hot coffee and blueberry muffins he'd brought them back for breakfast.

As she nibbled on her food she leaned her head against him and looked out the window where he looked. Together they stared at the brilliant red sky that was gifted to them that morning. The sun had risen with a fire and fury that flashed with light and heat. And there, sitting perfectly still in the red hot sky the full moon hung for them, the second full moon of the month, a rare moon made even more rare by its appearance in the morning. They watched it together and fell in love with it and began to fall in love with each other.

And as though it was time, her heart shifted from one that beat to the inconsistent and unreliable glow of the indigo ember, to one that danced to a ruby-red flame, strong, steadfast and eternal. She knew when the time came that she would choose to paint her world with a new hue, a colour that would last and never leave her alone to wonder if it would return. She would choose to live in the glow of a love that was hers and hers alone.

58

Days passed gently and evenly. Christianna and Stephen met often and began to love deeply. They never spoke of forever or permanence but each suspected this love would be such a one. Life settled into a rhythm that they created when they could be together. When they were apart it tortured them. It was often at those times that her mind drifted to Joe and what they shared, what hadn't ended yet and what she would have to end.

Joe still called almost every week while his wife played darts at the local bar with the other women. They talked about their lives and he promised to visit soon. When they talked no one else existed. He loved her as much as ever and he needed her as well. He would visit soon, she knew he wouldn't go much longer and when he did she would tell him it was the last time.

September brought a premature coldness to the land. The trees that surrounded her little home had begun to turn red and orange, cloaking her home with a natural coat of crimson beauty. It was an early fall and she shivered as she walked back towards her front door one windy day with Sailor.

Christianna stopped short when she saw the familiar car at the side of the house. Joe always came in the night, so no one would know. She wondered if her neighbours had seen him. She wouldn't want Stephen to hear about this. He'd never been spotted before so she started towards the house again. Her heart tore in half at the thought of what she had to do.

She entered the house, slipping the leash off Sailor. As she entered her kitchen she was grabbed from behind by strong arms. Her reaction to him was immediate. Her body knew his and wanted it. He turned her around and before she could protest he was kissing her with all of himself. He stopped and looked at her for a moment and she was lost. She knew then, without a doubt, that she still loved him. Tempered by time and distance, she had forgotten how precious he was to her but now his presence reminded her. He was her first love, her protector, her hero, her poet and he wanted her and she wanted him. So she took him.

The blankets on the bed lay at an angle as the couple that shared it were stretched beside each other in silence. How often she had seen their bodies together in this position, comfortable, complimentary, his so dark and male and hers exactly right beside him.

As the sun warmed the day, bringing happiness and peace to the outside world, Chris was inside with growing sadness and confusion. She knew she had to let him go but she still loved him so. She couldn't do it but she had to do it. She couldn't imagine this was the last time she'd see this man but it had to be.

She'd found something with Stephen that satisfied her in a way that Joe never could and she needed to give it a chance. Still, she couldn't even think about Stephen while lying here with Joe. She loved Joe as much as she loved Stephen, and since she couldn't have both, Joe was the one that had to go and her heart and soul protested at the thought.

"I better shower," Chris went to get up and he stopped her.

"You didn't ask," he said.

"Ask to shower?"

"No, you didn't ask me to read to you," he grinned. "I found you something special."

"No." Her voice broke.

"What's wrong?" He sensed immediately something was up with her and fear filled his heart, "are you okay?" What if she were sick?

"Get dressed Joe." She calmed herself. "I'm okay but we do have to talk."

Joe dressed quietly. He knew before she spoke that she was saying goodbye but he let her say it. He sensed that she was tired of this secrecy and this life that offered her nothing.

"We can't do this anymore." Her heart broke with the words she had to say. She couldn't look at him.

"It's not enough is it?" Joe asked moving close to her and forcing her eyes to look into his.

"It's not enough." She was given some hope that it would be easier than she thought. He understood and had seen this coming.

"I've been thinking about that lately." He confessed. Chris blinked at the pain that caused her.

"So you know what I'm saying?" She hoped desperately that she wouldn't have to say the words.

"I've been expecting it to come to this, I knew it would happen one day." He pulled her close. "I'll tell Tiffany when I get home."

Chris wrenched away from him. "Tell her? You can't *tell* her."

"I'll let her keep the house and come here with you." He was sad for his children but he had always known that one day he would have to do this to keep her and she was ready so he had to. He held her close again.

"No." Chris said, understanding dawning.

"No?"

"We can't be together anymore at all." She took a deep breath, decisiveness in her voice. "I've met someone else."

He let her go and she stumbled a little. His face had an expression she'd never seen on it before. It was anger and it wasn't just anger. It was shock and it wasn't just shock. It held fear and disappointment but these emotions too didn't stand alone. It was a combination of all of these that distorted his features and changed his expression from one of love to one of horror.

His body tightened. He'd never hit a woman in his adult life but he wanted to now. She had been seeing someone else. She was obviously in love with someone else or she wouldn't be letting him go. Yet she had just made love to him with her entire heart. He hadn't imagined the delight in her eyes when she saw him or the passion on her face as they loved each other exactly as they always had. He stopped his lips from uttering the word that first came into his mind-*slut*-and asked instead.

"Who is it?" His hands clenched in their eagerness to hurt *somebody*.

"You don't know him," Chris said. "It doesn't matter." Now she was the protector.

"And you love him?" Joe had to ask.

"Yes." She stepped back.

"I won't hurt you for fuck sake!" She was afraid of him and she had reason to be but he felt disappointed in her. It diminished their love somehow, that she would think he would hurt her though his hands itched to do just that.

"I'm sorry." She was completely and utterly honest.

"How long you been....?" Not that it mattered, but he wanted to know.

"Just a month or so but I've known him awhile." It felt like much longer and the thought crossed her mind that this might be a huge mistake.

"I'm too late? If I leave Tiffany now I'm too late?" He wanted to convince her, wanted their love back and it was slipping away from him and he didn't know what to do. He felt tears at the back of his eyes. He'd never considered she'd find someone else. It had never crossed his mind.

"Yes you're too late." Chris knew how cruelly that hurt him, and mourned for the heart she was breaking. His heart was hers and she felt his pain.

"If you had asked me to leave her I would have, before."

"You said you wouldn't and I didn't want you to hate me. I didn't want your children to hate you."

"I don't love her Christianna." And in that moment, however unfairly, he hated Tiffany. If it wasn't for her he could have been with Christianna.

"Maybe you would if I wasn't around."

"No, I just don't." Though he knew that the only real flaw Tiffany had was that she wasn't Chris.

"It was always wrong," Chris continued. "I always justified it because I thought you were mine first but that's not how works. We just stole something from your wife and we've been stealing it from your kids too and it's time to stop."

"What have we taken? No one knows. Nobody has had any idea about us."

"We stole you. We took any chance of you and Tiffany being together and in love, we stole the complete dad those girls deserve and we robbed me too, or any possibility of me having the partnership I deserved."

"So you wanted to get married? I would have married you later on, in time."

"No, I don't think that was how it was meant to be for us, not this time, not this lifetime, I think what we had, will always have, is perfect, exactly as it's supposed to be but it's not supposed to go any further."

"You have these strange ideas, these strange theories but the fact is we love each other. You are the love of my life." Joe's voice broke and he turned away from her. The cauldron of emotions simmered on a flame of hurt, tiny bubbles of hatred popping to the surface and breaking one after another until a rolling boil was reached.

"You are the love of my life too Joe." Chris said softly. "But it's time to let it go." She reached out and touched his hand.

"Shut up!" Joe croaked the words, the voice he used that of a stranger. "Goddamn it Christianna just shut up." He tossed her hand away, his hurt-blackened eyes flashing with an ebony light and his anger grew alongside a mental image of Christianna in bed with this other unknown man. As though painted on the canvas of his subconscious mind by Satan himself the images tore through breaking the threads of his sanity and he toppled over into an abyss of irrational rage.

When he emerged it was to find his hands around the neck of the woman he loved, her gasping voice pleading for mercy, the love he had always seen in her eyes replaced by fear and hurt. He pulled his hands away relieved that they were once again under his control and stepped back. Chris slipped to the floor weakly, unspeaking, never taking her eyes off him. The guilt that moved into the gaps created as the anger dissipated would not allow him to speak to her. He turned away from her with a wrenching, painful lurch and walked to the chair grabbing his coat. He let the door slam behind him with a soul-shattering bang.

59

The protected harbour contained the energy of efficiency and experience as the ships and boats entered and exited. Tourist schooners watched the humpbacks that had loyally come back to the waters just outside of St. John's Harbour and were playing their joyful entertainment to the delight of a packed ship.

Stephen and Christianna watched from above at the wall of the fortress named for the man who had discovered the province, Giovanni Caboto. Christianna had never been brave enough to walk the trail around Signal Hill but she liked to walk the back paths through Cuckolds Cove and beyond where it wasn't such a steep fall to the water below.

She spent more time in the city she loved now, Stephen lived and played there frequently and she stayed with him at his little apartment on Gower Street in one of the pretty-painted row houses that were lined like Lego blocks, one clipped into the other, pretty, original and defining the landscape of downtown St. John's. She liked his place. It was filled from top to bottom with musical instruments and music paraphernalia although he usually played her guitar as he referred to it. She would write and he would play and sing to her.

"It's like melted butter and home made bread," he had said to her once. "Playing this guitar is like coming home." She felt at home with *him*.

Then, weather permitting, in the evening when Stephen didn't have a gig, they walked the town, visiting O'Brien's music store where he bought much of his music materials and hiked up the hills. They would talk and dream and connect and their love blossomed and grew and matured as they started to realise that the other was not only exactly what they had always dreamt of but that they were more.

It was Autumn and the trail didn't have as many tourists as the summer months did and even on this beautiful day it was quiet. They walked together marvelling as they always did at the rugged beauty that nature provided, a view they never tired of and one that still somehow couldn't truly be carried in memories such that the awe of it struck every time as though it were the first. They sat beside a large boulder and watched as the sun began to set in the west flashing amber and red lights that reflected in the ocean.

"Someday we have to come for the sunrise." Christianna suggested her hand comfortably stroking the denim of his jeans.

"I would if they'd stop having it in the morning." Stephen joked.

"Well, just once. Perhaps we could just stay up a few more hours and watch it come up." They both tended to go to bed late each night.

"Someday soon." Stephen smiled and his smile held a promise of the future. He had never been in love before. He loved her so much, her spirit danced outside of her body, she was so alive and real. He was in awe of her much of the time, her success, her appearance and her essence. They spent most of their time in regular boring activities and she seemed to live very simply, completely unaware of her presence, her influence. She made the mundane spectacular.

"You'll have to tempt me to stay awake longer." He suggested raising his eyebrows and looking at her lewdly running a hand down her back and pulling close.

"Easy orders captain." Chris joked as she saluted and reached over to kiss him on the lips. She pulled back and looked at his face. He was so beautiful. Sometimes she was overwhelmed by him, his calmness and steadiness. He adored her and she wondered why. She was just a regular woman and he was incredible and young and talented. She was enamoured of him and revelled in having him around all the time. She'd never had both, the time and the love at once and the intensity of it all left her weak and scared but he was never unsure and it comforted her.

Her cell phone rang in her pocket and she tugged it out, her eyes apologetic as she answered.

"Hello?" She checked the screen and hit the end button.

"Nobody there." She shrugged, disturbed by the increasing frequency of the calls.

"Who was it?"

"Nobody, perhaps it dropped, they'll call back." She hit a few button and turned off the ringer, jamming the phone into her pocket.

Christianna looked into Stephen's worried face. She reached up and took it between her hands. He pulled her closer still and they became lost in each other for a moment until a seagull's cry nearby startled them apart.

"We need to go home," she whispered, all thoughts of disturbing phone calls gone.

"I can't wait, man I'm dyin' here." Stephen said, his eyes needy, reflecting the needs of his body.

"I can't either," she said. "But we have to." Chris glanced around. It was public, though no one was around.

"Come on then." Stephen jumped up, brushing some dust off the beige cable-knit sweater.

But instead of leading her back towards the tower he led her off the path until they were away from the main walking trail. It was rough and the blackberry plants with their thorny leaves made for an uncomfortable ground but Stephen was determined. He found a little alcove in a grassy area almost hidden underneath a tree. He pulled off the sweater his mother had knit so lovingly and laid it down on the ground underneath the bushy overgrowth, inside out.

"I can't wait m'love," he said again and his need was evident as he pulled aside her unnecessary clothing.

Chris was as eager as he was as she pulled on the button of his jeans. As they made love underneath the thicket where grasshoppers hopped, the sun set completely behind the horizon leaving them in a dusky grey heavenly bliss and creation waved an invisible wand and their love was celebrated in the heavens as it was meant to be. The stars waited to twinkle, their doing so superfluous to the moment. But the moon shone on the knowledge that creation had given them a gift more perfect than any man can create and smiled in anticipation of their acceptance of it into their lives.

60

Chris puttered around her house dusting and cleaning. Roxanne had come by and brought Sailor back. She was worried about her friend who looked happy and sad at the same time. She didn't say anything, Christianna had been evasive but Roxanne knew there was a man in St. John's. That only explained the happiness. But Roxanne had no idea as to her sadness. Her friend would tell her in her own time. Or maybe she wouldn't. Chris kept her secrets close. Chris was distracted and quiet and even her reunion with her dog that she loved so much didn't bring her back to life.

"Finally got the slobber off the walls and the hair under control and you're back," Chris teased her dog as she ruffled his fur.

For the first time since they had been friends Chris was uncomfortable around Roxanne. She was dating her son and although Roxanne was several years older than Chris, they were peers in most ways. It was just odd. Roxanne didn't see Stephen all that much and Chris had convinced him it was time to come home, that they had to tell her together and they had to soon. St. John's was really a small town and stories would come back.

"I have news," Roxanne chirped and Chris feigned curiosity. She knew what it was.

"My son is visiting for Thanksgiving!"

"That's wonderful." Chris had invited Roxanne for Thanksgiving dinner this year and she'd accepted. Chris and Stephen had thought it might be a great time to tell her their news but she was nervous about it. Stephen hadn't had a close relationship with his mother though she had started trying in later years, visiting him, bringing him things but he never came home. Now though, with Chris there, he had reason to re-establish himself in Rare Moon Tickle. He'd also finally forgiven his mother, getting to understand her better through Christianna. He was ready to try to reconnect with her.

"I suggested we have Thanksgiving dinner at my house since he was coming home but he said no, that we should still do it here. It's all right if he comes to dinner here isn't it?" Roxanne knew it would be and that her friend would welcome her son.

"Of course." Chris felt strangely weak and sat down on the couch but before she could say anything she jumped up and headed for the bathroom where she was sick.

"Up da stump or what?" Roxanne joked from the doorway, watching her friend lean over the toilet, concern behind the humour.

The earth seemed to stop, the shock in Chris's eyes at the possibility catching Roxanne off guard. She had been joking but now she suddenly knew too, "Oh my God, you *are* pregnant!"

"No." Chris whispered. But the Gods giggled and whispered *yes* and her heart immediately felt it. That day on Signal Hill, they had been impulsive and Chris had tossed her entire sensibility to the wind in the passion of that magic moment.

She started to shake with the shock and Roxanne saw her face and knew that the realisation was as new to Chris as it was to her.

"Come on!" Roxanne demanded, helping her up.

"Oh my God." Chris's voice was stronger. "This is crazy, I can't be."

"Have you had any of the sex then?" Roxanne's words made Chris chuckle.

"Yeah but..." It was enough of an answer for Roxanne.

"Well we're going to find out." Roxanne said. "I'm off to the drugstore for a test." And she was in her coat and out the door. Sailor barked and whined when she left without him and went back to the couch where Christianna lay in near shock.

Christianna placed a hand on her flat abdomen. She was too old. She had never wanted children. Her thoughts scrambled one into the other, her heart seeking something, any clue as to how this felt. She thought of the pregnancy test she'd taken once before back in university that had been negative. She had wept with relief that time.

She looked at her hand on her belly and knew with a certainty that she was pregnant, the time was right, she was off in a way she hadn't ever been before and as she lay there her heart was full of the wonder of it. What would Stephen think? They hadn't even talked of permanency. They had gone with the moment. Hell they hadn't even told his mother they were a couple and now they would have to tell her she would be a grandmother.

Chris closed her eyes willing herself to relax and suddenly she felt engulfed in a peace unlike any she had ever felt and the face that visited her was not Stephen's but Joe's. Now his memory came to see her, to taunt her but the face she saw held no pain, just the love he'd always had for her deep in those chocolate brown eyes. His presence in her thoughts was strangely peaceful and a tear escaped from the corner of her eyes.

The crash from the back of the house made her jump. Chris clamoured to her feet, and went towards the front by instinct, away from it. Through the glass panel at the side of the door she saw Roxanne's car and Roxanne walking towards the house. It must have been the car door slamming and Chris chided herself for being so jumpy. Roxanne walked in with a little white bag in her hand and gave it to Chris quickly.

"That nosey old biddy Chloe was there and she looked at the test when I paid so I told her I thought *I* was knocked up." Roxanne laughed. "That ought to set the tongues to waggin'!"

Chris laughed at her. Roxanne was in her forties, there was no way and the gossips would figure it out eventually but for now they would be wondering. She went into the bathroom and closed the door.

Christianna read the instructions. Then after she had followed them, she set the little plastic test on the edge of the toilet tank as she washed her hands. They shook a little. Her heart would be broken if it was negative. It would explode if it were positive. Three minutes she had to wait according to the detailed leaflet in the package. She left the bathroom.

"Well?" Roxanne was right there.

"It's gotta cook." Chris said. "But it'll be positive."

"Who is the father?" Roxanne had to know.

"I've been seeing someone for a while," she answered. *It's your son, your baby that you adore and I seduced him and now I'm knocked up.* Hell it sounded like a Jerry Springer episode. "You'll meet him soon enough, he's coming to visit on Thanksgiving."

"What's his name?"

"You'll find out then. Do you think it's been three minutes?"

"Good God Chris, you keep things closed up tighter than Mary's pussy." Roxanne genuflected and laughed. "Well 'cept p'raps yer own." She winked and laughed at her joke.

"Shut up." Chris said good-naturedly and headed into the bathroom and came back with the test in her hands seconds later.

"It's positive." She said and her calm voice hid her excitement.

"Yes!" Roxanne tackled her in a strong hug and Sailor barked and then put his head down again, tired from the exercise though he watched carefully as the women chattered, his doggie eyebrows volleying left and right as the women spoke.

"Congratulations mommy!"

"Thanks." Christianna said *and congratulations to you too Nanny* she thought.

"How do you feel? This guy, is he a keeper?"

"He's amazing, yeah he's a keeper, but you'll see."

"Is he the guy that was here last week?" Roxanne figured it was worth asking.

"No, he's never been here, at the house." Stephen had been playing in Corner Brook.

"Oh t'ought I saw a feller around here then. Can I be called Auntie?"

"You can be whatever you want?" Chris wondered who she had seen. The calls, now this man Roxanne was seeing around. Was it Joe? She remembered his violence the last time he'd been here, his hurt, his desperation. Perhaps it was time to do something, perhaps she should call someone. The hair on the back of her neck stood up with the chill in her soul. Joe wouldn't really hurt her. Would he?

"Well, Mary, Jesus and Joseph!" Roxanne's loud laughter shook her back to the present. She genuflected again, her grin wide and her heart filled with joy. "I'll spoil him rotten, just like me own." She declared.

Her fear forgotten for the moment, Christianna thought of the baby. She was excited for her friend as well. After herself and Stephen this baby would be Roxanne's.

Her parent's involvement would be minimal, they barely saw their existing grandchildren, still travelling and making up for the time they had lost. She now saw them twice a year and talked to them once a month. They'd be happy but they wouldn't be involved. Roxanne would be extraordinary and Chris was grateful.

Christianna checked the locks on all of the windows and doors and took her phone into her room with her, telling herself she was silly. She let Sailor climb on the bed making him the happiest dog on the planet for a night. She cuddled him and knew she was safe. He was nervous though, growling under his breath at something only he could sense and she wound up consoling him.

Chris wanted to tell Stephen this alone and in person yet it took all of her strength not to call him. She lay in her bed with her huge dog and smiled to herself at the miracle she had been given. She hadn't wanted children with Michael, she hadn't loved him enough to want his, she hadn't been ready in her whole life to give them what they deserved, until now. Joe had already had a family and though she would have loved to look into her child's eyes and see the indigo fire in their chocolate depths, it was not to be for them.

But now, with Stephen it was perfect. They were in love, and the fates had decided that the time was perfect. This time when she closed her eyes they danced with the face of the man who sang her beautiful ballads in his soft buttery voice and loved her as though she were a Goddess sent just for him. This baby would be perfect and she sent her grateful energy to the scarlet sky that had given her this greatest gift, the gift of creation.

61

Roxanne was nervous. She stood in front of the mirror that hung on the back of her bedroom door. Her hair was perfect and she had even applied a little make up. She wore a pair of black pants that hung loosely as though they were a skirt, dressy and practical. Her red chenille turtleneck fitted her thin body coming down over her waist and hips and she looked taller. She had probably over-dressed but it had been a long time. She wanted to look good for him. She pulled the clasp of the chain she wore to the back of her neck so that the cross pendant he'd given her was centred perfect against the soft red fabric.

Not only was her son visiting but she'd finally get to meet the mystery man who held the heart of her friend. Stephen would drive straight to Christianna's and she had told him she would be there around one. She finished her primping and headed to the kitchen to grab the dessert she was bringing.

Meanwhile, Christianna watched Stephen as he placed the turkey in the oven. It would be hours before it would be cooked Roxanne would be here soon and they would tell her. She had chickened out telling him the night before but now she had no choice. She knew that Roxanne would probably blurt the news about the pregnancy in the shock of seeing them together so she couldn't delay.

She had dressed simply in a long black dress that stopped just above her ankles. She wore large gold hoops in her ears and had left her long blonde curls down. She had needed the confidence the extra effort gave her but now she faltered.

"I have something to tell you." Chris said as he closed the oven door.   She took a deep breath.

"Wait," he held up his hand and then pulled two wine glasses down from the rack over the island. "Let's have wine."

"Okay," Chris agreed. This needed to be special she realised and the wine would give her courage.

Happy for the momentary reprieve she moved over to the couch where the midday sun heated the cool room. It was tastefully decorated for fall with ornamental gourds and butterscotch and red candles on the coffee table. Steven set the wine glasses down and pulled her close.

"What's up?" He knew she was nervous about telling his mother.

"Well," she reached for the glass of wine and took a sip and then she put the glass down sloshing the dark red liquid on to the table.

"I can't have wine." Her voice was sharp, her eyes wide.

"Why not?" Stephen's eyebrows raised. "It'll calm your nerves, Mom won't be that mad, have a sip." He wasn't worried about his mother's reaction at all. She would do anything to make up for all those years she'd neglected him including approving of whoever he brought home. He wasn't above using her guilt if he needed to for the protection of Christianna's feelings.

"No, I can't have wine." She inhaled deeply, this was the man who loved her and she needed to say the words. "Because I'm pregnant."

His reaction mirrored hers from the night before. His dark blue eyes widened and then narrowed and the initial shock was replaced by a flash of joy and excitement. His lips followed quickly and the dimples in either side of them deepened at her words.

"Pregnant?" When he spoke the word it was with a quiet reverence as though he'd been bestowed some great honour. It was how he felt.

His arms were around her and his embrace was warm and sweet and they held each other close.

Then he pulled back and looked at her, wondering if he'd been selfish, what if she wasn't happy. "Are you okay with this?" He asked, searching her eyes. He couldn't wait to see those eyes in their child.

"I am now." She smiled and their lips were together as the last of the words left her lips.

Lost in their own moment, their own joy, they stayed that way until they were interrupted by the gasp from the front door and turned to see Roxanne standing there, mouth agape holding a cherry cheesecake in front of her as though it were a life preserver. The large Newfoundland bounded over to his best friend and stopped to sniff the dish in her hand. Only food could stop him from attacking his favourite visitor with slobbery love.

"Oh Mother of Jesus." Roxanne said as her mind took in what she was seeing. "Oh Mother of Jesus." She repeated and the couple flew apart like two teenagers caught by an angry dad with a shot gun.

"Hello mom," Stephen said, the first to recover from the surprise a grin punctuated his face at her expression. Christianna turned scarlet red in mortification.

Stephen walked over, lips twitching, and took the shiny red cheesecake from his mother's hands and set it on the bench in the entryway. Sailor followed the scent, laying down on the floor in front of the bench, staring with pleading eyes and drooping jowls at the Pyrex dish, oblivious to the drama unfolding around him. Roxanne's eyes were filled with shock as her son turned to embrace her in a hug. He hadn't seen her in a long time and he realised he'd missed her.

"What is going on?" Roxanne was stunned but Stephen's hug had shaken her from her shock a little. He'd never volunteered the first hug before. It unsettled her in a happy way.

Christianna watched Stephen and her friend together, embarrassment leaving her. They had planned to tell her, not show her but Stephen's humour was contagious and she couldn't help herself. She stifled a matching snicker, not looking at him because she knew he'd set her off into a fit of laughter.

"Will somebody answer me?" Roxanne asked looking from one to the other.

"I've been seeing Stephen for a while." Christiana spoke from the couch and held up the wine glass as a prop.

"You can't drink that!" Roxanne almost screamed and then she thought of something. "Oh, the baby!"

"Mine." Stephen raised his hand. He looked exactly like the guilty school boy Chris had dealt with so many years before and this time she exploded in mirth.

Roxanne looked at Christianna who nodded, wiping tears from her eyes. She got up from the couch handing her the glass of wine. Roxanne looked from one to the other and drank the wine in one gulp and handed the glass back to Christianna.

"So this is the man I'm supposed to meet today?" She said, finally coming out of her shock and putting it all together. "The mystery man you've been seeing?"

"Yeah."

"So it's just the three of us for Thanksgiving?"

"Four." Said Steven walking behind Chris and placing his hand on her abdomen and she looked up at him, his sweetness deserving of the love in her eyes.

"Well then," Roxanne said with a deep sigh. "Guess I made too much frickin' cheery cheesecake." A joyful laugh burst from her at the entire situation.

Christianna and Stephen were then the recipients of a battery of hugs. Even Sailor caught the spirit and wagged his tail and snapped a low bark at them.

"The tongues will wag over this one." Roxanne's musical laughter bounded out of control.

"And you're knocked up and not married." She nodded at Chris and wiped the tears off her cheeks. Stephen took her empty glass and went to fill it up again. He let the women laugh. Roxanne hugged her friend who was making her a grandmother.

"So much for being a good Catholic woman." Chris joked as the mirth subsided to normal happy levels. "You're way too happy about the scandal of it all."

"Jesus he'll marry you I suppose." And that was all that mattered in her Catholic heart. "But it's just too perfect, the talk oh, my God, they'll have years from this one."

Their dinner was joyful and full of laughter and light and Roxanne was given permission to spread the news but first she would tell the priest.

"Proactive confession?" Chris asked.

"Yeah, best to get ahead on these things." Roxanne agreed with a grin. She knew father Doyle well. He would help her out, advise her.

The cool air brushed over Roxanne's face as she walked home with the leftover cheesecake in her hands. It was crisp and bright and a large moon hung suspended over the edge of the forest that backed on to her little house. She saw it there and stopped for a moment, its beauty enhanced by the clouds that drifted over, not quite concealing it in a layer of mist that changed the light from a grey to a deep purple-blue, a colour that reminded her of a time when she had been as happy as Christianna, the time when she'd discovered that she was pregnant with Steven.

This baby, this time would have all of the love that she'd failed to provide its father and she promised the moon and the stars that peeked out one by one as the mist moved along that she would be there to make sure of that. She thought of Christianna, her friend who had taken her without judgement, who trusted her and saw in her something no one else had bothered to look for and was happy that this was the person her son had chosen.

As the magnitude of the universe revealed itself in that clear perfect and infinite sky she understood that they had not actually chosen each other, that each had, instead, been chosen *for* the other and that both had been chosen for her. This perfect child who would join their family was a part of that divine plan as well. As this realisation came upon Roxanne, she slipped to her knees on the cold October ground and set the cake dish aside. She folded her hands together and spoke to her God with all of the sincerity in her heart.

"Thank you." She whispered to the night not even realising the significance of her timing that *Thanksgiving* evening. It would have been the same any day of the year. The rustling trees and the indigo moon whispered back that this joy was her reward and that it was well deserved.

62

Day rolled into day, the dominoes of time falling gently, one against the other, leaving a path, designed by the fates that the couple followed. The baby inside Christianna grew and the doctor she saw assured her it was healthy. Christmas that year was bright and happy. They decorated her living tree and sang carols and even attended the Catholic mass with Roxanne.

It was Roxanne's best gift of the year, not just the couple who stood with her, holding hands as the priest spoke of God and love and peace, not even the baby that was coming to them. It was the gift of forgiveness from her son for her weaknesses when he was a child and she knew that she needed to give back some of that good blessing somehow. She was eager to help in the church's Christmas Charity work and the people of the town whispered of the change in Roxanne Armstrong in a hushed, almost reverend way. They considered it a local miracle.

Later that evening, they dropped Sailor off with Roxanne because they didn't like to leave her alone. As the fire crackled and spit in the over-decorated fireplace, holding two stuffed stockings, Steven came up behind her as she stood looking into the scarlet and indigo flames. He put his arms around her, his hands rubbing her barely-there belly. "We probably should get married." He whispered.

"I don't do *shoulds* anymore," Christianna answered, though her heart fluttered at his words.

"Yeah, I guess I worded that wrong," he said, a nervous catch in his voice. Then he cleared his throat.

"I meant to say, would you like to marry me please." And although she rarely considered his youth now, he sounded very young.

"Are you serious?" She turned and asked in a hesitant voice and his eyes answered before his lips did. Her heart screamed then and Joe's face flashed before her and a craving washed over her soul for him as it did on occasion. She shook the image off quickly and looked at Stephen's face.

"Yeah," and he held out a little black box to her.

"Tell me it's not a diamond?" She wouldn't settle this time.

"It's not a diamond." He reassured her with a smile.

She opened the lid, her hand shaking a little. She was still a girl, still romantic and so in love. The box held a beautiful garnet, in a delicate ornate setting of sterling silver. Its glorious russet colour and perfect facets spoke of mysterious sunsets and reliable dawns. It was antique, non-traditional and perfect for their love.

"Oh." Christianna spoke, her voice a whisper, though it wasn't from the beauty of the ring. It was from the knowledge that she really was going to have the love she wanted, strong, secure and forever. She took it out of the box.

"Put it on then?" She said. "Oh and yes." Chris laughed. She hadn't expected this. Not yet. The pregnancy had been a surprise and they'd only known each other a few months but no wasn't an option. This was what she'd always wanted.

"Fish or no fish?" He spoke the old Newfoundland saying, his voice eager and a little less like a scared five year old.

"Fish or no fish." She agreed and she held her hand a little closer to her face.

The ring was perfect and the moment was perfect. The baby between them kicked its approval though they couldn't feel it yet. They were too caught up in the scarlet heat of their love and their new promise of a future together. She loved him so and he loved her as much and suddenly all of the hopes and dreams and promises of life were fulfilled.

The snow fell outside in gentle flakes, piling slowly, million upon million until a soft blanket of white covered the rooftops and created a scene of Christmas beauty that gave envious pause to any Norman Rockwell painting. And as the oblivious couple huddled warm in their bliss the moon that had shone full and round behind a wispy winter cloud, was suddenly bright and full and those who were outside marvelled at it's strange and delightful colour.

The atmosphere had combined in a perfect blend of light and dust to create a moon that appeared in perfect indigo glory. The stars twinkled and the rare moon shone its best wishes on a love as rare as its own appearance in the sky was. The heavens had blessed them and destined that their love, as much as the other, was always meant to be.

******

Joe opened the present and his eyes widened at the contents.

"Where did you guys get the money?"

"We saved and mom put in half, do you like it?" Merina's eyes were eager and she wasn't disappointed in his reaction.

"I love it!" He took the little black iPod from its box, flicking it on. He had wanted one, intended to buy himself one. He loved music, and had an extensive collection. He'd just bought the new Trinity CD when he attended their concert in Gander the week before. He'd load that one on right away. The girls had been full of the surprise for a month and Tiffany smiled at the pleasure on his face.

"Go ahead, try it." She encouraged. I put the songs on for the girls. She'd spent hours on the computer the last time he was out of town, filling it.

Joe put the little ear buds in his ear, smiling at his kids. He laughed out loud when the song that played was a favourite of his, from Trinity. He sat back and mouthed a thank you to his family as Tiffany walked back to the kitchen with their coffee cups. The girls drifted off to their favourite gifts and Joe closed his eyes to relax when the first few notes of the Jackson Browne tune began on the little speakers in his ears. As the words of the song that always brought Christianna's face to his mind's eye filled his heart with longing for her, he was hit by a renewal of the sudden and overwhelming sadness that had enveloped him lately. He didn't know what was wrong with him but he was finding it increasingly difficult to be happy and there was no real reason. He missed Christianna but he'd been trying to getting along better with Tiffany and his girls were still the centre of his universe. It simply wasn't working.

Tiffany watched from the doorway, the heavy emotional turmoil on her husbands face evident even from across the room. She was worried about him. He picked up his cell phone and stared at it for a few moments and then sat it back on the arm of the chair with an angry snapping movement that made her jump. In some ways they seemed to have grown closer but still, something was wrong with him and had been for a while. She pursed her lips wondering how she could help him. As the tears spilled down his cheeks, betraying the depth of his despair, she backed out of the room disturbed. She had never seen him cry before. She hoped that perhaps he was moved by his gift but inside she knew that wasn't it. He was simply sad and it was a sadness that she couldn't fix. She could only hope it was something temporary, that it would go away when spring came. She whispered a prayer for that as she walked away from the living room where the Christmas tree lights twinkled brightly, their colours dancing on the cheeks of the man who wept alone in a chair.

63

The image in the mirror satisfied Chris. She looked like a bride without the frills that station often called for. Her long hair was left down, flowing around her face in tender waves. Her skin was clear, glowing with the light of the life growing inside her and her eyes danced with excitement. When the cell phone rang she answered it on the first ring, expecting her mother or Roxanne. Instead there was a voice that she didn't recognise, distorted and almost inhuman. After the click to end the call it took a few seconds for the threat to register, her happy heart almost repelling the moment, as though she could step back over time and erase what had just occurred.

"You ruined my life you bitch, your honeymoon will be real short."

The phone lay on the dresser where she had dropped it. A knock came on the door.

"Who is it?" She jumped and turned. She was pale and there was confusion and fear on her face.

"Me." Stephen's voice answered from the other side.

"You can't come in." She warned him, torn between tempting the fates of superstition and her need to be held by him. It had to have been a mistake. Who would want to hurt her? She was unable to think the most likely explanation and chose to ignore the threat. For now.

"I know, the priest is here." Stephen's deep melodic voice said. "Are you ready?"

"I'm ready, tell dad to come in." She pulled her shoulders back and glanced at the phone one time before she shook off her dread. It simply couldn't be and she denied the possibility with a stronger determination and glanced back in the mirror, consciously removing the look of fear and heartache that had settled there. She missed Joe, ached for him at times and surely he hurt for her but she could not believe that he would harm her.

Her dad took her arm and led her down the two steps to her living room where the rest of the family waited. Roxanne had insisted on a bit of an entrance and had decorated the home beautifully in red and white roses. Still shocked by her parents' attendance at a Catholic wedding ceremony she'd been particularly giving to them and her father gave her away, his regretful eyes a little misty as he handed her over to Stephen.

Later they would further shock her by saying "Well we're all Christian, that's the main thing," and Christianna pondered the possibility of miracles, not for the first time in her life.

Somehow, in a manner known only to her, Roxanne had convinced the Catholic Priest to come to Christianna's house to marry her son and his fiancée. Christianna revolted at the idea of being married in a Christian ceremony until she met Father Doyle.

"I'm not Catholic," she'd informed him. "And I won't convert, it would be hypocritical."

"That's fine my darlin'," he'd told her. "The church leaves these matters up to the parish priest and I don't mind that at all, though I don't advertise it." He grinned, his eyes twinkling with mirth. He was a rare man, whose beliefs included the idea that others held their truths as dearly as he held his. She could see why Roxanne had returned to the church with this man as its leader.

"Well then, I guess it's settled." Chris was a little unnerved about the simplicity of the whole thing. All of her judgements about organised religion had, over time shattered. She had also realised that she was as guilty of judgement as anyone with all of her preconceived notions.

"I loves yer books." Father Doyle confessed after the ceremony and then shocked her further by asking. "Would you sign my copy of *Judgement*?"

"Yeah, sure." And in doing so she did discovering father Doyle's first name.

"Wilbert?" She wanted to laugh and her eyes twinkled, resisting the effort.

"Now you see why I became a priest." He joked "Everybody calls me Father Doyle instead of Wilbert Doyle." His eyes laughed as she signed her name to her new novel, a story of a young girl who had been banished from a small town for having an affair with her employer, a married man. It had explored the differences in how she was treated and wound up and how he did, though they had both committed the same sin.

The guests drank wine and beer while her parents drank sparkling non-alcoholic version that Stephen had provided. They liked him, and that thoughtful gesture was one of many that helped them do so. In the middle of the pleasure though, that things had gone so well, a niggling memory disturbed her happiness so when she had a moment she snuck into the bathroom and dialed the number she hadn't called in months.

When his machine answered, its deep voice stabbed at her and she hung up and sent a text instead, something she'd never done in the past for fear that his wife would see the message. In disbelief for what he was making her do Christianna hit the letters on the keypad one by one, wording it just right. *Joe, please stop with the threats, it's over between us and you are scaring me. I'm sorry I hurt you ~Christianna.*

She hit send quickly wondering if in fact she should have simply reported him. But this was Joe and she still loved him and she simply couldn't believe that he would hurt her, even though their last moments together told her otherwise and the messages were terrifying. Then, because she loved him and couldn't help but give him the benefit of the doubt, she sent a second. *If it isn't you can you let me know because then I definitely have to report this. I'm getting these threats and I think I'm in danger ~ Christianna.*

She left the bathroom hoping she had done the right thing. She knew that Joe had a violent streak and she hoped he took her message seriously. But it was her wedding day now and for the moment Joe was forgotten as she walked into her new husband's waiting arms.

The Hotel Newfoundland was luxurious and Stephen and Christianna basked in the beauty of the room gifted to them by her parents. Stephen brought along a companion, the guitar that Chris had given to him all those years before. Christianna was trying to learn to play and Stephen patiently guided her as she struggled over and over with the same chords.

"It's not fair," she whined giving up, sticking her sore fingers in her mouth.

"What?" Stephen pulled the guitar out of her hands and strummed it once, and even that was magic.

"I love music so much, it's such a big part of my life and I have no musical talent at all."

"I love reading and I can't write books," he countered playing beautiful music that laid a soundtrack to the moment.

"Yeah, I know, I know, the audience has a purpose too."

"Well I can play and you can write, perhaps we could work on something together someday," he suggested.

"Yeah maybe," she considered the idea. She had all that poetry she'd written years ago, perhaps there was a song in there.

"Meanwhile how's our other little project doing?" He placed the guitar reverently on the bed and leaned over to her, lifting her shirt up over her belly and as he often did, began crooning a soft lullaby against her skin"

"What are you singing?" The tune was familiar but she couldn't quite place it and she furrowed her brow and listened.

"Um, well, it isn't exactly a lullaby," he admitted and Christianna caught the guilt in his voice.

"What *are* you singing?" She pulled his head up to look in his eyes. He looked guilty and mischievous, his beautiful eyes watering with contained laughter.

"He likes it." Stephen explained not answering but still holding her stare brazenly.

"It's *Itty Bitty Titties*, you sleeveen!" She exclaimed. It was a raunchy song from a well known Newfoundland comedy troop. He'd slowed the tempo down and was singing it as a lullaby.

"He always moves though, he loves it," and he ducked and her swat hit him on the shoulder, not particularly hurting.

"You are singing dirty songs to our child." But her eyes flashed with laughter at his trick. "Wait, *always*?" Her mouth opened in disbelief and she closed it again, waiting.

"Well I sing really low and you never noticed, guess I got a little loud this time," he confessed his beautiful eyes full of mirth at his joke.

"I thought you were singing some nice lullaby and I was all moved by it, tellin' your mom how sweet you were and it's *Itty Bitty Titties*?" Her voice was full of mock indignation.

"Well I changed the words a bit." His grin grew wider, becoming a smile.

"I'm afraid to ask, to what?" She was laughing out loud now, waiting for his reply.

"Great *Big* Titties." Stephen cracked up along with her and moved away as she placed the guitar against a chair and came towards him.

Christianna caught him just outside the bathroom door and he grabbed her hands before they could slap him and pulled her close, kissing her soundly, still holding them. He tasted of the beer he'd had earlier and she pulled her right hand from his grasp and put it behind his head, pulling him closer, savouring him.

"So I'm forgiven?" He spoke briefly as he fumbled with her clothes.

"No, I'm just horny from all these extra hormones," she teased pretending to frown.

"I'm good with that." He shrugged and pulled her carefully to the bed, ready to begin their honeymoon. Christianna didn't protest.

64

The wind howled with a ferocious groan and the fireplace snapped back at it. The warmth created by the logs banked on there for the night was a soothing antidote to the storm. Christianna glanced at the deck, thankful Stephen had pulled the stuff off there the week before he went on his tour. She was trying to write a little and failing with writer's block hitting hard again. Christianna grabbed the phone quickly when it rang sitting up at Roxanne's voice.

"I'll keep the pup up here for the night, I can't walk in the wind, unless you want to drive over and get him." Roxanne informed her breathlessly. She had tried and had nearly blown over in the effort. Sailor had even had a difficult time.

"That's ok." Chris didn't feel like getting dressed and driving and Sailor spent nearly as much time there as he did with Christianna anyway.

Pulling her legs up on the couch, Christianna settled in to sleep, the wind, her favourite lullaby crashing in wanton gusts against the house, reaching a deafening crescendo then waning for a moment before building up again.

The crash that woke her wasn't the wind but she told herself it was. She looked around disoriented at first, unused to sleeping in the living room. The stars twinkled outside and the wind had faded somewhat, to a rippling wave over an ocean still black with the nor'easter's carnage.

Christianna pulled herself off the couch to go investigate grabbing the cell phone and sticking it in her jean's pocket as she walked towards the back. The door was wide open and she heaved a sigh of relief. She must not have locked it though she could have sworn she did. She was walking down the stairs to close it when he filled the frame and the scream that left her lungs was stifled by his hand smashing against her cheek, knocking her back against the steps.

She clambered up, and he slammed the door behind him. It didn't catch and swung back open, making a crash-bam-crash rhythm as the wind battered it again and again. His eyes were as cold as the last time she'd seen him and his smile came the second he saw that she remembered.

"Greg?" She whispered the question, her heart pounding as fear drifted through the room, palpable and thick.

"Hello *Christianna*." His voice was deeper with a layer of anger just underneath its calm tones and his eyes were wild, a deep contrast to his steady words.

Christianna backed up the steps slowly, her face stinging, her body taut with adrenaline and trepidation. Greg followed her, looking at her as though searching for something indefinable. As it had been years before, he did not see what he always hoped to see in her face. He decided to be content with what was there, fear.

"What are you doing here? Christianna's brain searched its depths for answers. She needed a way out of this situation. Her mind hoped that whatever he had planned it would be over quickly and it wouldn't harm her baby and pure self-preservation prevented her from hugging her arms around the front of her.

"I came for you." He said, his eyes flashing with the madness that had finally and completely destroyed his rationale. Here she was, the woman who had left him, the one who had treated him so terribly all those years ago and his life had been on a downward spiral since. He'd been ridiculed in Ontario, moved back home to Punt Cove only to feel himself shunned by everyone there because of what Christianna had told people about him and he'd never been able to make a go of his life again. She'd said very little but he believed otherwise. He'd lost his career, had been incarcerated for domestic violence several times and he'd battled addiction.

"Why?" Christianna had a notion that if she could keep him talking she might think of a way out of this.

"Because I hate you." He said, his voice calm. He reached out and touched her face and she flinched. He smiled at her fear, rejoiced in it. He had dreamt of this moment for a long while and now it was here at hand and the thought excited him. He grabbed her by the back of the head his mouth coming towards hers and she wrenched violently to one side to avoid his assault and at the same time threw herself backwards towards the landing, hoping to toss him off balance.

He growled a guttural, unnatural sound at her protest and pushed her hard so that she landed against the far wall with a dull thud, her head hitting the corner of the banister post. The blackness came then, closing in around her, and she was grateful for it when she saw Greg Kennedy walking towards her loosening his belt buckle. Before she passed out she heard a scream echoing in her ears and Greg's laugh as he disappeared in the bliss of the darkness.

The light burst against her eyes, blinding her and for a moment Chris was confused by the weight against her. She screamed at the face that loomed there and remembered what was happening. She tried to fight back but was pinned both by her own weakness and his strength. Consciousness seemed to be fighting a loosing battle and she drifted, feeling his weight against her and then seconds later in the haze of pain and fear the face was gone, replaced for a joyous moment by the concerned face of Joe Indigo. Her eyes shot opened in surprise at the oasis that was his dark flashing eyes and then she drifted back into a black ocean of peace.

Joe's voice called her from a great distance, begging her, pleading her to come back. She wanted to, she had missed Joe and her body ached for him as did her heart. It seemed a great struggle but finally she forced herself to open her eyes, her thought that this might be the last time she saw his face, inspiring a great effort. Perhaps she was already dead. Surely he would be in her heaven.

'Christianna!" Joe's desperate voice was inches from her face and when she finally found focus his dark eyes were terrified and grateful all at once. He sighed a great sobbing noise of relief and leaned forward and kissed her cheek, his tears unabashed and cleansing against her battered face.

"How did you know?" Christianna's memory was seeping in slowly and she knew Joe had saved her from Greg Kennedy somehow. In her slumbering mind was the image of Greg Kennedy about to hurt her and she glanced down to find she was still fully clothed. He hadn't gotten far.

"Where is he?" Her voice was frantic as she suddenly realised that was the most important information. Were they still in danger?

"He's gone?" Joe's voice was gentle.

"Escaped? We have to call the cops, they have to catch him." Her fear made her lean forward and she winced at the pain in her neck and head and felt herself drifting again. She struggled to remain conscious and Joe's hands held hers gently.

"Easy does it." He suggested, then carried on. "I killed him." He said the words lightly but the weight of them was tangible.

"He's *dead*?" Relief and horror were both in her voice. She looked at Joe, a question in her eyes that her lips couldn't ask.

"I went too far." He admitted. He looked at her, taking her other hand into his and holding them both.

"When I got the text message from you I tried to answer it but it wouldn't go through. Then I tried to reach you to let you know it wasn't me but there wasn't any answer."

"I was away." She explained avoiding the detail that she had been on her honeymoon.

"I panicked, I thought you were in danger and if it wasn't me then someone else was after you. I tried to ignore it but something told me to check on you. I came here yesterday because it was driving me nuts. I parked the car behind the trees and waited there and watched. I was going to come see you in the morning so that we could talk and then I heard his car and saw him coming into the house. I wasn't sure if it was your husband or not so I listened first. Then I heard you scream. Who was he?"

"You know I'm married then?" She looked at him sadly. How was it possible to still care so much for him and still love Stephen? Was it the lifetimes of love they had had before they reached this earth. Was it because he was her destiny?

"Yeah, I was talking to David." He'd wanted to die that day.

"It was Greg Kennedy, Joe." She realised then that Joe had never met Greg. "You still came to check on me? I thought you hated me." His love was as deep as hers and the connection as strong and as usual she was amazed by it.

"I thought I did too. But truth is, I still love you Christianna and I had to make sure you were fine, especially since you thought it was me threatening you. Not that I didn't deserve that after the way I behaved the last time." He was ashamed of himself for ever hurting her though it helped him understand a little of the madness Greg Kennedy had felt.

"You saved my life," her eyes were bright with gratitude and she smiled and reached up and touched his face. "You are still a protector."

"Will you come to see me *this* time?" He asked though he knew it would make her life difficult to do so. He just thought he could bear it better if he knew he'd see her on occasion.

"See you?" She was confused.

"I killed a man Chris, they're not going to let me get away with that."

He sat on the floor in front of her, defeated by the knowledge that his life was forever altered. He saw himself strangling the man he'd pulled off Christianna, saw the fear in Kennedy's eyes as Joe dragged him to the deck, knocking furniture and ornaments over in his attempts to escape. He remembered the pleading look on Kennedy's face when he'd realised what was about to happen and saw the light go out of his eyes when he bashed his head against the wooden rail of the patio and then tossed him over that same rail. He felt again the anger and disgust at the violence in his soul and knew without a doubt that he'd do it exactly the same if the moments were offered back to him. He also knew he deserved whatever punishment he received.

"It was self-defence, he came here to hurt me and you stopped him." Surely they would understand. This would ruin Joe and destroy his family. Their secrets would be out. She knew her life could survive, Stephen would understand, it was *her* past, but Joe would go to prison, his family would be alone without him. He was *their* protector too and they needed him.

"I went too far, they'll know I went too far, they'll investigate, they'll know we've been together in the past, phone records and then there's *my* record. I've got a history. I might get off but I doubt it." Joe's face was resigned. Even if he didn't end up in prison he'd lose his family, his business and he'd already lost Christianna. It *would* ruin him.

"Go then, go," Chris ordered understanding how right he was. "You have to get the hell out of here, I'll say I did it, if they ask for details I'll say I passed out, I have a head injury, they don't need to know there was another person here, nobody knows about you and me, Joe, I'll never tell and I don't think they'll suspect once they look into Greg's life." She knew from people back home that he'd spent time in and out of prison. *She* was the victim here and everybody would know it. The only other witness was dead.

"How did you do it?" Chris asked, glancing around for signs of a struggle. There was plenty of evidence, furniture tipped over, things broken but no blood. Her body protested. And her head throbbed.

"I hit his head." Joe didn't go into details, "He's on the ground below the deck.

"Help me out there." Chris reached for her phone, her arm screaming from the movement. Her shoulder felt broken or dislocated. Joe looked at her with wonder and concern.

"It might work, but you're hurt."

"It'll work and I'll be fine." Christianna smiled.

At Christianna's direction Joe wiped down any surface he might have touched just in case they did investigate the circumstances. There were few, he'd mostly just hammered at Greg Kennedy's body. Joe then carried her battered body carefully to the deck against his every instinct. He covered her with a blanket to keep her warm but she protested and made him put it back on the couch. It had to look real. Chris would say Greg already appeared beaten when he came to her door to explain away any other injuries that Chris wouldn't have physically been capable of inflicting. He'd chased her, they'd struggled on the deck, he'd hit his head then fell. No one would ever expect there would have been a third person there.

After she was on the freezing deck, the stars still twinkling, appearing oblivious to the humans below, Chris tried to send him away.

"You're freezing." Joe Indigo held Christianna close to warm her. "Will I see you again?" He was reluctant to leave her there, cold and alone, it went against his every instinct.

"The Moorlands in Whitbourne." She suggested, nodding. "I'll text you a date and time after we're in the clear."

"I'll be there." He promised and with a gentle kiss against her cheek he whispered, "I love you." and he listened with bittersweet agony as she whispered the words back. Then he stepped away, into the house and out the back door, leaving the door open as he'd found it.

As Joe drove off and out of sight, Chris dialed the number that would bring her help. She readied herself for her acting debut under a million twinkling stars that shouted their encouragement to her in the raw pre-morning light. When the sirens screamed around the corner and up the long laneway to her house and the officers stepped carefully out of their cars looking at the still form that lay on the ground, the trembling in her body was no longer completely from the coldness of the night air but from the chill in her soul that the words she spoke now would be sufficient to leave them both free.

65

Christianna watched the police car pull away and Stephen came up behind her, and looked out at the window.

"I'm glad that's all over, " he whispered in her ear, kissing her neck and holding her, wishing he'd been there that horrible night to do what she'd had to do herself. He was proud of her, though she couldn't remember much of it, what with the concussion she'd gotten in the scuffle, but she'd somehow fought the guy off and managed to toss him off the deck. The cops had concluded he'd been in a weakened state from the beating he'd already received just prior to attacking her. They traced the text messages from his phone to hers and chastised her for not reporting them but she'd told them she thought they were pranks or cranks and if they had continued she certainly would have. She'd gotten the worse one on their wedding day and Stephen was horrified that she'd managed to ignore it for the sake of their wedding. The police were completely satisfied with her explanations and closed the case within weeks.

She seemed fine, physically she was, and so, thankfully, was the baby which was her main concern in the early days. The doctors had run tests and she'd healed properly, suffering from a headache for days due to her refusal to take any pain killers. Stephen and Roxanne had fussed over her but now he was going away again and worried. Her next words eased his mind a little.

"I think I'm going to drive out home for a day or two," She smiled up at him. She was truly fine. She had a few nightmares but always Joe came to her rescue in them and for the past few nights they'd changed in their essence. Now he came before she was scared, reassuring her that he would always be there, always protect her. She believed in the truth of her dreams, she had proof.

Christianna pulled the car into the parking lot of the motel and took out her cell phone. She quickly sent a message to Stephen *Stopping at Whitbourne for a bite to eat, all is well.* Then scrolled through, looking to see if she'd received one. She hit the buttons and it opened on her screen. It said only *#12*.

She knocked on the door and it was opened in seconds. Chris smiled at Joe, her heart melting as it always did at the face that loved her so well. She stepped into the room and into his arms as naturally as if nothing had ever come between them. Somehow she couldn't feel guilty about this, she owed him her very life although that wasn't the reason she was here. She had promised *til death us do part* to Stephen only short weeks before but the fates had decided that it applied to her and Joe as well and she knew to fight it was to fight a losing battle. She loved him and though her mind said it was wrong, in her heart she needed to feel his body next to hers, hear his breath on her face and taste his lips. She needed to look into those eyes that held a supernatural attraction for her and see the bright blue crystals that flashed at her, for her and through her. Her resistance to his pull was futile and she gave herself completely over to the needs of her soul. With Joe she knew that even death couldn't destroy the connection of two souls that had found each other lifetime after lifetime.

"I can't stay long." Chris sighed and turned to his broad chest revelling in its familiarity and expanse. "But the investigation is closed and they believed everything I told them which wasn't much what with the memory loss and all." It felt surreal to joke about the death of a man.

"I'm glad you came...and surprised." Joe's eyes narrowed as he searched her face.

"I know, I never thought I'd do this. I love him...too." Chris was ashamed of this betrayal. Stephen deserved better. She'd judged Joe for this at times, though she'd been a part of it and here she was, doing this terrible thing to Stephen.

"Why are we like this?" Joe had always felt like an eel cheating on Tiffany. Now he'd dragged Chris down the same path.

"I don't know, it makes no sense, it's as though no matter how much we try, we somehow end up together and it always feels right. Since the first moment, way back when. All those years apart, I always thought we'd be together again and now, it's like I just always know you'll be there, know what I mean?"

"I always will be." Joe's eyes softened, their brown warmth heating her face, "I know how risky it is, how it always has been, but it's always been worth it."

"What about the others?" She didn't really believe in the *what they don't know won't hurt them* saying but there was no way she would devastate Stephen by telling him. And the love she felt for Joe in no way diminished her love for Stephen.

"They are as much our destiny as everything else is I guess." He stroked her cheek and pulled a curl loose from her wild blonde mop and let it spring back. He was starting to get what she'd always understood.

"You've always been my hero, my protector but what is my role in all this?"

"I don't know, keeper of the secrets?"

"Yeah, it's all I do, keep secrets. It's a little bit crazy."

"Isn't that what God does? Keep secrets? I've always considered all the mystery, that stuff we know nothing about, that's what I've always thought was God. Perhaps that's part of human nature, maybe it's even part of our divine nature, to keep things to ourselves that we're ashamed of, or to protect the ones we love."

"It's the second one for me. I can't feel ashamed for loving you."

"Me either." Joe grinned and kissed her hair, his hard hand coming up to stroke its softness, enjoying the scent of her, so familiar and perfect.

"You know what it's like, Joe? It's like we've always known each other. I love Stephen but it's like he's new, unfamiliar in some ways, worth every ounce of love he gets because he's an amazing man, but with you, I didn't even need to get to know you, I already *did*. I think we've always been together, before this life, and that we always will be, after..." She shook her head, waiting for him to laugh at her fancy.

"Yeah, that's it exactly. My aunt Mae used to tell me about this grand love, *the one* that is meant for everybody and she used to say, sometimes it doesn't work out, in this life but that it goes on into the next. I don't know what to make of all that foolishness but it's how it's been for me and you, right from the get-go." He put his arm around her and pulled her close, kissing her gently on the lips. He remembered the first kiss they'd shared so long ago and how he'd wondered how somebody new could be so familiar.

It wasn't as difficult for Joe now, thinking about her, with *him*. At least she was in good hands. Perhaps he wouldn't see her again, perhaps he would, the fates would determine that but he felt that their hearts were too intertwined to be pulled apart permanently. Their love had its place and was eternal.

"Your aunt made a lot of sense." She heard his heart beat under her hair and turned to kiss the smooth skin of his chest. "I wish we could have done it differently, but perhaps if we'd been able to be together, we would have ended up resenting and hating each other."

"You know, perhaps we would have. All I know is I'm just glad you are here now, Bonnie." He smiled kissing her forehead.

"Me too Clyde." Chris countered, getting his partners in crime joke while laughing and soaking up his adoration.

"Do me a favour this time." He sounded a little more serious, a little sad and she lifted her head to look at him.

"Anything." Chris offered, and she meant it

"Don't say goodbye." Joe helped the fates along a little, his eyes pleading. "I'm not saying we should see each other again, but don't say goodbye." .

She sat up, thoughtful and his arms were suddenly empty. She walked over, finding her clothes on the floor, then returned to sit beside him.

"Ok." Chris agreed and he pretended not to see the roundness of her belly and her breasts that had grown larger with the baby. He wondered and hoped but said nothing, feeling strangely connected to the child she carried even though it was most likely not his. Another secret for the keeping.

He sat up and reached over, pulling her hand into his own, holding it and picking up his cell phone he opened the flip, activating the camera. He snapped the picture of the two roses and showed the screen to her.

"Send it to me." She requested and kissed the hand that held hers and then let it go so that she could dress. He sent the picture to her phone and watched her as she walked around the bed again sitting back on the edge of it. She leaned over and kissed his lips and then smiled before she spoke.

"I'll see you around, keep in touch." Then she added recklessly. "I'll always come to you." Because she would and there was no point in pretending otherwise.

His heart leapt with happiness. He knew it would be painful for her to betray her husband and he would try to resist but it was only a matter of time before the need for her grew again, so strong he couldn't deny its existence, defeated by energy more powerful than his own. It was also nice to not hear goodbye because, for them, goodbye was simply impossible.

66

"Why don't you wait, my love, please." Tiffany begged Joe. It was foggy though it would lift soon. He'd been better lately, the weather had changed and the spring had brought a new light to his eyes. She wondered if he had that seasonal disorder everybody talked about.

"I've got to get-go, I'll call you from Whitbourne." Joe walked toward the motorcycle with his helmet under his arm. This bike was new and, it gleamed, shining in the mist that lay low. He was excited to ride and he hadn't been on it for a long trip, just around town. It was time to break her in.

"This fog is bad." Tiffany chewed her lip. She worried about him still despite his improvement in mood lately.

"I have to go, I'll be back tonight." He grinned at her.

"Well be careful." His wife couldn't help the warning. She didn't worry often but things had been so good lately, he wasn't as depressed, he was listening to her, paying attention to what she said, making love to her again.

He kissed her lips quickly. He still didn't feel the connection he thought he should with her but he was trying. He'd noticed she didn't nag him to stay home anymore. Of course that might be because he *was* staying home more. She was patient with him and she deserved better so he'd decided to try as Christianna had suggested.

He'd paid her some attention, bought her a present, made love to her with a little more attention to her needs but it wasn't there yet. Maybe, just maybe, with time, he would fall in love with his wife. At least he felt better now than he'd felt all winter. An early spring had brightened his mood and this trip was a pleasant reward for a dark winter.

He looked at Tiffany, her eyes full of love and worry for him. Her dark curly hair had been cut short. He reached out and pulled a curl and let it spring back on her head and he was reminded of Christianna. He shook the image away and concentrated on his wife.

"You should let it grow back." He suggested with a smile and he reached in to kiss her again this time with more feeling. "I won't be late." Joe promised. After she walked into the house he pulled out his phone and sent a quick message. He smiled as he hit send then put his helmet on and revved the bike.

The fog kissed his dark face with its cool breath. He loved riding in it, driving over the road as it unfolded in front of him in pieces. Joe picked up speed. Maybe he'd stay the night. He was undecided, work was busier now. They had a new big contract that would start in a week and he'd purchased some new equipment he wanted to play with.

He manoeuvred the heavy motorcycle through the grey. His warm jacket blew and bubbled around him. There was no traffic and he accelerated a little more. He would see the headlights of approaching vehicles anyway. The fog was light in some places but in some places it rose in giant banks, changing the look of the land. Joe knew this road by heart though. He sped along confidently.

Christianna's face arose in front of him then and he shook his head as though to shake off the apparition. Her long blonde curly hair danced around her beautiful face and his fingers on the handle bars remembered how it had felt as he curled a ringlet around them as he often did. He loved her hair. He closed his eyes briefly and then reopened them.

The vision was replaced. In its stead was a dark purple-blue shape that rose out of the fog before him as though placed there by the hand of some gigantic God when he wasn't looking.

The heavens cheered and the stars that were invisible in the early morning fog sang a quiet aria as in one cosmic instant Joe Indigo went from the moment of deepest earthly confusion to the brilliance of all encompassing profound knowledge.

The intensity of the light blinded him for only a moment and in the second that the Harley Davidson motorcycle hit the sharp invincible face of the granite cliff that bordered the turn in the road, all of the truths of the universe were his.

In that instant he became the recipient of the most precious gift life has to offer, the gift that is only given when all others are rescinded.

He was presented with the knowledge of all of the secrets of creation and non-creation as they were revealed to him and will be to all eventually. He was also given the gift of eternal and transcendent peace.

67

She held up the little yellow sleeper set and smiled. A little tiny person would fill this soon. She folded it and picked up the next one, pushing it against her face, smelling the sweet fragrance of the baby detergent she'd used to wash the tiny clothes in.

Life had drifted into a state of quiet domesticity and the uncomplicated nature of it pleased Chris. She sat in her over-bright living room, the sun shining through the large triangular windows leaving crystal patches of light on the floor, the couch, and the wall behind her. This day was perfect with the snow outside creating a picturesque wonderland. The view from here was perfect. Yesterday it had started out foggy but the afternoon had been 18 degrees and spring-like. Today a light dusting of snow covered the land courtesy of Sheila's Brush, as the late March storm was called by the locals. Stephen had recently repainted the entire house room by room and Roxanne had been concerned about paint fumes and she'd stayed with her until it was done. She'd missed this room in the mornings.

Somehow Chris compartmentalized her life. She felt as though her time with Stephen was her real life and that her rendezvous with Joe a few weeks prior was something entirely separate and justifiable. She took her risks, she knew it was selfish and reckless and sometimes she was brought up short by how wrong it was. But mostly she let it stay in the back of her mind, like the old shabby Michael Jackson t-shirt she kept tucked in a drawer, that she pulled out to sleep in when she was lonely.

Chris had not written a thing in the past months. She had not been inspired to do so. All of her thoughts were about the baby and Stephen and their life together as it was unfolding. She'd read books, joined online forums, entertained her parents and Roxanne with her philosophy of attachment parenting, extended breastfeeding and cloth diapering.

They all rolled their eyes and laughed at *the kids* behind their backs. Stephen however completely supported her and listened to her agreeing, this baby would not be neglected in any way and he would support her in any decisions that were best for the baby. Her parents and his mother thought they would change their minds once reality set in but they were determined to do things their way. This baby would be loved and well cared for and that was all that mattered to the entire family.

The phone rang on the coffee table in front of her. She checked the call display before hitting the talk button. It was David, a call she hadn't expected in the middle of the day. She placed the little pyjamas in the basket with the rest of the sweet-smelling newly washed clothing.

"Hey." But something in David's voice tipped her off. Something was wrong. His mom had been having some tests.

"What's up?" She was worried now.

"Bit of bad news today." He said and his deep voice was sad. "From out home. Joe Indigo was killed in a motorcycle accident yesterday."

The black in front of her eyes threatened to consume her but there was a pinpoint of light that danced in the distance and she reached for it as a drowning man might reach towards the sunlit surface. Climbing upward in her mind, the sound of her voice surprised her in its normalcy.

"Oh no!" She spoke as though he were telling her of the death of some stranger instead of the man who shared her soul. She took a deep breath before speaking again.

"What happened?" She didn't want her cousin to suspect anything and her voice cooperated while her heart shattered in a billion tiny shards.

"It was foggy, he was probably going too fast and he missed a turn and hit a cliff, died instantly."

"His poor family." Her heart broke a little more, each original shard breaking again for the wife and two little girls who had lost everything this day. This was their grief and though she shared it, she had no right to it.

"Yeah, they're devastated." David was devastated himself. Joe was one of his best buddies. He would miss him.

"How are *you*?" Christianna asked, knowing this.

"Pretty shocked, he was a good buddy." His breaking voice did her in and her tears flowed for both of them, all of them.

"I'm so sorry." It was the complete and inadequate truth.

"I'd better go. I have some more calls to make. How are *you*?" His buddies in Ontario would want to know, but he thought he should ask about her.

"I'm good, until now." She confessed that much.

"Yeah, it's hard." And he listened for a clue as to how she really was. He knew she'd cared for Joe but she seemed to be fine, upset of course but everybody he spoke to was.

"Take care." She spoke, a sad whispered condolence.

"Thanks m'love, bye." The click of the phone was final and profound.

The sun that shone through the large windows continued to shine in complete innocence, as though it still had a right to. The basket of sweet smelling baby clothes remained piled beside the couch and the telephone sat silently on the coffee table.

Christianna remained on the couch in shock, the only movement the baby inside her as it rolled and then eventually that subsided as well. Her tears fell in silence and the grief held her with giant pincers, holding her heart in their grip.

The bleeping from her cell phone pulled her upright for a moment. It had been dead for two days and now it sat charging. She hadn't been going too far lately and hadn't needed it. She picked it up off the table. The screen said *charge complete*.

Shaking, Chris flipped it open to the text messages and a sob escaped her lips when she saw it there. The picture of their hands entwined, two indigo roses etched so long ago in a moment of youthful impetuousness. She'd programmed it against his cell number to identify him in case he ever called her. She selected it inhaling the pain quickly. Their secret was still the priority and the message was merely a number. The message said *# 12.*

Christianna had always had to bear the secret of their love alone and that was difficult enough, but what was unbearable now was the thought of being alone with the secret of her grief. She didn't know if she could do it. If they had not lied, if they hadn't held so tightly on to their secrets perhaps Joe would be alive now.

The pain was excruciating and in her agony, in the despair that brought endless tears and trauma Christianna recognised one truth that crushed her heart completely and tore her soul entirely to shreds. It was entirely and irrevocably her own doing.

68

Stephen's brow furrowed in thought as he watched her on the couch. He knew something was wrong and fear gripped his heart. It had been going on for a while now and he watched her there in the sunlight, asleep, tearstains on her cheeks that she explained away as allergies. Perhaps she wasn't well and his heart tightened in fear. He didn't know what it was but he had been startled to see the change in her when he returned on Monday morning from the trip. She insisted she was ok. .

"Is it the baby?" He had asked her and she'd smiled and placed her hand on her abdomen where their child kicked.

"He's been keeping me awake all night." She told him and it was true but there was a lie hidden in there.

"I'm worried about her, did something happen while I was away?" Steven had gone to his mother's house to talk to her.

"Nope, pretty quiet, she asked me to take the dog, said she was tired and that's probably it. Perhaps low iron, I read that happens at 7 months." Roxanne had read a lot about pregnancy lately in a book that was full of all the terrible things that could happen. She'd diagnosed Christianna with several maladies already which hadn't proven correct in the long run.

"She seems more depressed than tired." Stephen was disturbed by the sad look in her eyes. He had a lot of work lined up until the baby came and they needed the money. He wondered if maybe she should come with him.

"Perhaps she has postpartum?" His mother suggested.

"Mom everybody gets postpartum *after* the baby comes and anyway it's postpartum depression you're thinking of, postpartum just means you had a baby." He was quick and annoyed and his mother sensed his stress.

"I'll check on her." She had reported back that she too was now worried.

"She's low-minded me love, something sad about her."

"I'm fine," Chris snapped. She was irritated at his fussing and urged herself to try to put on a better show for him. But once Thursday passed, the day Joe was to be buried, it did get a little easier. When Roxanne suggested that she was still traumatized from the attack she pretended that was it.

She sent a card to Dar and that helped some. She sent another to David. She wept in the card aisle and stopped reading and grabbed two alike. It felt good to do something. Dar probably wouldn't even remember her name but that might be for the best.

She went to St. John's for the weekend with Stephen and tried to be normal. Being pregnant was a blessing with the baby constantly reminding her that life goes on, that something new was coming. Her heart lifted in the cool misty mornings of the city she loved and on the Saturday night she felt well enough to accompany Stephen and the band to their gig. The city was still blanketed in snow, piled in little edges alone the streets. It had been a good year, not too much, just enough to define the harbour, framing it with a trim of white.

Stephen watched her from the stage, her blonde hair down around her face. She smiled at him from her seat laughing with Lisa and Carrie, the weight of her grieving heart lessened by the happy surroundings. The girls at the front of the stage screamed at the three handsome young men who entertained them and she was proud of her husband in that moment, of his success. Then the music started and she forgot he was hers. She was mesmerised by his presence, his talent, his beauty. She loved to watch him perform. He was brilliant and owned the crowd easily. What a gift he had. He would soon be the famous one of the family. Trinity was taking off and she would be the one following along.

She looked forward to it. They had planned that she would follow along until the baby was of school age. She entertained the idea of homeschooling at the back of her mind and thought she could follow him forever if they needed to. She could write anywhere and would likely write better with some travel under her belt.

The song, that had worked the audience into frenzied excitement, ended to deafening applause. Christianna and her friends joined in, screaming their approval. Then Stephen stepped forward and looked briefly at her, pulling a guitar from the rack of several that stood to one side of the small stage.

It was the old Gibson Hummingbird she'd given him years before.

"This guitar was given to me by the most important person in my life." He said as he strummed and checked the tune of it. The audience hung on his every word.

Stephen's eyes found hers and he smiled then looked back over the audience. He ran a hand through his hair, searching for the perfect explanation. He didn't care that the words didn't matter to the audience. They mattered to him.

"I wrote this music for the person who gave me this guitar. If it wasn't for this gift I likely wouldn't be sitting here, and for a long time I didn't know who it was. The words to the song were written by Christianna Cormack-Miles, my wife and the love of my life."

The music swelled behind him as his band mates started their instruments. His voice married the music perfectly with lyrics that melted the heart of all in the room but particularly one blue-eyed woman who had pledged her heart to him forever. Christianna wept at the corner table as the words he sang reached her. Written for another, he had rearranged the words using the first verse as a chorus. He had no way of knowing it was a tribute to Joe Indigo and it didn't matter to her. His love was in the gesture and her appreciation was for that and that alone and his timing was perfect. He had no way of knowing how much it healed and hurt at the same time. She would protect him from her secrets. She'd keep them hidden if only to save this man who now loved her and whom she loved. She would have to find a way to deal with her guilt. Perhaps their child would bring healing. But for now the words he sang to her started the process.

You live in the dreams of my heart
you walk on the floors of my mind
Whispering "always we are the same
we're the ones we were each meant to find"

The earth bears the steps of our fathers
worn smooth with the pace gone before
I walk that old path for the others
and they'll tread that same path once more

We are the same you advise me
with the voice you send on the breeze
Whispering "I left you there to make room for
the dream that we made in the trees"

Underneath my feet are the ashes
of one who whispers my name
remember my darling forever
we'll always be one and the same.

As Stephen finished the song he blew her a kiss and motioned for her to join him back stage. When she found him she fell into his arms and wept for the beauty of his gift to her, the gift to her life that he was.   She also realised that the only secret that is pure is one that gives such as the one she kept so many years ago when she gave the guitar to a troubled young boy. The universe balances itself by rewarding the keeper of those most precious lies. The proof to her was this same boy in her arms, grown into a strong and loving man, who shared with her a slow burning, red hot love built on the sweet foundation that secret set. Now, with his song, her lesson was learned. All that was left for Chris now was healing.

69

Christianna stepped into the smell of baked bread cooling on a rack in her aunt's immaculate kitchen. The golden buns were off limits no matter how tempting. She was in the back busy working on some sewing. Chris opened a bag with older but still delicious bread.

She quickly made herself a cheese sandwich cleaning up every crumb behind her. The baby made her hungry. A glass of ice water and with a few grapes added to her fare and she left quickly guiding the sliding door inch by inch to remain undiscovered.

Some early flowers danced in the mild warm late May wind. The tastefully decorated retreat welcomed her, beckoned Chris in fact, to write. Her uncle must have been napping. He wasn't around. He worked long hours and he spent a lot of time resting when he was home. The backyard was hers.

The plate sat empty on the table to her left as she opened the pink book yet again. The words flowed including the secrets, the memory of their love, onto the pages. In all of her life she had only written fictional characters. This was real and difficult. This was his story, their story and the outline filled the white paper quickly. A chipmunk scurried by. She let out a squeal and then laughed at herself.

"Hi little guy." She said to him. The day she got it, a memory as brilliant as sunshine, crossed her mind. Its clarity was a pleasant gift. Her writer's block was gone but instead of imagination and inspiration the words she wrote were the secrets she'd lived with for so long. They need to be shared even if they only ever saw the pages of her journal.

She looked at the rose. A youthful impulse she told people and it was true but it was also so much more. She heard a voice calling her from inside.

"Out here," she answered her aunt.

"Oh, did you have anything to eat my love?" She asked kindly. Never would anyone go hungry in her Aunt Maisie's home, her hospitality was boundless and infinite.

Aunt Maisie pressed on. "Don't go hungry, there's something to make sandwiches in the fridge, though I don't know what you eat if you don't eat meat, do you eat cheese, you do eat cheese right, you want me to make something? Don't the baby need meat?" Chris hadn't eaten meat for a while. It had made her sick early in her pregnancy. She and Stephen had decided together to give it up at New Years as a resolution.

"I made a sandwich earlier." Chris replied. "Thank you."

"Oh, you cleaned it all up, I didn't even know, I could have made you something." Aunt Maisie went on. "But I'm glad you're not hungry, did you have a good walk?" The subject changed again.

"Oh yes, I had a great walk." Then aiming to be casual she added. "I walked by Joe Indigo's house, what a tragedy." Glancing up she saw her aunt hadn't noticed anything too obvious in her statement.

"Some sin my dear, poor family is lost since he got killed, he was bad as the devil one time you know, when he was young and then he turned his life around. He was going to run for council you know and he would have got in. Smart as could be and such a good guy, took care of his family, his mother never had to worry about nothin' while he was there, his wife put up with all his foolishness, and was so happy he smartened up. She's lost without him, haven't got over it, crying all the time, on nerve pills for it." Her aunt Maisie was free with the details.

"What happened? What caused the accident?" Her heart ached for an answer.

"Nobody knows, drove off the road on a curve and hit the face of a cliff, nobody's fault the mounties said, foggy morning, couldn't see, died instantly thank God." She said with a shake of her head, as though to shake out the visual of the collision. "He was some han'some in his coffin, not a mark on him but beat to pieces, internal injuries, never had a chance." She carried on with the gruesome details.

Christianna's heart broke with every word but the train wreck was in front of her and she couldn't turn away. She asked. "How was the funeral?"

"Oh, yes, big crowd, they had a nice speech, nice poem somebody wrote about him was read, they didn't say who, one of the family I guess about the Indigo Sky. Everybody was bawling. He was always good, come here with David, best kind to have around but full of the badness." She grinned at some memory of mischievous teenage pranks.

"Only ever hurt himself, and must have been hard on his wife and family when he was in trouble, but that was years ago, he was good lately, since they moved back home, never heard a bad word about him." Aunt Maisie hesitated. "They're all talkin' about if it was an accident though."

Chris acknowledged a flipping feeling in her stomach. "What do you mean?" She hoped her voice was calm.

Her aunt lowered her voice, a sign she was about to share gossip. "Tiffany said he'd been different for a while, sad, stayed home a lot more, quieter, she thinks it might have been deliberate."

"Suicide." Chris whispered, her voice struggling with the word as her mind considered their pain at this possibility. The guilt rose like bile and she swallowed quickly to tamp it down. "But they don't know for sure?"

Christianna knew for sure. His destination was known only to her and it wasn't to his death. How she wished she could reassure them but her confession would only cause them more grief.

"Well he was sad, depressed." Her aunt said. "But the cops said it was an accident and that's what the family is sayin', you know, *fishally.*"

She was off plucking a dead flower from a planter and it gave Chris a moment to breathe and then she offered words that rung fake in her ears.

"Time will make it easier I guess." Chris said, her mind still on the revelation of the moment before.

"Better get the clothes on the line." Aunt Maisie shuffled off, she rarely stopped moving and had been pulling tiny weeds furiously from her garden during most of conversation. She stepped off the deck, back into the house, the sliding screen door scraping noisily as she did so.

"This door gotta be fixed." She said working it roughly across its track until it closed.

Guilt laid a familiar net over Christianna's head, trapping her in its mesh, tangling her with the idea that she had caused this, that she had been the reason he was on the road that day. The reason he had died. She was caught in the idea, the thoughts repeating themselves, dragging her under, drowning her with the possibility that because she had not been able to let him go he had now gone for good.

.

70

The day bloomed bright and warm, a light mist hung low on the ground but the sun was quickly burning off the moisture. Chistianna's sadness hung like the mist and she set out for an early walk to see if it would burn the pall from her heart. It was still warm for May. Christianna was grateful that the snow was gone and the ground was drying up. This pilgrimage had to be made before the baby came.

The night before had been difficult. She'd cried with the grief that had filled her after her heart had been poured on to the pages of her note book. The catharsis she had been hoping for had not appeared. Replacing the grief was a heavy guilt that pounded on her organs and made her brain weak with the weight of it. For the first time in years she felt that she might be getting sick. Chris knew she needed to go to that place, to be with him again. She had to make sense of it all somehow, before she could move on with her life.

Stephen had called. She'd claimed exhaustion which was the truth and she regretted being unable to ask him to support her in this. He loved her, she loved him. He was her future but she couldn't journey towards it with the past so unsettled in her heart, particularly since the secrets of that past haunted her into physical illness. Then there was the baby to consider. He needed a whole and healthy mother when the time came.

Christianna made her way to the corner where his marker stood and stared again at the stone , reading the words that were written there, words that she had written for him over twenty years before. How had they gotten there? Who knew of that poem but Joe? The mystery tore at her and she sat on the ground in the little hollow of a bush that rose just beside his resting place.

Grass had already grown long around the sides of the stone. The sun had shone there evidenced by the basket of flowers on the top, their edges already fading to a pale grey but the deep blue at the centre indicated the original color of the plastic petals, the cold north Atlantic weather not conducive to delicate natural blooms. The words danced before Christianna's eyes. The cold marble gave no clues though her eyes searched as though somehow the mystery of how they got there would be revealed by the mere act of her staring at them.

The wind will dance with the leaves

When we meet again by and by

I'll come to you when I can

And we'll love in the indigo sky.

The impact of the words hit her with blunt force. The prose she had written to Joe so long ago as a reflection of their blue-flamed love, had been etched in cold stone. They were the words from the song Stephen had sung so sweetly a few weeks prior that had moved her and helped her heal a little. Heated tears stung her cheeks. Her anger upended her sadness and was directed at herself. The baby rolled inside her, a reminder to be gentle with its mama.

She thought the tears would bring relief but instead she ached with the agony of the loss. The wound pained both her body and mind and new tears formed, following the path of their predecessors down her swollen, heart-broken cheeks.

Tiffany might have been his wife, shared his life, but it hadn't made one shred of difference to how much Christianna missed him.

"He t'ought da world of you." The voice made her jump and Christianna wiped her tears away. The face that looked down at hers was familiar and warm and the smile the woman gave her was the smile of her brother's.

"Dar, oh my God, Dar." Chris hurled herself into the arms of Joe's sister. She wept again and Dar wept with her, not so much for her brother as she'd wept all these last weeks, but for the broken-hearted woman she held.

"Das fine, ma love, yer a'right now, yer a'right." She consoled Chris who wept now with relief that she could share her grief with someone. Chris didn't know what Dar knew, but she knew she understood and understanding was what was needed.

She pulled herself together and wiped the tears from her face with an apology. "I'm sorry, I'm so sorry, he was your brother and here I am weeping in your arms like a fool when I should be consoling you." But Dar brushed her words away.

"It's good to help someone else get by." She said patting Christianna like a child. "Lard knows I was a mess for a few weeks and I've a lot of cryin' left, years p'raps but your just startin' wi' dis idin ya?"

"I've know since it happened but I couldn't get here until now. I didn't know it would hit me like this." Chris shrugged, her eyes welling up again.

"I t'ought maybe you'd make it to the fun'rel but den I figgered it'd be a bit awkward and dat?" It was question.

"I didn't think it was right." Chris dried a last stray tear and asked. "What do you know, how much do you know? About me and Joe I mean?"

"I knows it all my dear, he tol' me everyt'ing. I knows you broke up with him way back and I knows you got together again in the years later. I knows you wuz the love of his life and dat he only married da other one 'cause she looked somet'ing like you." This made Chris raise an eyebrow. She hadn't known that.

"I knows it all." Dar reaffirmed. "He worshipped the ground you walked on. He gave me your poems to hang on to. They was some beautiful. I gave Tiffany dat one after the accident and told her it was 'is favourite and she put it on dat stone, dat was me done dat," She said proud of her artifice.

"Thank you." Chris whispered, the tears coming close to the surface again. "I wondered how..." She tapered off.

"He was so good as gold, smart, he's my baby brother." A soft sob broke from Dar's lips and quickly Chris moved close. "His second girl, the baby, her middle name is Christianna."

"What?" The question was whispered. "That was risky." Her heart glowed at the thought in spite of how wrong it was.

"He had me suggest it. The second one was born just after you two met up again. He was starting to think about, you were on the news and television a lot, gettin' known and he, well, asked me to tell Tiffany that it would make *me* happy. So I did. Then she asked Joe if it was ok and he said sure but for a middle name only, he had a way about him. She thought he was doing *her* a favour." Dar smiled the grin she knew so well, as devilish as her brother when it came to getting things to go her way.

"Wow, I'm floored, I thought that when he came to see me it was a coincidence, he happened to be down here and invited the same weekend." He *had* said he had known she would be there but she hadn't known he'd been thinking of her even longer than that.

"Oh he kept up on everything you did, they had satellite up there on television and he watched you on NTV when you was interviewed about the poetry and when you won that award that time. He was at my place and we watched that together and he said. "I still love her so much." She looked at Chris with a nod.

All of this information warmed Christianna's heart and like the sun burning the mist lingering over the early morning fields, the knowledge that he'd loved her that much, enough to share that love with his sister, helped lift the pall of despair that she'd woken with in the morning. The truth, like the sun, bore heat and was healing at its rise.

"Come on m'love." Dar said. "Let's get on over to my place, we'll have a cuppa tea and chat and warm you up, tis only May for Jesus sake."

"I'm coming down with something I think." Chris confessed.

"Not a good time to get sick." She must be nearly due but Dar didn't ask. Instead she wondered when the last time she'd seen Joe.

"Not a good place to be then, doe 'tis a good day." and she blew a kiss towards her brother's grave. Chris reluctantly got up and followed her.

They were installed in a large neat kitchen in a sweet little salt box house with windows on the ocean and clean clothes on the line. It was the family home, just up the garden from where Joe's family, his wife and his daughters lived.

"When did you move back?" Chris inquired.

"We come back when dad got sick, years now." Dar said. "We all moved back. Joe built his new house in the garden and dis is mudder and fadders house, we took this one, then dad passed on. Now it's just Mudder and me and Tom. They're in to Gander this morning. In her seventies, smart as a whip but got her heart broke sumpin' fierce. Joe was her baby and this might do her in." She worried. "He took care of us all you know." The sad look touched her features and she sipped her tea for comfort.

"It's good you're all home for the family now."

"Well now I guess he didn't tell me everything" Dar said, taking Chris's hand and looking at the little rose that looked more blue than purple as it faded. "I always wondered why a blue rose." she said.

"It's indigo, the colour changed, and Rose is my middle name. We had them done together." Dar had guessed that when she saw it.

"It was a grand love he always said. You were his grand love." And she touched the rose gently and felt closer to her brother. She'd not thought she'd see that little rose again, but here, its twin was, on the hand of this woman he had loved. She got up and went to the next room.

"I got something for you." Dar came back and placed a corrugated cardboard box on the table. It had three faded flowers, the Carnation milk symbols, on the sides and she reached in and pulled out a large brown manila envelope. She handed it to Chris. Her movements were slow and deliberate as though to give Chris a chance to adjust to the package in her hand.

The writing on the front was in Joe's familiar hand and one word. Christianna. She opened it up, revealing all of the copies the letters they'd exchanged over the past years and a little worn, brown book that he'd read to her so many times. She held it in her hand and kissed it feeling his love for her and the words inside through the soft leather cover. Dar smiled.

"That's everything he told me belonged to you." Dar said."I was gonna look you up and mail it to you if you didn't come."

Chris looked up. "Dar, do you think it was an accident?"

"I heard what people is saying but I knows different, he *was* sad after you said it was done, he told me that you were getting married and that you couldn't keep secrets anymore but he understood that it was time."

"He was coming to see me" Chris blurted. "I didn't know it until after but he was coming to see me, I couldn't give him up. I know it was wrong, I do love my husband but Joe was, well he was *my* love and I couldn't let him go. It was like it was out of my control, like I had no say, we had to be in each other's lives."

She waited for her reaction and when Dar was quiet Chris went on, telling her about the death of Greg Kennedy, how Joe had risked everything and saved her life and how she had returned the favour by taking the blame. Then she told of how they'd met again and decided they would see each other, occasionally at least, that they would never say goodbye.

"Wasn't that just Joe all over then? He'd die for the ones he loved without a blink. You know I heard about that attack, wondered how you was doing and even asked Joe if you were alright and he said he didn't know. I can see why he didn't tell me dat, if it was found out I'd be as guilty as you two. Now, don't worry m'love, I won't breath a word of it to anybody but it settles me mind a bit. It was an accident for sure then." Dar looked at her and then smiled a sad little smile.

Chris held the book in her hand and turned it over. She opened the inside and saw writing in there that hadn't been there before. It was dated for March 18 of that year, a day after they'd met at the Moorlands.

Christianna, I'm no poet but I wanted to tell you that I get it now. I am always yours, you are always mine, you inhale, I exhale, your heart beats and mine skips one to make room. I am not a poet but I listen to the rhythm of the song we make when we are together and know you are right. If we can't be together in this life I'll catch you in the next, just like I did in the one before. We'll never say goodbye, Joe Indigo.

She felt the tears on her cheeks and Dar handed her a Kleenex box quietly. She passed the book to Dar who was moved to tears as well.

"Should say he *was* a poet, writin' that." Dar said sniffing.

"Yeah,' Chris whispered." He was."

"This was his favourite poetry, you know that?" She said holding up the little brown book as she sniffed back her tears.

"No it wasn't." Dar disagreed and got up from the table and looked in the envelope. Realising it was empty she reached into the carnation milk box sitting on the table. Neatly folded and wrapped with an elastic band was another stack of papers.

"This was his favourite poetry." Dar handed them to Chris. "They must 'ave fell out."

Chris looked at the collection of poetry in her hand. He'd hand written a note as a wrapper for the poems. *"The poetry of Christianna Cormack"*.

"Oh." And her heart knew this woman was right. "He made me write a poem for every time he would recite one back when we were first together all those years ago in Kitchener. We were so young and foolish, it seems like only yesterday but it seems like a lifetime ago too. He was good at reciting."

"I didn't know that, but he talked about your writing to me, never mentioned the udder fellers, though I've heard the name me self but that wasn't Joe's favourite, nope. He quoted your stuff to me all the time, it was right pretty."

"Oh." She repeated. Joe had kept his own secrets from her and they were all sweet.

"In later years he would walk in the house and take out the envelope and kiss it and put it back, for good luck he would say. I read them lately, since he passed," she confessed. "Only the woman who loved him best could have written of him so well."

"Oh Dar, what a loss, I feel better for me but so sad too, you will miss him so much." Christianna's heart tore in two for this sister who loved Joe Indigo. But her own heart had healed a little, the guilt of her possible part in his death minimized by the words he had written. She also knew, they *would* be together again.

Christianna walked away from the little house, careful to walk around the back where she couldn't be seen from the newer house, Joe's home, down from Dar's.

The little box under her arm was a blessing and when she returned to her aunt's home she put the little pink booklet that chronicled the time she'd spent with Joe Indigo inside it too. This was where her memories and her secrets would stay. There was nothing to be gained by sharing them now. She would put it behind her and move forward, the spirit of Joe Indigo ever- present in her heart. Stephen was her future and she would forgive herself and give the rest of her life to him. He deserved nothing less.

71

She saw his face and it didn't surprise her. His dark brown eyes with the indigo sparkles in their depths held the love of eternity. His dark skin was flawless and perfect and his onyx hair was held back in the pony tail he'd worn when they had first met.

Her heart leapt with joy that he was here and she moved towards him but his eyes told her no. He smiled the grin she knew so well and handed her a blanket wrapped bundle. It was pink and moving and she looked down at her flat abdomen with wonder. She held out her hands and he placed the little package in the crook of her arm.

The little round face in the blanket was perfect. But she was more fascinated by him for the moment. She looked up and he smiled down on her with utter peace on his face. He spoke no words, simply fading away as the dawn's light pulled her from her perfect dream. She awakened to complete bliss which was instantly replaced by heartbreak at the realization that he was truly gone, that they no longer walked on this earth together. She placed her hand on her abdomen and the baby rolled, reassuring her even as her tears fell.

At first the dreams had bothered her. During her entire pregnancy her dreams had been vivid and sometimes scary but lately they had shifted.

They were always a variation on the same theme. Joe would be there, he would hand her the baby. Sometimes the blanket was blue, sometimes it was pink. She would see the baby's face but could never recall it upon awakening.

She would come out of the dream in a moment of perfect bliss. Then Chris would remember that he had gone and be sad again. She never realised as she dreamt that it was a dream. She wondered at its message and marvelled at its return each time. What was he trying to tell her?

Christianna didn't believe in due dates but sometimes wished the baby did. She had enjoyed her pregnancy, her full round belly a miracle that sometimes captured her breath with wonder at the whole process.

Stephen had been as awestruck as she was but as they went day after day past the date that the doctor had suggested he was getting more and more nervous about the actual event.

One Monday the Obstetrician had suggested an induction and Christianna's entire body rejected the idea. The doctor had pressured her with all the fearful words that doctors use and Christianna had walked out of his office. She hadn't returned though she had been advised to make an appointment for a week later.

When the contractions started it was ten days past that arbitrary date and exactly perfect timing. She felt completely confident in her body, in her heart and the dreams that foretold of a perfect outcome.

She took her time, walking a lot with Stephen, calming him with her reassurances that this was not imminent, they had time.

The little hospital was not equipped with pain management options but she had decided to go there anyway to have this baby. She would be transferred to the larger hospital twenty minutes away if necessary. Most people opted for the larger hospital and the maternity ward was generally only occupied with those babies that made sudden appearances. They were equipped for childbirth but it was not often used.

Christianna laboured at home, wanting a birth that was as natural as possible. She found labour intense and painful but manageable. When she finally felt ready to go to the hospital she was almost ready to deliver and half an hour after their arrival the baby slid easily into the world where he cried briefly and then captured the hearts of the couple who had created him. There was little for the medical staff to do and Christianna refused all testing to the chagrin of the nurses and doctors who were a little put out at her rejection of their care. Roxanne was firm and Christianna knew nothing of the battle that had raged outside her cozy hospital room door after he had come to them. She had mentioned law suits and malpractice and they'd all gotten quiet and left the couple alone after that.

Roxanne peeked her head around the door, not wanting to disturb them but so anxious to see her new grandson that she couldn't wait.

She wasn't intruding. They had been waiting for her. Stephen looked at his mother with tearful eyes and said. "I have a boy."

Her tears came hot and quickly as she embraced her son first. "I am so proud of you." She said as she held her boy. Then she looked at her best friend on the bed, holding her grandson and could no longer contain herself.

"May I?" Roxanne held out her aching arms, her eyes almost afraid to ask, afraid that maybe she didn't deserve this.

"Yes, of course." Christianna said and she indicated that Stephen should take the baby.

He did and handed him to his grandmother who waited. She looked down at the brand new little person in the blue blanket, forgetting to breathe, forgetting everything but the tiny perfect face that looked up at her.

As her eyes met his bright alert ones she inhaled and breathed one whispered word that filled the entire room.

"Indigo," Roxanne said and her voice was full of wonder.

As the word drifted across the room to Christianna she sat up. She had wondered if people would see it. His eyes were a dark, black blue but in them, in the depths of them were the sparkles of the indigo eyes that had been Joe's and she had been confused by the mystery, knowing it was impossible, yet it was there. She hadn't mentioned it to Stephen and he hadn't mentioned it to her.

"Yes." Christianna whispered.

"I noticed that." Stephen said. "I've never seen anything like it before."

"I have." Roxanne said and both Stephen and Christianna waited for more.

"It's funny how genetics works." Roxanne seemed to be almost talking to herself. They'll be a dark black brown eventually but you'll still see the purple in there, like little bits of glass, deep and mysterious and rare."

"Where did he get them?" Christianna needed to know because the obvious reason wasn't possible.

"From his grandfather, Stephen's father."

Stephen's face paled. It was the first time his mother had ever mentioned his father to him and he was afraid to move, afraid she would stop. He had craved for this information his whole life and he needed to know. He kept still afraid to break the silence. He felt Christianna's hand on his and it gave him the strength to wait.

"He was a guitar player, a musician, in a band that came through here occasionally. He was part Indian but he never spoke of that but you could tell. We were in love and when he came here we would be together. We would walk and he would sing beautiful songs to me. One day he told me about being Indian. He had grown up teased mercilessly about it. He even changed his last name to Indigo."

"But my last name is Miles." Stephen finally spoke.

"That was his *first* name, I didn't want you to be able to find him but I wanted you to have your father's name somehow." Roxanne looked ashamed. She had done so much wrong.

"What was his full name?" Christianna had her own reasons for her curiosity.

"Miles Joseph Indigo." It was a comfort to Roxanne to be able to say it without pain after all those years.

"What happened to him?" Stephen needed this story as much as he'd needed the air he breathed. He needed it more than ever now that he had a son to share it with.

"When I found out I was pregnant with you I drove out to his home town to tell him. I hadn't ever been there before. When I knocked on the door of his house, a woman answered the door, his wife. He was married and had at least two children. I left and never looked back." Roxanne had been looking at the baby in her arms the entire time, mesmerized by his eyes. Now she looked up at his father.

"He never knew about you and he never came back again, and I heard he died a few years back." Her broken heart still held a wound but she had healed enough to finally be able to put her story into words. Stephen had the features of his father but carried her colouring and eyes. She had never thought she would look into those indigo depths again.

Stephen walked to his mother and wrapped his arms around her and his son. They stood like that for a long moment, an embrace of healing and forgiveness. The child between them drifted off into a deep baby sleep, warm and secure in the arms of one who would love him unconditionally forever.

Christianna watched the scene unfold but she was in other places. Her mind was at the cemetery she had visited, the tombstone next to the one that had marked Joe's grave had held the words *Rest in Peace* and the name of his father was also etched in cold marble. Miles Joseph Indigo was *her* Joe's father and her son's grandfather.

Stephen and Joe were half brothers and now, though she had not seen it before, her eyes were clear and certain that this was the truth. Her heart danced with the gift that she had been given, the gift that was from Joe and Stephen, both of the loves of her life. And the colours of her life once again shifted and she realised that the red and the indigo were a part of the same essence.

Her heart beat with the rhythm of the earth and the patter of the rain that fell outside of her window, a gift from the fog they had come through to bring her here just two hours before. And as usual the bounty in the fog was precious and priceless and a gift from both the heavens and the earth.

When Stephen asked if they would name the baby Indigo Raine Miles, though he would be called Raine, Christianna smiled a secret smile of one satisfied that all was as it should be.

72

Life passed well and happiness graced the long and happy life of Christianna. She thought of Joe often and saw him in her son who wore the indigo spark in his dark brown eyes.

She celebrated the birth of a daughter and then grandchildren, and she surrounded those children with the stories of romance and poetry she carried in her heart from her long ago love. She never wrote the story of her love for Joe but he was in every story she wrote. Her love of Stephen burned with a deep hot red glow and they celebrated it in the ordinary days and extraordinary moments of family life.

Christianna lived a long life with Stephen. But one early summer morning, in her eightieth year, as a foggy mist hung over the grass and the sun entered the sky with a red and golden hello, she walked out to the back of their property. There she found a comfortable place under a large shade tree and settled beneath the canopy of its branches. She wrapped herself in a warm blanket and pulled out the little brown book from the box she'd brought along. She saw the aura of the early morning sky, and the reflection of the ocean and its purple sparkle brought a melancholy to her eyes.

The exhaustion of life danced in her bones and as she often did she whispered to the wind that played music in the branches of the trees. This time, instead of reading from the book of verses that she referred to for her poem she heard the voice of the man himself, strong and familiar

speak to her. Her eyes widened at the sound and she
repeated it again

"I love you Joe Indigo." And her heart listened in a
frequency ears had never heard.

Then she tossed the little book into the container it
had come from. She took a match and struck a flame that
danced with red and blue lights and touched it against the
little box with the three faded carnations on it. She
watched the flame grow into a fire and then, as the fuel was
consumed, die into a pile of hot ashes. Then, the secrets of
her life blew away with the aid of a cooperative breeze into
the brilliant blue waters of Rare Moon Tickle.

She heard his voice again. He answered her with
words familiar and welcoming, a gift from the wind and
the earth and the sky. Timeless words from the little book
his aunt had givin him so long ago. A gift that had been
promised to them in that little tree house where they'd
made their love and cemented their destiny was now theirs.

"And stood by the rose-wreathed gate. Alas,
We loved, sir -used to meet:
How sad and bad and mad it was -
But then, how it was sweet!

And she slipped off the burden of the body that was
too tired and walked toward his voice. She saw him
standing there, in that familiar fog, hand extended, waiting
for her. She answered him as she always had, with the
verse she'd written for him in the eternity that had been
theirs in the life before.

The wind will dance with the leaves
When we meet again by and by
I'll come to you when I can
And we'll love in the indigo sky.

She left behind the red sunrise, the adoration she held for her other love, knowing he would come when it was time and she would be there to welcome him. She walked towards that indigo flame once again returning to the place that she was destined to be, to one she was destined to love.

The words came from her soul and danced with the mist and the wind and filled the spirit of Joe Indigo with the happiness he had found in the moment he met that blue cliff and discovered that this moment was inevitable. That is the peace of heaven.

Their hands touched, their lips met and eternity kept its promise.

As they met where the universe begins and ends, in the universe that has no beginning or end, the secrets of all of the ages were revealed. And they didn't matter.

The End

Or is it?

Epilogue

"Time to go back"

"I'm excited!"

"Me too!"

"I'm only two years behind you this time"

"It'll be easier, we've learned so much"

"Have you seen the plan?"

"Yes, it's perfect"

"It always is"

"Yes, you're right, it always is"

"See you earth side"

"Yes, see you earth side, I love you"

"I love you too"

Thank You and Acknowledgments

The Poets

In no particular order

Edgar Allen Poe

Emily Dickinson

Robert Frost

Elizabeth Barrett Browning

Robert Browning

Pablo Neruda

About the Author

Carolyn R. Parsons was born and raised in
Change Islands, Newfoundland and currently
resides in Tavistock, Ontario. She is a published
poet and her first book, Wind Rhymes; Poetry
from the Breeze was published in December,
2009. She credits growing up in an isolated island
community as the number one contributing factor
to her development as a writer. Without the
distraction of movie theatres and organized
activities she was left alone to read Shakespeare
and the classic poets to her heart's content. It
instilled into her a love of poetry which she calls
her first love. When asked to describe The Secrets
of Rare Moon Tickle her response was *"I simply
wanted to write a beautiful story. This was the
story that begged to be written and Joe and
Christianna were the characters I had to write
about. I wanted to tell a love story that was unlike
any other and I wanted it to be airy and spiritual
and beautiful and poetic. I hope I've
accomplished that."*

Cover photo Credit; photo by Tenisha Saunders. Tenisha lives on Change Islands with her fiance Jamie Porter and their son Carson. Most of her photography is landscape and scenic Change Islands is her favourite subject. This photo was shot from the causeway looking down the main tickle between the North Island and South Islands of the community.